SOVIET POLITICS

Legitimacy and Convergence

The Johns Hopkins University Press
Baltimore and London

The Johns Hopkins University Press, Baltimore, Maryland 21218
The Johns Hopkins University Press Ltd., London

Library of Congress Catalog Card Number 72-4017
ISBN 0-8018-0710-7

Library of Congress Cataloging in Publication Data will be found on the last
printed page of this book.

BRITISH AND SOVIET POLITICS

Jerome M. Gilison

BRITISH AND

Acknowledgment

I would like to thank Professors Milton C. Cummings, Peter H. Melvin and Francis E. Rourke, who read portions of the manuscript and offered valuable suggestions. I am particularly grateful to Professor Stephen V. Stephens for his careful and perceptive reading of the entire manuscript; such deficiencies that remain are largely the result of my stubborn resistance to his suggestions. I am also in debt to members of The Johns Hopkins University Press, Mr. Jack Goellner for encouragement and support and Mrs. Linda Vlasak for improving the readability and accuracy of the text. Finally, and most importantly, my thanks to my wife Margot, for her patience, understanding, and encouragement, and to Kenneth and David, who cooperated (most of the time) while their father worked on into the evening.

Contents

Introduction

The comparative study of communist and non-communist politics is a neglected subject in political science. The study of communist systems, as a separate species, has advanced along its own track. Specialists of this species have provided some interesting studies of communist systems,[1] but their work has remained an appendage, without links to the larger body of literature on comparative politics. There are several reasons for this unfortunate neglect. The earlier emphasis on "totalitarianism" as a model for communist systems tended to place these systems in a separate, incomparable category, and the "area studies" approach also tended in this direction. Paradoxically, the advances made in the behavioral study of politics in Western countries have further increased the separation, for many of these techniques could not be employed in studying the relatively closed communist societies.

Perhaps most important, these distinctions in approach, added to the ever-increasing volume of required reading for "minimum acceptable expertise," have led to a divergence in career patterns. The discipline has been separated into many groups of experts, happy enough to ramble on their own chosen turf, but not inclined to cross the border into a colleague's territory. The terrible demands of expertise have had an inhibiting and intimidating influence on the study of comparative politics, and most particularly on the comparative study of communist and non-communist systems.

Mastery of foreign languages, histories, and cultures has been the stock-in-trade of specialists in the communist world, while facility with statistics,

---

[1] Among others, one could include: Chalmers Johnson, ed., *Change in Communist Systems* (Stanford: Stanford University Press, 1970); H. Gordon Skilling, *The Governments of Communist East Europe* (New York: Thomas Y. Crowell, 1966); Donald W. Treadgold, ed., *Soviet and Chinese Communism: Similarities and Differences* (Seattle: University of Washington Press, 1967); Ghita Ionescu, *The Politics of the European Communist States* (New York: Frederick A. Praeger, 1967); and John N. Hazard, *Communists and Their Law* (Chicago: Chicago University Press, 1969).

computer programming, and survey research techniques has increasingly become the trademark of specialists in American and West European politics. More recently, some attempts have been made to apply mathematical techniques to communist systems, but with considerably less success than has been the case in the study of Western political systems.[2] Even without the new mathematical emphasis, the information explosion in political science has led most practitioners to narrower definitions of their specialty or to highly abstract theorizing or cross-national data gathering. All this implies more than a slight disparity in mental horizons, style of work and technique, leading ultimately to an unsettling difficulty in communication. Clearly, something has been lost by this compartmentalization of the field, and, conversely, there is something of value to be gained by stretching conceptual links across the abyss that exists between communist studies and the study of Western "democratic" systems. That, essentially, is the purpose of this book.

In the following chapters, a comparison is made of the structure and functions of two important and influential political systems, one communist and one a Western democracy. The method that is used is basically structural-functional, in that certain functions of both systems are compared in relation to the political structures that perform them. This approach tends to underline similarities rather than differences, partly because the functions are, by definition, common to both systems. Consequently there is a tendency to emphasize similarities in those structures of government which perform the defined common functions.

This emphasis on similarities can serve as an antidote to the conventional view that the politics of the Soviet Union and Great Britain are polar opposites. The very words "totalitarian, autocratic, closed, monolithic" widely used to describe the Soviet system, contrast starkly with the usual descriptions of the British system: "democratic, representative, open, pluralistic." Judging from such descriptions one would imagine that there is nothing comparable about the two. The picture is sometimes displayed as a contrast between evil and good, morbidity and health. That is not the approach taken in this study. While recognizing that there are significant differences in these two systems, primarily in the relationship of the individual to the regime, we have put the primary emphasis on the less obvious similarities. The hope is that this book will serve as a corrective to the "common sense" exaggeration of differences between East and West.

One of the central themes of this book is legitimacy, and how two regimes with different histories, different traditions, and ostensibly different

---

[2]See Frederic J. Fleron, ed., *Communist Studies and the Social Sciences: Essays on Methodology and Empirical Theory* (Chicago: Rand McNally, 1969); Roger E. Kanet, ed., *The Behavioral Revolution and Communist Studies: Applications of Behaviorally-Oriented Political Research on the Soviet Union and Eastern Europe* (New York: The Free Press, 1970); and Milton E. Lodge, *Soviet Elite Attitudes Since Stalin* (Columbus, Ohio: Charles Merrill Publishing Co., 1969).

values have achieved a consensus adequate for maintaining their stability. In other words, we are seeking an explanation for the fact that in both countries the large majority believes that the regime ought to exist and that its generalized, over-all goals ought to be achieved.

Some may argue that political legitimacy has not been achieved in the Soviet Union, that the people there are cowed into silence, that they fear their government and grudgingly obey it rather than suffer suppression by the omnipresent KGB. This is a misreading of the nature of contemporary Soviet society. It may be depressing, or paradoxical, or simply incredible, but contemporary Soviet society is built upon a solid foundation of regime support. Coercion by the secret police cannot explain the wide acceptance of the regime's platitudes and promises by the Soviet man-in-the-street. For this one must turn to the regime's tight control and regulation of school curricula, supervision of the entire output of the mass media, isolation of the entire Soviet society from most outside (foreign) influences, and effective penetration of group activities to force individual conformity to regime-sponsored group norms. Of course, everyone knows that there are dissidents in Russia, that there is a *samizdat* (the underground, carbon-copy "press"), that writers have been tried and condemned for their "anti-Soviet" prose, that there is a Solzhenitsyn, that there was a Pasternak. We do not wish to disparage the importance of this phenomenon. Quite the contrary, we wish to stress the courage of the individuals involved, for they must fight not only the secret police, but also the orthodox indignation, or mere indifference of the vast majority of their fellow citizens. The small minority of dissidents, who have escaped the web of indoctrination, are isolated and rendered ineffective by the vast net of regime legitimacy which surrounds them in the "working masses."

Although coercion cannot explain consensual legitimacy in the Soviet Union, it does serve the Soviet regime's purposes in many ways familiar in the West. In general, it channels individual behavior into socially approved patterns, by providing a series of increasingly severe sanctions for increasingly non-normative behavior. For the most part, this involves social behavior not connected with regime legitimacy. Even after regime legitimacy is widely accepted, some people will be tempted to pilfer public property, get uproariously drunk, or think that the Soviet regime's massive aid to Egypt is a great waste of rubles. In such cases, the not-so-secret Soviet police (the so-called "militia") can be very helpful, or perhaps social pressure will have an influence on the miscreant. In any case, such "anti-social" acts, whether committed by a Soviet or British subject, have little bearing on the question of legitimacy, or the way in which a regime gains the acceptance of its subjects for using coercion on those who break social rules.

Even the slightest penetration into the legitimizing doctrines supporting the Soviet and British systems reveals that they are both built upon concepts of representation. The use of people's representatives in the framing of socially binding rules serves as a justification for obedience. Whether the representative is claimed to be just like the ordinary citizen or is claimed to be wiser or abler than the common man, the point is that the use of representatives is of primary importance in stimulating regime-supporting consensus. This fact has led to a somewhat unusual stress on the organization and role of representative structures in this book. On the other hand, very little space is given to describing the organization of the executive or administrative functions of government because they play a far less significant role in legitimizing government, whether in Great Britain or in the Soviet Union.

The conventional view of representation in the two countries once again tends to exaggerate the differences. The usual contrast is between the "sovereign" Parliament and the "powerless" Supreme Soviet. On the one hand, Soviet specialists, who ascribe to the Supreme Soviet "purely symbolic" importance, have not sufficiently considered the extent to which other legislatures, such as the British, have become purely symbolic. On the other hand, British specialists who emphasize the (mostly theoretical) constitutional power of Parliament, or even its actual influence on the opinions of policymakers, fail to consider the extent to which even a communist legislature is constitutionally powerful or actually influential in making policy.

Of course, in claiming greater weight for similarities, we are not suggesting that the situations are identical. All we are suggesting is that the representative process in Great Britain and the Soviet Union, when examined for symbolic support of regime legitimacy and for actual power or influence in policy-making, have more in common than is usually supposed.

The political parties also play a part in the representative process, by organizing leadership teams and by organizing the public in support of them and their policies. In a sense, the political parties legitimize the "wisdom" of the political leadership, thus providing a rationale for popular acceptance of its programs. Obviously distinctions must be made between the one-party system of the Soviet Union and the 2½ party system of Britain, but even with these distinctions clearly in view, similar functional patterns emerge. Also some structural similarities in the organization of parties and in the psychology of party membership are brought out in the discussion of the role of the political party in the political process.

Another major topic of this book is the clear disparity between legitimizing theory and political practice in both systems. This difference between theory and practice, between patriotic myth and political reality, appears disturbingly similar in the Soviet and British cases. The divergence is no doubt wider in the former than the latter case, but in both it is still fair to say that the effect is the same: to provide a rationale for popular acceptance of the political structure and its acts while permitting a relatively small, self-selecting group of men to run the governmental machinery. This gap has been a primary target for most critics of the Soviet regime, but for the most part they have tended to contrast Soviet reality with an ideal of democratic mass participation that has never been applied in the real world. The limitations of Soviet-style "democracy" can be seen much more clearly by a comparison with the set of practicable compromises that comprise the British system, than by comparison with a set of ideal principles.

British observers have also been concerned with the gap between theory and practice in British politics, but for the most part they have taken a very parochial view of the matter, looking for solutions within the specific context of British institutions. Various writers have called for reform of the House of Commons, reform or elimination of the House of Lords, better use of the communications media to inform (or "educate") the public on political issues. Far less consideration has been given to the question of whether this admitted gap in British politics can be likened to the well-known and oft-condemned falsity of Soviet pronouncements on "socialist democracy." If it is true—as indeed it seems to be—that the stability of government in the modern mass society depends on the widespread dissemination and acceptance of democratic myths, then the entire process of institutional reform could only have the effect of creating a popular impression of "citizen competence" that is belied by the actual practice of politics. Too often one meets condemnation of this process—as it is practiced in the Soviet Union—without adequate reflection on the extent to which it is found in the West.

In Chapter V this theory-practice gap is analyzed through a schematic model of the policy-making structure in both countries. The model is designed to be equally applicable to both cases, and almost equally divorced from currently approved notions of legitimacy in the U.K. and U.S.S.R. It is an attempt to describe modal patterns of interaction in policy-making through a structural model of leadership "tiers." Using this model, policy-making in both systems can be analyzed in terms of typical "scenarios" of leadership interaction.

Thus the major thrust of this book is the illumination of similarities: similarities in principles of legitimacy, similarities in the symbolic institutions of government which support legitimacy, similarities in the actual policy process, and similarities in the divergence of those policy processes from the established legitimizing principles. Does this mean that the two countries have converged, are converging, or will converge into a single form of "post-industrial" society with a single political process appropriate to its needs? Although the materials presented here are confined to two countries, they do tend to support (by implication at least) the image of a converging world. Yet they also point to certain, perhaps ultimately decisive, limitations on convergence in the specific context of Soviet and British politics. Some factors which have stimulated convergence are:

1) the content of legitimacy principles;
2) the establishment of consensual legitimacy based on these principles;

3) the effective separation of the mass public from direct participation in political activity through the intervention of party organization and legitimacy;

4) the process of policy formulation, including the growth of bureaucratic norms and the oligarchic structural integration of leaders.

On the other hand, the conceivable inner boundaries of convergence seem to be limited by the following factors:

1) In the Soviet Union open competition between organized leadership teams is absolutely prohibited. In Great Britain such competition is traditionally considered a vital part of the political process.

2) In the Soviet Union there is no limitation on the scope or method of government involvement in the life of society. In Great Britain there are well-accepted limitations on government activity.

3) In the Soviet Union the government is committed to achieve a set of broadly defined goals, which involve substantial restructuring of both the social order and the human personality. In Great Britain such far-reaching goals are beyond the understood limits imposed on government.

It is highly unlikely that these convergence-limiting factors will be substantially changed in the foreseeable future. The common structural features generally seem to be connected with organizational imperatives in the management of modern mass society. The common functional features are connected to the bureaucratic "rational" order, described so well by Max Weber. Beyond this, there is certainly no reason to believe that the two systems are converging completely—a thought which would equally horrify most British and Soviet citizens!

This brings us to the ultimate problem: to what extent the "limited convergence" of the Soviet and British systems can be taken as an indication of a universal trend toward East-West convergence. The reliability of generalizations from a study of two countries always depends on the extent to which these countries are actually typical of a larger class of countries. Yet in many respects, the similarities brought out in this study depend on seemingly unique aspects of British and Soviet institutional arrangements. Apparently, this limitation was in the minds of Samuel Huntington and Zbigniew Brzezinski when they wrote their landmark comparison of American and Soviet politics.[3] In summing up the evidence in their case, they concluded that on balance "the evolution of the two systems, but not their convergence, seems to be the undramatic pattern for the future."[4] Yet in their discussion of the policy-making process, Brzezinski and Huntington found "differences between the United States on the one hand, and *the Soviet Union and Western*

[3] Zbigniew Brzezinski and Samuel Huntington, *Political Power: USA/USSR* (New York: Viking Press, 1964).

[4] *Ibid.*, p. 436.

Europe on the other."[5] Thus the evidence for or against convergence to a considerable extent depends on the particular test countries compared, as well as the methodology of comparison. The evidence presented here would tend to support the Huntington and Brzezinski inference that British politics is much closer to Soviet norms in policy-making, selection of leadership, and legitimization of leadership than is American politics.

In some respects, however, other Western countries, including the United States, share characteristics with the Soviet Union much as Britain does. The question of convergence in all these cases cannot be answered by a simple "yes" or "no." It requires careful investigation of functional similarities and differences which may underlie the surface of structures, styles, and forms peculiar to the traditions of individual countries. That has been attempted in this book. It is hoped that this study will encourage others to carry comparative analysis beyond the barriers imposed by convention.

[5]*Ibid.*, p. 207 [emphasis added].

BRITISH AND
SOVIET
POLITICS

Note: Translations of Russian sources were obtained from *The Current Digest of the Soviet Press* in cases where *CDSP* is cited in the footnotes. In all other cases, the translations were made by the author. Russian words have been transliterated according to the Library of Congress system (without diacritical marks), except where common usage has established a variant form (as in the use of "Politburo" rather than the technically correct "Politbiuro").

I

Legitimacy

A State may come into existence because a small num-
ber of men climb into a position from which they can
control a large number; but when this majority start to
ask "Why should we obey?", it becomes necessary to
show that certain advantages follow from obedience, and
this will only be true if those who control the Govern-
ment do so for everyone's advantage, and not solely for
their own.

Michael Stewart,
The British Approach to Politics

Political systems exist in social and economic environments. The political system provides a mechanism
through which the activities of individuals are coordinated, through which their energies are directed toward
achieving economic and social goals. The political system
also provides the mechanism through which immediate
and long-term goals are defined, and repeatedly re-
defined.

In choosing Great Britain and the Soviet Union for
comparison in this study, an assumption was made that
the social and economic environments of politics in
these two countries are sufficiently similar to provide
similar (but not identical) "loads" on the political systems. On the other hand, the ideological "superstruc-
ture" of politics in the two countries (traditions, values,
"national characters," dominant political attitudes, etc.)

1

are sufficiently different to suggest dissimilar solutions for the similar problems that confront the political systems. The essential question is: do the common environmental influences perforce require similar adaptations in the political systems, despite ideological differences?

We start from an assumption—an admitted simplification—that we are dealing with two "mass industrialized societies," i.e., two large populations, each having a common culture and economically organized for industrial production and consumption. We assume that the society is largely urbanized, organized for factory production, well-developed in communications and transportation facilities; and that the individual citizen is engaged in production or services, is often divorced from the end-product of his labor, is specialized in his work, and is a consumer of other people's work.

The simplifications are not too difficult to detect: the Soviet Union does not have the same standard of living and is not as highly urbanized as Great Britain; there is a different pattern of consumption in the two countries; there is a greater difference between urban and rural life in the Soviet Union, and, of course, it is a much larger and more diverse country than Great Britain in extent and population. The list of differences could be expanded without much difficulty. The point we wish to suggest here—we shall assert it with less timidity later—is that these recognized differences do not have a significant impact on the development of certain patterns of political activity, and that where they seem to exert a subtle influence on such activity, we shall be alert to this possibility.

Despite the differences, it can still be said that a great many British and Soviet citizens are engaged in large-scale economic organizations in which their work must be coordinated with the work of others, for they perform only a small part of an over-all productive process. Their whole life-style—including leisure, travel, recreation, nourishment—is highly organized, and thus limited, patterned, and routinized. The scale, the complexity, and the productive activity of these two industrialized mass-societies impose outer limits on the range of conformable life-styles, making them more similar than their historical traditions would indicate. To the totally objective, disinterested observer it would not seem that the average day of the average Soviet factory worker is too terribly different from the typical day of the typical British factory worker. But even this observation is not essential to the succeeding argument, for certainly in aggregate terms we can state with assurance that both societies contain a large mass of people who are specialized in production (and thus diversified), who are largely secularized in values (i.e., do not place primary stress on transcendent, "otherworldly" values) and who are consumers of other people's labor. For our purposes, these attributes are sufficient as a common basis for analytical comparisons of the political systems.[1]

[1]No attempt will be made here to catalog the many works which contain analytical descriptions or typologies of society or the political system, nor will any attempt be

The focus of this study is not the economic performance or the social organization of Great Britain or the Soviet Union. We are primarily concerned with the political systems of these two countries or, to be more precise, with the interaction between the operational reality of these political systems and the theories and attitudes which support them and contribute to their stability. We are confronted with this primary fact: both systems have gathered a high degree of support from their populations, have achieved a high degree of stability (i.e., continuous, gradual development rather than sharp, discontinuous change), and have apparently experienced no breakdowns in their continuing efforts to cope with the rapid social and economic changes inherent in modern society. This success gives these countries membership in a very select group, for the list of failures in this effort is very long.[2] Their success must also be explained, for it seems to have been achieved by quite different routes.

We focus, then, on the simple assertion that the survival of regimes is directly related to their ability to instill (by purposive action or propaganda) or to inspire (as the result of professed values or goals) attitudes which support the continued existence of the regime or which do not—at least actively—oppose its existence.[3] When such attitudes do not exist in sufficient

---

made to discuss these works or compare them with the comparatively modest scheme presented in this chapter. Such a discussion would either be an unwarranted digression or it would be too short to be adequate. The only previous full-scale attempt at analytical comparison of a communist political system with a non-communist system is *Political Power: USA/USSR* by Zbigniew Brzezinski and Samuel P. Huntington (New York: Viking Press, 1964). Those works which I have found most useful in preparing this chapter are: Gabriel Almond and G. Bingham Powell, *Comparative Politics: A Developmental Approach* (Boston: Little, Brown and Co., 1966); David Easton, *A Systems Analysis of Political Life* (New York: John Wiley & Sons, 1965); Max Weber, *The Theory of Social and Economic Organization* (New York: The Free Press, 1964), and "Politics as a Vocation," *From Max Weber: Essays in Sociology*, ed. and trans. by H. H. Gerth and C. Wright Mills (New York: Oxford University Press, 1958).

[2] Aside from the many breakdowns of regimes in Asia, Africa, and Latin America, some major continental European powers have also experienced discontinuous change in this century: Russia in 1917, Poland in 1926, Germany in 1933, Italy in 1922, France in 1958.

[3] The words "regime," "government," "state," and "political system" are so variously interpreted in the literature that definitions are required to make them useful. For the sake of clarity, these words will be used in this study as follows: (1) *regime* refers to the continuous long-term structures of the political system, to the sum total of the relatively persistent processes and organizations which characterize the system; (2) the *Government* refers to a specific group of men, who in a parliamentary system head ministries or administrative departments and, at the same time, are elected representatives. When the word is not capitalized, it has the more general meaning of the entire body of men who at any given time occupy the authoritative, official positions of the state structure. When it is not preceded by an article, the word is used in the more general, dictionary sense of "direction, control, rule, management"; (3) *state* connotes the legal, constitutional definition of the political structure as a set of specific organizations and processes; and (4) *political system* will be used in the sense employed by Gabriel Almond and G. Bingham Powell when they say that it concerns "the entire scope of political activities within a society, regardless of where in the society such activities

numbers, such as in Tsarist Russia or Weimar Germany, the regime cannot survive any crisis brought about by its own mistakes or inefficiency. When such attitudes are present in sufficient degree, as in present-day Britain or Russia, the regime can proceed from blunder to blunder in relative security. Whatever factors may be involved in individual cases, men ultimately support, or reject, or remain in some intermediate range of indifference to a political regime; and the entire complex of attitudes within the population must contain sufficient amount of support and "benevolent" neutrality to preserve the regime. We do not know what that sufficient quantity is. There is probably no general answer. We know that both the Soviet Union and Great Britain have attained it, and probably exceeded it by a substantial margin (although this is primarily an observation from outward appearances in both countries and some opinion polls in Great Britain). In other words, both regimes have attained a high degree of political legitimacy and have, therefore, become highly stable.

LEGITIMACY, CONSENSUS, AND AUTHORITY

A legitimate political organization, role, or process is defined as one which people feel ought to exist because it conforms, in whole or in part, to principles which are considered morally good. Such a feeling has no immediate connection with the efficiency of the organization or the benefits of the process. The use of secret police may be widely condemned as "illegitimate" even though (and perhaps because) the secret police is highly efficient in its work. Similarly, an act of foreign aggression may be condemned as illegitimate by the aggressor's own citizens even though the act was militarily successful and brings benefits to the aggressor's population.

Clearly this definition excludes attitudes toward particular political personalities, political acts, or specific leadership groups. When a man assumes a political leadership role, he may already have a following of supporters, but he cannot be legitimate in himself. Only the role, seen in terms of a political "office," may have legitimacy, and only that office can entitle the individual to take actions which effectively control the actions of others. A political leadership role is considered legitimate if:

    (a) the process by which a person has assumed the role is considered legitimate;

    (b) the role itself is considered justifiable in moral terms.

---

may be located" and that it includes "all structures in their political aspects" (*Comparative Politics*, pp. 17, 18). An interesting (and caustic) critique of this term, as it is used by Almond and Powell, can be found in S. E. Finer's article, "Almond's Concept of 'The Political System': A Textual Critique," *Government and Opposition* 5, no. 1 (Winter 1969-70), pp. 3-21. The definitions of regime and the government are essentially quite similar to those offered by Richard Rose in "Dynamic Tendencies in the Authority of Regimes," *World Politics* XXI, no. 4 (July 1969), pp. 602-3.

Thus it is perfectly consistent for a British citizen to dislike Edward Heath intensely and yet accept him as the legitimate Prime Minister of the country, because the office and the process of becoming Prime Minister conform to principles considered morally good.

In the same way, a political act, such as a judicial decision, may be considered absolutely reprehensible in its content, and yet legitimate, because the process by which the decision was made and the role of the judiciary in society are felt to be morally justifiable. A person feeling this way might very well obey the offensive ruling, while simultaneously striving to overturn it by legitimate procedures.

Since the moral connotation of legitimacy is inherent, the question of which moral values are being used as a standard is extremely important. An action may be illegitimate to some people and quite legitimate to others. In fact, the legitimacy of an act can only be determined, as the definition implies, by reference to a particular group (here meaning people with shared values). The clearest example of this is the case where two groups are in conflict (say, a labor-management dispute). A strike by government employees, for example, may be viewed by some as "blackmailing the public," while the strikers view it as a legitimate means of securing redress of their grievances.

In a society where the subcultures are relatively more distinct, discrete, and discordant, the sense of shared values is weakened. The question of legitimate political ends and means is not easily resolved in such "political cultures," and the long-term stability of the regime is uncertain. The critical question here is not the mere presence of pluralism in society, or the actual number of identifiable groups, but the degree to which they are set apart from each other in separate value systems (or at least separate value priorities). It is generally accepted, for example, that pluralism in France implies much more intergroup hostility in values than pluralism in Great Britain.

Because legitimacy is related to values (i.e., propositions about right and wrong) and moral judgments, it is very difficult to determine empirically the extent of its presence or absence. Because legitimacy is related to basic feelings about the morality of acts, it changes only slowly and requires time and favorable circumstances to become firmly attached to particular organizations or processes of government.

Within each society, there are some values which are shared and which derive from the national culture and historical experience, but there are also subgroups in society which have additional, parochial values not completely shared by the wider society. Newly established political regimes must build upon this complex of values and orientations in society in order to achieve legitimacy. If an organization conforms to the existing values of a group and is accepted by the group as morally justified, we can say that a *consensus* has been reached in that group about the legitimacy of the organization. If it does not, it may try to establish a consensus by use of propaganda, programs or promises which conform to prevailing values. Or alternatively, it may try to change those values through propaganda and "educational" techniques while relying on its monopoly, or near monopoly, of the means of coercion.

Some organizations and processes come into being with a preexisting consensus concerning their legitimacy because the organizations were created in response to previous pressures from society. This is more often the case in a stable, developed political system, where the major organizations of government have achieved legitimacy and where the political system is responsive to pressures. The introduction of the National Health Service in Great Britain is a good example of this ready acceptance of a new government function where a prior consensus on the general outlines of government involvement already exists. Pressures for change are not simply the result of material conditions in society. It has been noted in many different circumstances that the most deplorable conditions of life are not necessarily deplored by those living under them. Extreme poverty may be apathetically accepted or even embraced as the way to a moral life.[4] Not even extreme inequality in material wealth necessarily leads to pressures for change, for this inequality may conform to prevailing values and thus be considered legitimate. Pressures arise only when these conditions are *perceived* as susceptible to change and morally wrong—when people perceive a disparity between existing conditions and their moral values, and when they feel that they can affect these conditions through coordinated activity.

Within developed societies, such as Great Britain or the Soviet Union, pressures for change are the result not only of social values, but also of group values, which may be in conflict with each other. These societies have placed, within their values, a great emphasis on material living conditions. Pressures for change in material conditions are often articulated in moral terms. In the Soviet Union (as we shall see), the current goal of "building communism," a positive moral commitment of the regime, is often virtually equated with raising the living standards of the Soviet working people. In Great Britain, wage demands, strikes, and even government budgets are often justified in terms of people's rights to certain specified economic conditions. Thus, in these societies even "bread and butter" issues have moral content and much of the contention concerns the ethical premises of the division of wealth and reward in society.

The moral basis of pressures subjects political organizations to a continual test of their legitimacy. The moral basis of their legitimacy may be undermined if they are not responsive to the moral content of new pressures. Thus, even though values do not change very rapidly, political organizations must be continually responsive to pressures if they are to maintain their legitimacy.

---

[4] The traditional Hindu social system of India can be cited as one example of legitimizing (giving positive moral content to) poverty and inequality.

The need for responsiveness can be viewed in another perspective. It can be said that people have either *affective* or *instrumental* orientations toward political organizations and processes. An affective orientation implies an emotional bond, an attachment of loyalty and allegiance based upon a moral commitment by the individual to the organization's goals or purposes. An affective attachment may be the result of tradition, but such traditional connections are in themselves based on moral judgments transmitted from generation to generation by society—a process often referred to as "political socialization." This affective bond is the substance of legitimacy, and emphasizes the comparative strength and durability of the relationship, once established. Instrumental orientations, however, are based upon an evaluation of the organization's effect on the individual. If the effect is perceived as beneficial, the individual supports the organization, but always provisionally, subject to continued "good behavior." An instrumental orientation does not accord the organization legitimacy, for its support is based upon a continual evaluation of its effective output, and can be withdrawn relatively rapidly.

A good example of the consequential distinction between affective and instrumental orientations is the contrast between the Weimar and Nazi regimes in Germany. The former achieved only an instrumental bond with the population, and was swept away by its own failure to stem economic and social disintegration. The latter achieved an affective bond of loyalty and pride, and survived through the most dreadful days of deprivation in modern German history, only to be brought down finally by outside forces.

It is true, however, that good performance over a period of time may—it's not a certainty—gradually change the basis of support from instrumental to affective and thus build legitimacy for the organization. Thus legitimacy may be attained by long-term performance of wanted functions. In order to achieve this level of performance, however, an organization must be responsive to needs and the pressures arising from them. Responsiveness implies channels of two-way communication between the organization and the group subject to its actions, for the organization can achieve legitimacy only by performing *wanted* functions for the subject group. Thus the secret police may achieve high legitimacy for a leadership group by being responsive to its desire for security from real or imagined enemies, but it may be illegitimate to the wider population unless the people too can be made to feel threatened by enemies from within. It can thus be seen that efficiency and responsiveness to needs can lead to legitimacy in societies, such as the British and Soviet, where prevailing values prescribe that government should serve the people's needs.

When an organization achieves a consensus about its legitimacy within a subject group, it achieves *authority* over that group. *Authority is the quality inherent in a legitimate political organization or process which predisposes individuals to conform to its rules.* This predisposition is an internalized moral commitment to conform, and is quite different from obedience based on fear of penalties or retribution by the regime. Authority speaks to the individual as the inner voice of conscience: "Thou shalt" or "Thou shalt not."

It is the authority inherent in legitimate organizations and processes that makes legitimacy so desirable for government. After all, government exists to control, channel, and limit some portion of the activities of its citizens. As such, it imposes restriction and relative deprivations on some, while opening advantages to others. On most matters, the self-interest of some groups would dictate a refusal to conform to the imposed rules. If only an instrumental relation exists between the political organization and the subject group, the group may indeed refuse to conform through a wide range of reactions, from violent attacks to quiet sabotage.

In both the Soviet and British mass industrial societies, there exist many functional groups (such as doctors, lawyers, machinists, electricians, etc.) performing needed occupational functions for the society, and containing a virtual monopoly of expertise in the area of their specialities. These functional groups are as necessary to the regime as the regime is to them. Their cooperation is required if the regime is to succeed in its tasks as economic coordinator and regulator of society. The relationship must, therefore, be harmonious, a "good working relationship." Yet the relationship must also be between unequals, for the authority of the political organization must be so well established that the inevitable relative deprivations meted out at times to practically all functional groups do not bring the groups to reject the rules or the regime which issued them. Therefore, under conditions of the mass industrial society, political organizations with authority are a requirement for long-term stability of the regime.

INSTITUTIONS AND POLITICAL POWER

A political institution is defined as a political organization, role, or process which has attained authority. Since authority is a quality of legitimate organizations, we can also say that an institution is a legitimate part of the political system. The word connotes an authoritative relationship between a subject individual or group (which may in some cases be as large as the entire population) and some part of the political system.

The process of acquiring legitimacy and thus authority over individuals and groups is the process by which an organization becomes an institution, a process which is often called *institutionalization.* This is a crucial process for a regime in the mass industrial society, for it is undoubtedly the most effective and "least-cost" method of attaining stability. Clearly both the Soviet and British regimes have attained a high degree of institutionalization, or, put another way, they have achieved a wide consensus on the legitimacy of their political organizations.

Ultimately, a regime must have a preponderant power over the population within its state boundaries. If power is defined as the ability to control actions of others, it would seem that there are only two ways of achieving it. One can control the actions of others either by inducing beforehand a specific response to the command, or one can use rewards and punishments to induce the required response. The first type of power we have already defined as authority, the power intrinsic to legitimate organizations (institutions). This implies an affective bond between the institution holding power and the individual or group subject to this power. The second type implies an instrumental orientation toward the holder of power. This instrumental power can either be negative, that is, coercion by the threat or use of force or deprivations; or it can be positive, the use of rewards in the form of physical or mental benefits, advancement, honors, etc.[5]

In actual practice these two kinds of power do not exist in isolation from, or opposition to, each other. They form two extremes of a continuum of means which regimes use to exercise power. In both the Soviet and British cases, the two methods are employed, although perhaps to different degrees. The important point, however, is the tendency of both these regimes—and other regimes as well—to seek affective power rather than instrumental power, and to reduce their reliance on instrumental (especially coercive) power to the lowest acceptable level.

One can summarize this entire process by saying that these regimes are continually engaged in legitimizing their organizations and processes and thus institutionalizing them. They have both achieved considerable, although not identical or consistent, success in acquiring legitimacy. In this process they have both used the following techniques:

1. reasonable efficiency of the regime in performing functions (in the most recent period, primarily functions of economic management);
2. retention of political organizations (components of the political system) over time so that they can become institutions;
3. conformance to prevailing societal values;
4. education which inculcates supportive values and supportive communications through the mass media;
5. sufficient responsiveness to needs of subjects.

While we can observe that these regimes have become legitimized over time and can detect efforts by both regimes to enhance legitimacy, the ques-

---

[5] It is in this sense that Max Weber's definition of a state as "a human community that (successfully) claims the *monopoly of the legitimate use of physical force* within a given territory" is insufficient, although certainly necessary. The emphasis in Weber's definition is on the very element of a state's power that a really successful state uses least of all. See "Politics as a Vocation," in Gerth and Mills, *From Max Weber*, p. 78. The subtle distinctions between different varieties of power are analyzed by Anthony De Crespigny in "Power and Its Forms," *Political Studies* XVI, no. 2 (June 1968), pp. 192–205.

tion of *why* these regimes should strive for maximal legitimacy is more difficult to answer. It seems clear that coercive techniques—mass terror, purges, executions, forced labor colonies, and the like—involve a considerable wastage of the society's resources. The machinery of coercion is expensive, and poses a potential threat to the government which ostensibly directs it. In addition, there are probably losses in social production caused by the mysterious disappearance of skilled personnel and the anxiety of those still left. Of course, some governments, notably Stalin's, have been content to pay this price for a time, but even Stalin seems to have found that these extreme measures are time-limited; they apparently cannot be sustained indefinitely. The demonic energy called up by mass purges and terror is a self-destructive energy, the beast gorging on its own flesh. It must eventually subside into relative quiescence—certainly a "permanent purge" in the literal sense would be virtually impossible to sustain in any but a benign form.

In any case, there is a more compelling reason why a government would prefer to hold affective rather than instrumental power: affective bonds are more enduring, more supportive during the regime's crises of performance, more resilient when the regime suffers a loss of confidence caused by poor performance. In an age when mass populations are mobilized into politics, the need for affective bonds between regime and population acquires greater significance. Since it is likely that most groups and individuals in society will be frustrated by the regime in achieving their maximum goals, the regime is bound to lose purely instrumental support from time to time as an inherent consequence of its functions. A regime in this position will have to bargain with groups and try to balance them against each other. Such a regime, based on instrumental power, is therefore based on limited power; it is weak in comparison with regimes which have achieved strong affective bonds with their citizens.

Finally, we must add the possibility that leaders of governments are continually engaged in a process of self-legitimation, or justifying their possession of power to themselves, as well as to their citizens.[6] One will search in vain through the writings and speeches of twentieth-century leaders for an admission that they are driven by personal gratification acquired from wielding power over others. Leaders, whether Gandhi, Winston Churchill, Franklin Delano Roosevelt, or even Hitler and Stalin—all saw themselves (or at least *said* they saw themselves) as working to improve the life of their citizens. One may, of course, simply disbelieve these statements and assume that they are

---

[6]This is, essentially, the argument advanced for the Soviet case by Alfred Meyer in his insightful article, "The Functions of Ideology in the Soviet Political System: A Speculative Essay Designed to Provoke Discussion," *Soviet Studies* XVII, no. 3 (January 1966), pp. 273–85.

part of the ritual which leaders perform to please their followers and to gain their support. It may be that some leaders are conscious and cynical manipulators of their publics, and the best one can say in such cases is that they are very good actors indeed. There *seem* to be more cases, however, where leaders appear to be genuinely driven by a desire to implement a general program (modernization, democratization, socialization, etc.) or a more specific program (free medical care, old age pensions, lower prices, etc.) all in the name of the people's interests. There is no need to mention some specific cases, for in no case can the assertion be proven or disproven by the public record alone. One finally has to assess the inner state of mind of the leader, an always difficult and uncertain task. Still, one can say with certainty that service to the society is the *professed* goal of both Soviet and British leadership. This is the natural concomitant of the political mobilization of a mass public.

LEGITIMACY PRINCIPLE OF THE STATE

Both the Soviet and British states are founded on the same elementary doctrine of legitimacy: *the people rule.* The state, according to this doctrine, is ultimately in the hands of the people, who are, nevertheless, still subject to it. Thus the rules (limitations on action) made by the state are given authority (i.e., made into law) because they are theoretically *self-imposed.* The laws express the will of the people—at least in the long run—because they are made by the people, acting indirectly through their chosen representatives. The legitimacy of law is, therefore, the consequence of the legislative actions of representative bodies of the state. The people's representatives, standing for the people as a whole, must approve all provisional rules before they become law.

In neither country is this doctrine that law expresses the people's will ever tested empirically by requiring a referendum on the text of a specific legislative proposal. In fact, both systems occasionally adopt unpopular laws. Popular acceptance of a particular law cannot be assured in advance by reliance on the legitimacy of the political system, or the corpus of law as a whole. But this generalized system legitimacy can assure widespread application and acquiescence even when the law is unpopular, whereas in the absence of system legitimacy, an unpopular law may invite not only widespread evasion but also attacks on the state structure itself.

The representative assemblies thus provide legitimacy for laws by providing symbolic verification of the people's acceptance of them. We have already defined power as the ability to control actions of others. In this sense, law can be seen as an instrument of power, since it is a way by which the state controls the actions of its subjects. Here too, we can observe two different bases for this power: authority or coercion. Law attains authority when both of the following conditions prevail:

1. there is a consensus that the process and the organizations which created the law are legitimate;
2. there is a consensus that the ends or goals of the law are legitimate.

The second prerequisite requires some amplification: it is not necessary that the law be approved in all its details or provisions for it to attain authority. It is sufficient that the law be based on certain principles that are considered legitimate, or that it establish a legitimate goal or purpose for it to be accepted as authoritative, even by those who object to various specific details of its formulation. It is quite possible, and especially in a stable political system, to be opposed to a law while readily conceding its legitimacy. But in an unstable political system, people who oppose laws often deny their legitimacy, primarily because there is little or no consensus about the legitimacy of the regime or about the goals of governmental action.

When a regime has failed to achieve legitimacy, its laws do not have authority and it therefore must resort to physical coercion as an available technique to ensure conformity to its rules. This technique is, however, the hallmark of an unstable regime, and it cannot be applied to large numbers of people indefinitely. Even in stable regimes, however, physical coercion is used against the relatively few people who fall outside the consensus on legitimacy: criminals, revolutionaries, and such.

The regime's claim to legitimacy is based not only on procedures which symbolize the involvement of the public in formulation of policies, but also in the instrumental claim that the government is efficient in responding to the people's wishes concerning proposed policies and in implementing policies that have been adopted. The legitimacy principle of the regimes in Great Britain and the Soviet Union can thus be refined as follows: *The regime is legitimate because it is responsive to the needs and best aspirations of the people and is organized efficiently to carry out the policies required by the people.*

In both countries the regime is said to be responsive to the best interests of the people, but this often means "what the people would want if they were in possession of the best information and if the matter were carefully explained to them." It is not often claimed that the system is responsive to what the people—in their present imperfect state of knowledge and discernment—are actually thinking. For the British case, Nigel Nicolson makes the point quite succinctly:

Owing to a remarkable combination of restraint on the part of the electorate, and of tact, vigour and innocent deceit on the part of their leaders, British democracy has hitherto emerged successful from its most important test: unpopular decisions by a Government are, in general, accepted;

and popular clamour weighs no more than an ounce or two in the scales of its judgment.[7]

For the Soviet case, the claim is made that the system embodies the people's will at any given moment—as long as everything is kept nice and simple so the people can understand what is happening:

> In higher representative organs of the socialist countries, the people, through their all-powerful elected representatives, decide all the most important questions concerning social and political life. In this connection, the activities of the people's deputies and of the representative organs themselves are arranged so that they are understandable to the mass of the people and accessible to them.[8]

British party leaders are also aware that political issues must be presented to the public in simplified and vivified form, as the following comment by a Labour Party publicist makes clear:

> We must not expect these people [i.e., the voters] to follow closely reasoned arguments or to be automatically interested in the great issues of the day. Unless our propaganda can immediately echo a feeling or strike a subject close to their hearts, we have lost them and all our further effort will be wasted.[9]

Although claims to governmental legitimacy are not couched in such frank terms, these statements are an obvious indication that the leadership is expected to mold public opinion as well as to follow it. This, however, is generally considered a primary legitimate function of the party rather than the government, both in the Soviet Union and Great Britain.

The claim of governmental legitimacy is based upon an essentially instrumental assertion. The government must be *responsive to inputs* from society and *efficient in translating them to outputs* for society. Generally, the responsiveness of government is identified as a property of its representative assembly, although in recent times, the quite obvious growth of administrative rule-making has shifted some attention to this sector as well. It is now generally accepted in Great Britain that the bulk of actual rule-making is handled by administrative departments in consultation with interested outside groups and with the support (or disinterest) of the government in power. Nevertheless, responsiveness to the undifferentiated public—to the "grass roots" of politics—is still supposed to be the special property of the represen-

---

[7] Nigel Nicolson, *People and Parliament* (London: Weidenfeld and Nicolson, 1958), p. 11.

[8] *Verkhovnyi sovet SSSR* (Moscow: Izvestiia Publishing House, 1967), p. 24.

[9] Brian Murphy, "The Purpose of Propaganda," *Labour Organizer*, March 1965, p. 45. As quoted in Richard Rose, *Influencing Voters: A Study in Campaign Rationality* (London: Faber and Faber, 1967), p. 76.

tative body. This body exerts pressure on the Cabinet, sets outer limits on policy and occasionally causes the government to retreat.

In the Soviet Union, while the claim for the representative assembly is much greater, the reality is much less. The claim is that the representatives are directly linked to the people, because the membership of representative bodies (primarily the soviets) is a cross-section of the population—the representatives don't have to respond to the people because they *are* the people. But the legitimizing assumption that the people are always and forever united behind the decisions of the leadership means, in practice, that the representatives must demonstrate the unity and loyalty of the people rather than play an independent role in decisions. For the most part, this is what they do as representatives. (For the other part of their activity, see Chapter IV.)

LEGITIMACY PRINCIPLE OF THE RULING PARTY

Without in any sense attempting to ignore the important distinction between a one-party and two-party system, it can be said that both systems make essentially identical legitimizing claims for the ruling party, whose leaders either temporarily or permanently hold the most important positions in the government. The legitimacy principle of the ruling party can be stated as: *The people support the party's control of the state because the party puts forward programs which are based on the true interests of the people.*

In both systems, the party cannot directly hold legitimate political power, the power to make binding rules for society. In both systems, this power is exercised by a party acting through the legitimized state structure. In both systems, the state structure is the mechanism of legitimate political power, but the machine does not operate unless the controls are firmly in the hands of a single party leadership for a sufficient space of years. In both systems then, the party provides the leading men and (hopefully) the leading ideas which, when blended with the authority of state institutions, are capable of sustaining a functioning political system. Finally, in both countries, there is a sufficient consensus behind this combination of party and government to make it legitimate.

Parties are multifunctional organizations in the political system, and in a number of these functions, the Soviet Communist Party differs markedly from the British parties. This is particularly the case in terms of mass membership and political mobilization of the public. But in terms of their specific function of providing leadership for the political system, they are much more similar. The leadership functions of the parties can be divided into two components. As ruling parties (leaving aside the opposition functions of the British parties) they provide:

1. a means of organizing a coherent and cohesive leadership team;
2. a means of legitimizing an elite leadership principle.

Clearly, there are some important differences in the *structures* by which these functions are accomplished in the two systems, but in both cases the functions are inherent facets of the role of parties in the political process. Thus, even though the Soviet Politburo is a party institution, while the British Cabinet is a governmental institution, they share many functional and even procedural characteristics.

The function of organizing a coherent and cohesive leadership team is obviously extremely important for the stability of the regime. Just as obviously, it cannot always be said that this function is accomplished with complete success in either country. What can be said, however, is that parties establish a predisposition to resolve, or at least reduce, conflict. Parties, like other organizations, tend to develop certain ideal leadership types and to recruit and advance members who most closely conform to the ideal. Leaders who advance over years through the same hierarchy and selection process are likely to have similar values and perceptions of the world, as well as mannerisms and dress. Furthermore, this experience provides a continuous background of interaction between members of the emerging leadership team, and this interaction establishes an informal set of superordinate-subordinate relations between the leaders, a loosely defined "pecking order." Since the pecking order is loosely defined within parties, it is subject to partial breakdowns in the form of personal rivalries. Still, there is no question but that parties help to reduce the level of leadership conflict below what could reasonably be expected in a less structured group of highly ambitious men.

In addition, these parties create a shared loyalty to the symbols of party identity, to its public image, to some vaguely defined purposes and goals which are the party's presumed raison d'être. Party loyalty is internalized by those who rise through the organization, and in addition to the psychic restraints against deviance, there are real sanctions (demotion or expulsion) which the party can employ against those who too strenuously or too often challenge the prevailing sentiment of party loyalty. The constraint of loyalty is a powerful (but not always decisive) influence over the actions of those who desire to rise through the party. The party always strives to present a united face to the public, and those who publicly divide the party ranks embark on a risky course. Private and gentle persuasion is thus the preferred technique. As we shall see in the next chapter, the parties (and particularly the British parties) are usually willing to forgive their erstwhile errant sons, but the way to the top is usually barred to such troublemakers.

The other leadership function of the party, legitimizing an elite leadership principle, is of crucial importance to the stability of the regime. This legitimizing principle helps to resolve the tension between the legitimizing principle of government—that the people rule—and the undeniable fact that in reality a relatively few people rule, and acquire power in the name of the ruled. This would be difficult to legitimize if leaders were presented as mere average people, as "no better than" sailors, secretaries, or shoemakers. Such an admission would more readily legitimize a system of regular rotation of governmental leadership amongst all citizens. Instead, the business of government is described—and with some justification—as a speciality requiring experience and expertise. Secondly, the party is described as being composed of particularly capable people. This quality gives the party special capabilities for creating and initiating optimal policies, while at the same time maintaining close contact with the people so that public needs and opinions are given full consideration in formulating policy. In this sense, the party is defined as simply another one of countless specialized agencies in a modern, complex, structurally differentiated society.

This legitimizing doctrine of elite leadership rests upon precisely the same foundations as the legitimacy principle of the state described previously. In both cases the claim rests on *responsiveness* to inputs from society, and *efficiency* in translating inputs to outputs for society. In both countries it is claimed that elections are a way of assuring the responsiveness of leaders and that in the process citizens will form judgments on the efficiency of the leaders; thus elections are a check on the two essential attributes of leadership legitimacy. To what extent this claim is empirically justified in either country will be discussed later, but even without empirical support, the claim for elections can be seen as a closing of the circle of legitimacy which surrounds the creation of authoritative positions of leadership in a state structure legitimized by democratic theories. This is as true of the Soviet Union as it is of Great Britain.

In this case, as in others, claims for legitimacy need not accurately describe reality. It is sufficient that enough people *believe* them. Legitimacy can be based on widely accepted myths, but it cannot be based on widely rejected facts. A well-established, stable government can generate supportive myths and simultaneously suppress subversive facts. When the government has a monopoly over the channels of communication, as in the Soviet Union, the power to select only supportive information and to build legitimizing myths can greatly enhance the survival powers of the government. In a relatively open society such as the British, the government must compete with other sources of information and cannot as easily survive when its efficiency falls.

Still, even in Soviet society, citizens can and do measure the claims of government against reality. In the next three chapters we will examine these legitimacy doctrines in the light of their actual operation, first in connection with the parties and then in regard to the representative organs of government.

Leaders,
Followers,
and the Parties

In the literature on political parties, the assumption is often made that they are democratizing organizations, mobilizing the mass population for a more active—even if intermittent and limited—political role. If one has in mind a "state of nature" consisting of an amorphous, unorganized mass of people without institutions providing regular channels of access to the political system, the parties can certainly be seen as "democratizing" improvements. But parties, as all organizations, exist to channel, to order, and thus to limit the actions of men. In this sense, parties exist to provide some political activity for all citizens, but the over-all effect is to provide very little activity for very many citizens and much activity for very few. The party, in the age of the mass public, can be seen as manning the interstitial boundaries between society and the political system. The party is the way in which the public is organized for politics. This is not to say that the public must be drawn into its work or even become members. Far more significant, the party mobilizes public opinion, and organizes public responses to the actions of government. The party in power, the party which provides the leadership of the government, attempts to mobilize support for government policy and performance. In Great Britain, the opposition party attempts to mobilize discontent and rejection of government policy.

The parties, then, attempt to be mass organizations. They develop a network of local branches and attempt to attract people to their work. Even the Soviet Communist Party, which maintains rigid formal entrance requirements, simultaneously carries out massive propaganda to attract increased numbers of enthusiastic members. But the party's claim to being *of* the people as well as *for* the people rests on extremely shaky foundations—and not only in the Soviet case. If one discounts the over seven million indirect members of the Labour Party (whose mere membership in an affiliated trade union automatically makes them members of the Labour Party), not one of the parties in either country can claim a membership in excess of twelve percent of the adult population.

The actual membership of these parties, while being better educated and apparently having higher average income than the population, cannot be pictured as an "elite" in any reasonable definition of that term. The major and intractable factor seems to be that these partisans are distinguished from the population mainly by their curious and inexplicable desire to participate in political activity. Some members may only be lukewarm, may only give a minimal part of their leisure to matters of party organization. But the general level of political activity is considerably higher than that of the population at large. In fact, in British and Soviet parties alike, one of the major activites on the local scene is to stir the lukewarm bodies of the indifferent members into a more active role.

Lethargy may be a problem of party organization, but loyalty rarely is. The member is almost always a dependable follower of his party. With remarkable fidelity, he zigs with its zigs and zags when it zags. The relatively few who become disenchanted fall away from the party, but the usual outcome of party work over a period of years is to confirm partisan prejudices through closer identification with the party's record and goals.

Since all of these parties place such high value on unanimity, occasional defections or "deviations" from the approved party position achieve far more notoriety than a much more remarkable fact: that amongst such a large group of politically involved people, the parties can maintain a very high degree of agreement on an endless succession of complex policy questions. Perfect unanimity is not achieved by any of them, although its surface appearance is more nearly preserved by the CPSU than by either of the British parties. Nevertheless, the striving for solidarity is one of the most important activities of all three parties, and absorbs much of the energy and attention of the internal party bureaucracy.

MASS MEMBERSHIP

Membership in either the CPSU or the British parties is a voluntary act. However, the requirements for membership and the significance of belonging are quite different in the two countries, a fact which flows from the quite un-British role of the CPSU in Soviet society. There really are no stated prerequisites for membership in either the Conservative or Labour parties, save a totally untested affinity for the party's approach to political affairs. One joins the Conservative or Labour party simply by becoming a member of a constituency organization, or in the latter party, by being a member of an affiliated trade union or cooperative association. There are residency and minimum age requirements but no check is made of past political fidelity and no promises are exacted. The annual dues are quite reasonable and ward meetings are not so frequent as to become a burden—and one need not attend them anyway.

CPSU membership is quite another matter. Tests of character, motivation and endurance are interposed between the neophyte and the cherished party card: three recommendations from party members (of at least five years' standing each) for entrance to a year of probationary membership before one can become a full member of the Party; and then submission to a continuous series of checks of one's character and deportment, measured by standards that are purposely set higher than those established for the average Soviet citizen. Dues are certainly not onerous, but obligations of membership cumulatively amount to a considerable expenditure of time. Among the ten duties of party membership mentioned in the Party Rules there is a litany of adjurations such as: "to put Party decisions firmly and steadfastly into effect . . . to take an active part in the political affairs of the country, in the administration of State affairs and in economic and cultural development . . . to master Marxist-Leninist theory . . . to be an active proponent of the ideas of socialist internationalism and Soviet patriotism . . . vigorously to protect the ideological and organizational unity of the Party . . . to implement undeviatingly the Party's policy . . . to observe Party and State discipline . . . vigorously to assist in the strengthening of the defensive might of the U.S.S.R."

It all amounts to a formidable combination of activity, forbearance and steadfast loyalty, which must be added to the normal burdens of Soviet citizenship: fulfillment of production quotas despite relatively low pay and a perpetual shortage of recreation facilities, consumer goods, and amenities of all kinds. It should not be assumed that all party members faithfully adhere to these rules of conduct; the Party Rules establish ideal standards against which many members would be found wanting. Still, these standards do represent the kind of party which the leadership would wish to have, and for this reason the Party engages in a ceaseless campaign to "improve" the conduct and qualifications of its members along the prescribed lines.

This is one important reason why the Party maintains a much tighter organization at the lower levels than the British parties. The network of "primary party organizations" (of which there are now over 350,000 in the CPSU) is designed to affiliate the party member with a small, face-to-face group, a most effective organizational technique for enforcing conformity to established standards. These primary organizations are the descendants of the party cells established by Lenin to avoid infiltration by the Tsarist Secret Police during the days when the Party was an underground revolutionary organization. Since that time, the growth of the CPSU to over 14 million members and the development of large industrial plants has caused some primary organizations (470 in 1967) to swell to over 1,000 members. There is thus a great disproportion in primary organizations: while almost half have less than 16 members, the mean (inflated by the presence of the unusually large units) for industrial enterprise organizations is 83 members and 74 for state farms (1967 data).[1] Of course, in these large units the opportunities for monitoring the "party spirit" (*partiinost'*) of the members are considerably reduced.

Still, it is fair and quite accurate to say that the large majority of primary units in the CPSU are small enough to permit each member to know all the other members rather well. Since these party units are organized in work places or dwelling places, there is a high probability that the party members also know each other from other social roles: they may be members of the same work team ("brigade") or residents of different rooms in the same over-crowded apartment. The possibilities for surveillance of conduct to assure conformity in such conditions are enormous, and undoubtedly helpful to the Party in enforcing its standards. The Party, wishing to make the most of such collective living conditions, continually attempts to inculcate a feeling of so-called "community-spirit" (*obshchestvennost'*), which essentially legitimizes the activities of those who would only too gladly be their brothers' keepers—even if this means listening to their neighbors' hushed conversation through a tumbler pressed to the wall.

On the other hand, the Party standards can be undermined by the development of close friendships among members. There is a natural and understandable tendency to reduce tensions among members by relaxing the standards of surveillance, since laxity is beneficial to all the lower-level members and detrimental only to the interests of higher levels of the Party. Despite the constant urging from above to maintain vigilance and to weed out undesirables from the party ranks, laxity seems to be a pervasive and perhaps growing problem for the Party. To counteract this tendency, the rules for expulsion and readmission to the Party were tightened at the Twenty-third Party Congress.[2] Still one reads in the Soviet press of particularly egregious cases of a "forgiving attitude" by lower party cadres toward the sins of their fellow party members.[3]

---

[1] *Partiinaia zhizn'*, no. 7, April 1968, pp. 26–28. [*CDSP* XX, no. 16, p. 11].

[2] The changes in the party statutes can be found in *Pravda* and *Izvestiia*, April 9, 1966 [*CDSP* XVIII, no. 15, p. 9].

[3] See "Law of Life for the Party," *Pravda*, June 6, 1966. [*CDSP* XVIII, no. 23, pp. 44–45.]

The Party's insistence on model deportment from its membership is drawn mainly from the emphasis in Lenin's writings on the necessity of a small, dedicated and "conscious" revolutionary elite. Lenin drew a distinction between the "spontaneity" of the masses and the "consciousness" of the relatively few who thoroughly understand the development of social historical forces. The spontaneity of the masses, according to Lenin, is a necessary primal force for social change, but is incapable of sustained effective action without the guiding hand of consciousness provided by the leadership elite. The elite in Lenin's concept, however, is guided by a new revolutionary *noblesse oblige* which requires of it a most abstemious personal life and a dedication and selflessness which legitimizes its position—and which, incidentally, Lenin himself observed with rare fidelity.

The contemporary derivative of this Leninist notion states that the Party leadership is fully conscious and therefore enabled, and legitimately entitled, to develop plans for society, but it is often noted that the Party rank-and-file falls short, in some degree, of the leadership's level of consciousness. From this recognition flows the constant stream of appeals to Party members to strive toward self-improvement. The Party ranks are now 565 times larger than at the time of the October Revolution. Systematic, large-scale purges are no longer fashionable as a means of weeding out insufficiently conscious and devoted members. Although a system of sanctions against individuals is still available to the leadership to achieve this end, the application of sanctions seems too sporadic and unsystematic to prevent the swollen party ranks from including many lukewarm members. In a society which does not contain strong hereditary class distinctions, the Party membership card can be used as a channel of influence to further career goals, particularly in the ranks of the intelligentsia. The Party actually enlarges the careerist element in its membership by encouraging and even pressuring its achievement elites in economic management, military leadership, the sports world, science, and the arts to join the Party as a sign of over-all loyalty to the regime.[4] The dilution of zeal in Party membership can be traced to several sources, but primarily it stems from the use of the Party member as a model of loyal orthodoxy and conformity, an attribute which is not likely to attract the most creative, talented, or even ideologically ardent citizens. The obligations of Party membership involve the rank-and-file in a round of activities for the leadership, mobilizing the population and instilling enthusiasm (however shallow it may be) for current policies. In the days of the forced industrialization and collectiviza-

---

[4] A well-known example of this honorary granting of party membership is the case of German Titov, who at the time of his space flight was only a candidate member of the Party. Shortly after he landed, he talked by telephone to Khrushchev, who told him: "As of now you are no longer a candidate member of the Party. Consider your period of candidature to have expired, because each minute of your stay in space counts for one year." (*Pravda*, August 7, 1961.)

tion of the 1930's, the Party was cast in a heroic, if oppressive, role: the agent of dynamism in a rapidly changing society. In the last decades, however, the Party has settled down to incremental growthsmanship and has become enmeshed in the relatively mundane problems of economic management. It no longer is the magnet for youthful idealism and zeal which it was even during the dark days of Stalinism.

Thus in the membership of the vast network of Party primary organizations one finds a mixed picture of enthusiasm shading off by degrees to indifference and passivity. Even enthusiastic Party members may find the burden of Party work too heavy to bear, for Party obligations are added on to an already heavy schedule for many of them. This is particularly true because such additional burdens tend to accumulate on the shoulders of those who are known to be conscientious and capable activists. As one activist remarked in a conversation reported by *Pravda*: "You may notice that it is a fairly narrow circle of people who are bustling about on Party business. Always the same ones. Why? Simply because it is easier and more convenient to rely on them. They have been tested and will never let you down."[5] Since there are many Party assignments to be filled, it is not surprising that the more reliable activists can be overworked, as is evident from the following complaint written to the editors of *Pravda* by a taxi driver who had been "active as a public-spirited person for almost fifteen years":

> Judge for yourselves: Consider me and my colleagues—chairmen of shop committees, secretaries and members of Party Bureaus; you will find that each of us is obliged to attend in the course of one month: two sessions of the Party Bureau, one meeting for all Party members in the garage, two sessions of the People's Control Group and one general meeting each of Party shop organization's Communists, a column trade union and the brigade. To this we must still add quarterly meetings of the People's Control Groups and of the Party organization *aktiv* [activists], conferences, etc. Add participation in ad hoc commissions and people's control inspections—sometimes lasting several days—and there goes your week! All our month's free days turn out to be taken up by volunteer work.[6]

In addition to these practical problems of Party organization and "instilling enthusiasm," there is the fundamental and ineradicable problem that the Party structure, day-to-day operation, and original historical purposes are all contradicted by its current legitimizing doctrines. The Party organization under Lenin was a command structure, a paramilitary organization, well-suited to do battle in revolutionary conditions. Lenin was contemptuous of parliamentary democracy and other such "debating societies," and had no intention of instituting such forums within the Party. Since the Revolution,

---

[5] *Pravda*, December 7, 1967 [*CDSP* XIX, no. 49, p. 16].
[6] V. Ovchinnikov in *Pravda*, May 11, 1969 [*CDSP* XXI, no. 19, p. 21].

however, and particularly since Stalin, the Party has increasingly legitimized itself by assuming all the slogans and symbols of democracy, even within the Party structure. Party officers at all levels are "elected," and there is much insistence that frank and open discussions precede decisions taken by all Party organizations. One often finds statements such as the following in the extensive legitimizing literature of the Party:

> Internal Party democracy has significantly increased. At the present time, there is not a single important political question which has not been widely discussed in the Party, nor a decision taken which has not been an expression of the collective wisdom and experience of the membership.[7]

Despite such repeated assertions, it is clear from many reports in the Soviet press that the Party's internal norms of operation are far from democratic. The Party press treats such undemocratic practices as aberrations from the norm, usually placing the blame on local Party leaders for such malpractices as "excessive ostentation and pomposity" or "dictatorial methods." In trying to instill the norm of "collective leadership"—as exemplified at the highest level by the Politburo of the CPSU—the point is made in the press that "the secretary of a party committee is not a boss, he is not invested with the right to command. He is merely the senior person in an agency of collective leadership elected by Communists."[8]

All these claims to the contrary, the reality is that the Party has not forgotten its Leninist origins. The Leninist organizational principle of "democratic centralism" (which is formally defined as the right to discuss all matters before a decision is taken, and the obligation to obey all decisions after they are taken, plus the election of all Party officers) has been interpreted for many years to mean simply that Party decisions taken by the leadership should be thoroughly explained to lower echelons so that their full and sincere support can be elicited. The Party structure is still hierarchical and as inflexibly centralized into chains of command as in Lenin's day. Since the Tenth Party Congress (1921), there has been a prohibition against "factionalism," i.e., any attempt to organize dissenting opinions, but more important than such formal prohibitions is the hierarchical nature of the organization.

The chain of command is also the career ladder for those who wish to pursue a career in the Party bureaucracy (or "apparatus"). These budding *apparatchiki* are fully aware that their progress up the ladder is dependent upon the good will and efficiency reports of their superiors in the chain of command. They will be very anxious to preserve the appearance of success— an atmosphere of quiet unanimity, if not ardent loyalty, within their Party organizations. The rank-and-file also understands that it is not prudent to

[7] R. S. Shikov, "Partiia i narod v period stroitel'stva kommunizma," in *Partiia i massy* (Moscow: Publishing House "Mysl'," 1966), p. 93.

[8] F. Petrenko in *Pravda*, July 20, 1966 [*CDSP* XVIII, no. 29, p. 26].

rock the boat, either to raise objections to policies or to raise indelicate questions about the performance of local Party leaders. The former is more dangerous, for it is of questionable legitimacy under current applications of "democratic centralism"; the latter is merely foolhardy (in most cases), for the local leaders who are criticized have the power to make life miserable for their critics.

Because of the basic ambivalence of Party doctrine, the Party member receives conflicting signals from authoritative sources, caught between the Scylla of "party democracy" and the Charybdis of "Leninist norms of party life." As a dialectical counterpoint to the call for greater Party democracy, the Party also urges its members to strengthen Party unity. As one writer put it: "The Communist Party can solve the problems before it only through maximum unity, a unified, single will, and iron discipline."[9]

The legitimacy of this call for unity—which in practice amounts to a call for unanimity—is supported by two doctrinal assumptions. The first is that the "victory of socialism" in the Soviet Union and the "liquidation of the exploiting classes" has "eliminated the fundamental internal causes, which would give rise to some degree of wavering in the solidarity of Party ranks or cause a split in the CPSU."[10] The fundamental cause of social conflict, according to Soviet Marxism-Leninism, is the existence of classes with contradictory goals—a situation that cannot exist in the socialist system of the Soviet Union.

The second assumption is that Marxism-Leninism is a "scientific" body of knowledge about the development of social systems, that the answers it yields about social development are not based on human preferences, but are "neutral" in value terms, calculated from data, and, in a sense, inevitable. The Party legitimizes itself as the single authoritative source of such scientific calculations. The "theses" published by the Central Committee of the CPSU for the one-hundredth anniversary of Lenin's birth make this clear:

> Based on the theory of Marxism-Leninism and the accumulated experience of struggle, the CPSU works out the political line, guides the masses and manages the economic, social and spiritual life of society; unites, coordinates, and directs the activities of all chains of the managerial system. . . . Analyzing the character of social processes and generalizing the experience of the masses, showing the way toward forward movement, the Party reveals new possibilities, works out the means for conquering all difficulties and contradictions.[11]

[9] A. E. Ekshtein, "Ukreplenie edinstva partii—odno iz vazhneishikh uslovii uspeshnogo stroitel'stva sotsializma i kommunizma," *Voprosy istorii KPSS* 1969, no. 2, p. 113.

[10] *Ibid.*, p. 117.

[11] *Izvestiia*, December 23, 1969.

It is all put in neutral, problem-solving terms, as though the collective Party wisdom were a form of scientific genius.

This theory clearly legitimizes the authority of Party policies developed by the leadership, but it also creates special obligations for the ranks of ordinary CPSU members. As conscious students of Marxism-Leninism they must "understand" the "correct solutions" to problems handed down by the Party leaders. As members of a socio-political elite—those given the grace of Marxist-Leninist consciousness—they must display model behavior toward the non-Party masses. For Party members, the message is quite clear: "People can see with their own eyes that actually Party members do not have any special privileges except one: to be always and in everything more advanced, to be the first to tackle the most difficult tasks."[12]

Despite this assurance, there are special privileges that attend Party membership. The special, yellow-curtained shops of the Stalin era no longer distribute scarce goods to Party members, but the Party card still carries important advantages for members of Soviet society. For those who wish to pursue a political career, it is a *sine qua non*; for acquisition of sensitive posts in internal security, the military, or the diplomatic corps, it is well-nigh indispensable; for ordinary careers in the professions or in management, it is extremely advantageous, and for anyone in Soviet society, it carries special status in the community. In more concrete terms it may mean special opportunities to travel, even abroad, more frequent vacations at government-controlled resorts, and better prospects for acquiring new living quarters, which are still in short supply.

In almost all of the foregoing respects, the significance of membership in a British party is quite different. This is because the mass membership of a British party is primarily an electoral device, a structure whose primary function is to fight and win elections. Historically, the mass organizations of the British parties arose as a response to the gradual introduction of universal suffrage, as the parties realized that they had to compete for the votes of millions of electors rather than the patronage of socio-economic elites. In the roughly one hundred years since their inception, the mass organizations of the British parties have remained true to their origins, coming to life with the announcement of a General Election, and then relapsing into a state of relative dormancy for the intervening period until the next election.

In contrast to the Soviet case, the Britisher who joins a political party makes a minimal commitment of time and energy. The party establishes no model of the ideal party member, nor does it make demands on the member to conform in his public and private life to the established model. The British party asks—it does not and could not demand—only that the member pay his

[12] N. Rusakov, "Kazhdyi partiets—obshchestvennyi deiatel'," *Partiinaia zhizn'* 1969, no. 5, p. 43.

minimal annual dues, possibly attend ward meetings occasionally, and be ready, willing, and able to join in the party's campaign effort. Since the campaign customarily lasts only one month (from the announcement of the election until the polling day), and since General Elections occur approximately once every four years on the average, the demands of British party membership are quite slight when compared with the Soviet case. The evidence indicates that in both the Conservative and Labour parties, only a very small proportion of the total membership remains active between election campaigns, and in fact only a small minority bothers to attend monthly ward party meetings. According to R. L. Leonard,

> In areas in which parties are weak, local and ward parties often have an ephemeral existence depending for their existence primarily on the enthusiasm of one or two members who provide the impetus for the others. A loss of interest on the part of one or two individuals, or their removal from the neighbourhood, may cause the branch to collapse altogether and go out of existence. Then, after an interval of perhaps several years, an enthusiastic newcomer will start things up again and with the aid of old and unreliable records will call on long dormant members and try to rekindle their interest.[13]

Since local party organizations are primarily electoral, the balance of party preferences in the area has a great effect on the strength of local party organizations. In constituencies which are in a state of precarious balance between the two major parties (so-called "marginal" constituencies) both major parties are likely to have strong, active, and highly motivated organizations. In constituencies which deliver consistently large majorities for one of the parties (so-called "safe" constituencies), neither the majority nor the minority party is likely to have strong and active local groups. When habitual voting patterns produce a predictable result in a constituency, the result is apathy in the party organizations, since their essential raison d'être is to wage the electoral battle where a real contest exists. Where there is no real contest, either in Great Britain or the Soviet Union, the result is likely to be a very sensible and well-founded lack of enthusiasm.

Local party organizations may also supply some non-political needs of their members, as Leonard points out:

> It is not unusual for a local party to spend more time discussing who is to look after the sweet stall at the party's jumble sale than it devotes to considering possible resolutions for the annual conference of the party. It follows from this that local party branches are as much social as political affairs and the sense of comradeship at this, the lowest level of party politics, is strong.[14]

---

[13] R. L. Leonard, *Elections in Britain* (London: Van Nostrand, 1968), p. 55.

[14] *Ibid.*, p. 54. R. T. McKenzie describes local Labour party activities in a similar fashion: "It seems fair to conclude that, between elections at least, the great proportion

In functional terms, there is a very significant difference between the British parties and the CPSU. The mass organizations of the British parties exist primarily as a basis for conducting election campaigns, an activity of very low significance in the CPSU's scale of priorities. On the other hand, the CPSU is continuously involved in providing leadership for all aspects of life in Soviet society. The CPSU's legitimate role is to supply the so-called "leading core" or nucleus of every public organization, whether it be a trade union, professional organization, or amateur sports club. The Party, in a sense, legitimately infiltrates every organized social activity in the Soviet Union. This role is totally foreign, both literally and figuratively, to the British parties. Except for some latent social by-products of their political structure (as mentioned above), the British parties define their role as "purely political," within a definition of the political sphere that is limited to matters of major public policy and the acquisition of elective positions in the government.

Keeping these important differences in mind, it is still worthwhile to note that the primary attribute expected of the party member in both countries in unswerving and enthusiastic loyalty to the party leadership. This solidarity of party ranks is the goal of party leaderships in both countries, although the British parties, having relatively weak sanctions and less docile members, suffer more open discord and indignities than the CPSU would tolerate. Of the two British parties, the Labour Party has had more than its share of open discord. Yet even the Labour Party has had on the whole little trouble in keeping its ranks in file. The Labour Party leadership has been defeated by its mass membership only once (in 1960–61) in its entire history, despite the fact that the structure of the party was designed originally to permit the membership continuous control over the actions and policies of the leaders. The Labour Annual Conference, which on paper is the controlling organization of the party, has authority to determine policy on a one-member-one-vote basis. In 1960, the Conference voted for unilateral nuclear disarmament against the wishes of Hugh Gaitskell and other party leaders. However, the voting at the Annual Conference is controlled by the large trade unions affiliated in the TUC, and the extraordinary reversal of the Gaitskellite leadership in 1960 can be attributed to Gaitskell's inability to hold a few key union leaders in their normal respectful position (in non-union matters).[15] In

---

of party members are content to play no part at all in the work of their ward or constituency party. Those who do take an active part are mainly concerned with the pleasantly complex task of maintaining the party organization in being, a task which involves an extensive social program and a great deal of routine internal party administration." *British Political Parties*, 2nd ed. (London: Heineman, 1963), p. 548.

[15] Membership in the Labour Party can either be indirect (through membership in a trade union affiliated with the Party) or direct (by joining a Constituency Labour Party). Since the great majority of Labour Party members are indirect members, trade union representatives arrive at Annual Conferences with huge and decisive blocs of votes to cast. At the 1960 Annual Conference, the trade unions had 5,513,000 votes out of a total of approximately 6,328,000.

fact, Gaitskell managed to reverse this adverse decision at the following conference by persuading several key unions to switch their bloc votes.

The Labour Party has had for many years a left wing (the Bevanite wing during the 1940's and 1950's), a dominant moderate group from which the leadership has generally been drawn, and a more vaguely defined right wing, trailing off to views which would fit comfortably in Conservative Party programs. This persistent internal division of the party creates a continual friction between the extremities and the center. Evidence of this can be found at every Annual Conference, as left-wing resolutions are brought up, debated heatedly, and invariably defeated by large margins. The heat and noise of these debates should not lead to the false impression that the leadership is in serious difficulty.[16] Even within the Labour Party, where identifiable divisions exist, the extent to which left-wing attitudes characterize the party activists can be easily exaggerated. Maurice Duverger, in his classic *Political Parties*, suggested that a fundamental problem of party organization is that the party activists at lower levels (whom he calls "militants") are naturally inclined toward more ideologically extreme philosophies than the party leaders or the electorate.[17] Several eminent British writers have examined this problem as it pertains to the British case.[18] The Duverger description seems particularly disturbing in the context of the British political tradition, which is characterized by moderation, compromise, and a decent tolerance for conflicting views.[19] Fortunately, the evidence does not entirely support the conclusion that Duverger's danger is applicable to the British parties. Richard Rose's study of resolutions introduced at the annual meetings of both parties concluded that "attitudes on questions of policy are randomly distributed among constituency parties, and it may be tentatively assumed, among party activists as well."[20] Rose proceeds with the following description of the relationship between the party activists and the party leadership:

[16] *The Economist's* judgment of one such Conference seems on the mark: "The Labour Government is almost a separate party from the one which meets in annual conference. There is no real dialogue between the two, and neither has much influence over the other. This is the reality. Promises made and attitudes struck at the conference need last no longer than the week, and the Government can then get back to governing in its own sweet way" (October 5, 1968).

[17] Maurice Duverger, *Political Parties* (New York: John Wiley and Sons, 1963), pp. 109-16, 190-92.

[18] D. E. Butler and R. T. McKenzie, among others, have apparently subscribed to this view. See Butler's "The Paradox of Party Difference," *The American Behavioral Scientist* IV, no. 3 (November, 1960), pp. 3-5; and McKenzie's *British Political Parties*, pp. 196-97.

[19] For empirical evidence of these attitudes, see Gabriel Almond and Sidney Verba, *The Civic Culture: Political Attitudes and Democracy in Five Nations* (Boston: Little, Brown and Co., 1965), p. 315. See also James B. Christoph, "Consensus and Cleavage in British Political Ideology, *American Political Science Review* LIX, no. 3 (September, 1965), pp. 629-42.

[20] Richard Rose, "The Political Ideas of English Party Activists," *American Political Science Review* LVI, no. 2 (June 1962) p. 369.

An immediate consequence of this diversity [of party activists' political views] is the flexibility which it gives to party leaders. At annual party conferences leaders are not faced with a mass of extreme-minded activists, demanding the adoption of socially divisive policies as the price of continuing to do menial work. Opposition comes from only a fraction of the rank-and-file. Another portion is likely to support the leadership and a significant group may have no clear views, or even interest in questions of party policy. . . . Lacking firm anchorage in an ideological position, constituency parties may be willing to trust their leaders wherever they lead.[21]

Rose's conclusion, supported by several cases outside his study, is that "factional disputes divide parties vertically, joining some Privy Councillors, MPs, lobbyists, activists and voters into a faction which is in conflict with another which also contains members drawn from all ranks of the party."[22]

In contrast to the Labour Party, the Conservative Party has never made any claims nor spread any illusions about inner-party democracy—a concept which would fit rather awkwardly with its political philosophy. The Conservative Party has been and is still the defender of a hierarchical, harmonious order in society. According to this philosophy, leadership is a skill; it requires a rare combination of talents, fortitude, and character, and those who have these traits *should* lead, while others should recognize the legitimacy of the leaders' position. The attitude of Conservative Party activists toward their leaders, as characterized by Austin Ranney, is:

Whatever their personal political views . . . most Conservative activists undoubtedly place great value on such virtues as loyalty to the national Leader, solidarity in the face of attacks by Labour, public silence about internal party conflict, and solid character and reliability rather than flashiness or brilliance as prime qualities for party leaders.[23]

Unlike the Labour Party, the Conservative Party is not divided into more or less permanent wings, or factions, with identifiable, persistent differences in political viewpoints. It is perhaps possible to make a vague differentiation between the tradition-oriented Old Tories of the Establishment, and a new group of business-oriented Conservatives who advocate changes designed to increase managerial efficiency. One study of the parliamentary detachments of the parties explains that "by their very nature the internal quarrels of the [Conservative] party are temporary. They subside as the issues which gave

---

[21] *Ibid.*, pp. 370–71.

[22] *Ibid.* However, Leon D. Epstein cites some incomplete evidence that party activists "not only . . . have less incentive to modify their views than do office-seeking politicians, but . . . also tend to have more rigid personalities and find fixed, unaccommodating, partisanship congenial." *Political Parties in Western Democracies* (New York: Frederick Praeger, 1967), p. 117.

[23] Austin Ranney, *Pathways to Parliament Candidate Selection in Britain* (Madison: University of Wisconsin Press, 1965), p. 70.

them birth are resolved. The absence of two clearly drawn camps means that the man who deserts on one issue may be a staunch party man on another."[24] This relative fluidity of opinions in the party ranks is appropriate for a party which has eschewed, and in fact habitually distrusted, formal ideologies.

The party is also not burdened by institutions or traditional doctrines which give the mass membership the authority to determine party policies. In contrast to the professed doctrines of the Labour Party (but more in keeping with its actual practice), the Annual Conferences of the Conservative Party are occasions when the party leaders present the party line to the accompaniment of enthusiastic applause of the faithful. Despite differing theories, and the appearance of greater oppositional activity by factions in the Labour Party, the evidence of recent history shows that both party leaderships are equally and solidly in control of their mass memberships, and can normally count on their substantial loyalty. Intense feelings in the mass memberships—which are generally an indicator of intense feelings in the mass electorate—can and do strongly influence the leadership, but the leaders can usually carry party opinion with them. R. T. McKenzie's justly acclaimed study of the British parties makes this point quite clearly:

> Setting aside the party myths and the inter-party propaganda it is clear that the primary function of the mass organizations of the Conservative and Labour parties is to sustain two competing teams of parliamentary leaders between whom the electorate as a whole may periodically choose. . . . Their followers outside parliament become little more than a highly organized pressure group with a special channel of communication directly to the leader, the Cabinet and the parliamentary party. Any disposition to take advantage of this special relationship is normally more than neutralized by feelings of pride and loyalty to their leaders and by an anxiety not to embarrass them in the execution of their duties or to provide aid and comfort to the rival team, who are eagerly preparing to overthrow them at the forthcoming election.[25]

In fact, the unstated guiding principle of British party organization is remarkably close to the Leninist doctrine of democratic centralism. In fact, if one considers the existence of large nationality-based subparties within the CPSU (which tend to decentralize it), it appears that the British parties are indeed more structurally centralized than the Soviet Communist party. As for the "democratic" part of democratic centralism, it can be said that the leaderships of the British parties and the Soviet party strive for the same sort of democracy within the party. The freedom to speak is formally granted to all members of the party, while the leadership strives (with varying degrees of

[24] S. E. Finer, H. B. Berrington, D. J. Bartholomew, *Backbench Opinion in the House of Commons, 1955–59* (New York: Pergamon Press, 1961), p. 123.

[25] McKenzie, *British Political Parties*, p. 642. See also Peter G. J. Pulzer, *Political Representation and Elections: Parties and Voting in Great Britain* (New York: Frederick A. Praeger, 1967), p. 77.

success) to assure that the speakers all support the leadership and its policies. The norm of democratic centralism is that free discussion ceases when the party reaches a decision, and to the extent that there is ever free discussion within the party concerning important policies, strong pressures against dissent appear once a party commits itself to a position.

Of course, the CPSU leadership has many more sanctions to impose on its errant members than the British parties, but the unanimity that is achieved is not so much the product of stern punishments imposed from above—far more important are the self-imposed limitations willingly accepted by the members. Membership in all cases is a voluntary act and implies at the outset a personal commitment to the party. Even where such commitment is lukewarm at the beginning, the commitment is likely to grow for those personally involved in party work. The active member has, or develops, a personal stake in the success of the party; he wants it to conquer its objectives, to vanquish its real or imagined enemies. He may be called upon to defend the party to people outside it, and he may spend many hours of his free time in unexciting chores, chores that could only be justified by one's personal feeling of involvement in the party's fortunes.[26]

Since the party member is committed to the success of the party in achieving its stated goals, he will be highly reluctant to weaken the party's chances for success by openly disagreeing with the leadership. Since the member's commitment to the party is psychologically supported by a feeling of personal achievement resulting from party success, he is normally highly reluctant to criticize past actions of the party leadership, striving instead to find sound justifications for even the most dubious or disastrous démarches. With the possible and partial exception of the Labour left wing, all the parties have achieved within the membership a high degree of consensus concerning the legitimacy of party goals. Therefore, the most significant and persistent cause of disaffection within the party is the clear failure of the party leadership to achieve stated immediate objectives in social or economic policy when in control of the government. In such cases people outside of the party are more likely to turn away from the party *in toto*, but members, fundamentally committed to the party, even as it passes through hell and high water, are more likely to demand the heads of the party leaders responsible for the party's plight. In Great Britain, since the party organizations are primarily concerned with winning elections, there is no greater hell than the loss of successive elections. In the Soviet Union, the party's great concern (in fact, obsession) with efficiently managing the economy makes management the chief area of responsibility for the leaders.

---

[26] One very interesting explanation for this growth of loyalty could be Leon Festinger's concept of the reduction of "cognitive dissonance." In this case, disagreement with the party position on an issue would be dissonant with the knowledge of one's past activity in support of the party. See *A Theory of Cognitive Dissonance* (Evanston, Ill.: Row, Peterson and Co., 1957).

PARTY ORGANIZATION

In all three cases the officers of local party organizations (secretaries of primary organizations in the CPSU and officers of constituency associations in the British parties) are elected by the membership, but the elections are rarely contested. In all cases the selection of parliamentary candidates is accomplished by local party organizations although guidelines and occasionally candidates are sent down from the party center.[27] In all three parties the involvement of the member is almost totally contained within the lowest level of party organization. In fact, the lowest levels—the ward parties in Great Britain and the primary organizations in the Soviet Union—are the only party units which are primarily concerned with the ordinary rank-and-file members.

The next step upward on the CPSU's organizational ladder is the *raion* party committee. There are somewhat less than 3,200 such committees (commonly called *raikoms*) in the Soviet Union, and since each has between 50 and 70 members, the number of party members directly involved in *raikom* work is less than 220,000, or under two percent of the total party membership. Although the *raikom* controls and supervises the work of the primary party organizations, it is far more concerned with the local economy and social order. At this level, only one step removed from the bottom, we find the Party fulfilling its other important functions as part of the party-state administrative structure, and at this level the professional bureaucrats of the Party, the *apparatchiki*, are already dominant in party work. Indeed, the most important men in the *raion* are the two or three secretaries of the *raikom*.

The British case offers contrasts and similarities. In contrast to the CPSU, the British parties play no direct role in the management of the local economy or social order. The local constituency parties in Great Britain, therefore, do not have and do not require permanent paid staff workers. In fact, constituency organizations are generally kept alive during the uneventful years between elections by the devotion and energy of a relatively few local volunteers. The officers of constituency party organizations are often those who are most ready, willing, and able to devote time to nurturing the morbid, but not quite moribund, organization. This leads to the similarity: that in the British party organizations, as in the CPSU, the national party leadership is dominant, acting indirectly through local activists.[28]

---

[27] This procedure is examined in more detail in Chapter III.

[28] Austin Ranney's study of British constituency parties concludes that "they are manned by activists primarily loyal to the national parties' leaders and causes." (*Pathways to Parliament*, p. 281.) There is also some evidence that the local leadership of both British parties is more middle-class than the population, a fact which might suggest a certain kind of bias toward middle-class attitudes—whatever they might be—or middle-class parliamentary candidates. See J. Blondel, *Voters, Parties, and Leaders: The Social Fabric of British Politics* (Baltimore: Penguin Books, 1963), pp. 94–103.

Since the primary function of a British constituency party is to nominate and elect a Member of Parliament, it is extremely important to the cohesion of British parties (which is normally high) that those activists at the local level who choose candidates for the House of Commons are motivated mainly by feelings of loyalty to the party's national leadership. Constituency parties (particularly in the Conservative Party) have a high degree of autonomy in selecting candidates. The fact that conflicts between local leaders and the national headquarters are very rare may be an indication that local party leaders see their legitimate role primarily as support of the national leadership. In choosing candidates, they are guided by the same kinds of considerations and objectives as the party headquarters—although their preferences may be flavored by stronger prejudices. On the other hand, the local party leadership appears to be as little influenced by the ordinary party members' opinions of potential candidates as is the typical first secretary of a *raikom.*

Both major British parties maintain a staff of paid agents. The agents have a responsibility for coordinating and supervising the activities of all the constituency parties in a designated region. The Conservative Party has twelve Provincial Areas, each containing from 28 to 80 constituency organizations. Similarly the Labour Party has established eleven Regional Councils. The paid agents in both cases are responsible not to the local parties but to the national headquarters (specifically to the Party Leader in the Conservative Party and to the National Executive Council [NEC] in the Labour Party). The national headquarters are also staffed by professionals, but by surprisingly few of them. The Conservative Party headquarters, known as the Central Office, employs about 39 administrators in its national office, and another 60 in its regional offices, plus 49 for research and publicity. The Labour Party headquarters, Transport House, employs about 12 for national administration and about 21 for research and publicity.[29] The small staffs of the major parties reflect the minimal role of the national parties outside the Parliament between elections.

The Soviet party apparatus is quite another matter. It has been estimated that there are between 1,300 and 1,500 administrators in the national headquarters of the CPSU (i.e., the Secretariat, or the apparatus of the CPSU Central Committee).[30] The apparatus of the Central Committee is divided into approximately 25 departments, with the nine secretaries of the CC supervising their work. This relatively massive organization at the party center is understandable in view of the continuous and important role of the Party in the economic and social life of the country. In addition, since the Party has

[29] Leonard, *Elections in Britain*, p. 33. The figures are from 1963, but according to Leonard, "although the actual figures are no longer correct the general picture which it conveys is still valid."

[30] Abdurakhman Avtorkhanov, *The Communist Party Apparatus* (Chicago: Henry Regnery Co., 1966), p. 209.

special roles as the defender and developer of the ideology, and since the Party itself at lower levels is a part of the party-state bureaucracy, the central organization must undertake special, additional tasks in these realms. Thus special departments for ideology and party organizations—which would be as strange as they would be unnecessary in Great Britain—are found in the central apparatus.

Below the central headquarters of the Party, the Party organization is divided regionally, in steps that parallel the organization of the Soviet state. The pseudo-federal structure of the Soviet state is replicated in the organization of the CPSU. Thus the CPSU itself is formally a combination of 14

Table II.1

CPSU ORGANIZATION AT LOWER LEVELS
(As of Jan. 1967)

Level	Number of Party Committees*	Approximate Number of Members of Committees
Union Republic	14	25,000
Oblast'	133	
City	743	300,000
Raion	3139**	

*There were also party committees in some special administrative units, such as the 6 krais and the 10 okrugs.
**Of this total, 413 were in urban centers, the rest rural.

communist parties (each coterminous with a union republic of the U.S.S.R.) and the massive Party organization within the Russian Republic (the R.S.F.S.R.), which does not have its "own" party. The Party organizations in the Russian Republic come directly under the national CPSU headquarters, because the R.S.F.S.R. contains 64 percent of all party members and 55 percent of all party organizations, and, according to one Soviet writer, "in these conditions, the creation of a [Great] Russian or Russian Republic CC would bring about the existence of two centers in the Party, and would be contrary to the requirement of centralized leadership of all activities of the CPSU."[31] Each of the union republic parties has its own Central Committee with its set of secretaries, organized in similar fashion to the Party leadership at the center (which we shall examine in Chapter V). Below the union republic party one finds party organizations at the oblast' level (the obkom), at the city level (the gorkom), and finally the raion level (the raikom). The number of party committees at each level and the large number of people who become Party committee members are shown in Table II.1.

[31] B. N. Moralev, Respublikanskie, kraevye, oblastnye, okruzhnye, gorodskie, i raionnye organizatsii partii (Moscow: "Mysl'," 1967), p. 8.

As previously mentioned, the large corps of Party activists is a result of the special legitimizing roles undertaken by the Party. Generally, the Communist Party accepts two legitimizing roles which clearly distinguish it from British parties, and indeed from all parties in the Western democracies. One of these roles is as the director of the entire social, political, and economic life of the country. The other is as the model of character and personal deportment which all Soviet citizens should emulate. Both of these roles come from the Party's ultimate claim to legitimacy, its claim to be the agent, the inspirer, the scientific planner of a conscious, coordinated social development toward an ideal, future communist society. It is this undertaking which justifies—at least to those within the consensus on the Party's legitimacy—the Party's involvement in every and all areas of social life. A good, and in no way unusual, example of the Party's involvement in economic management on all levels is given by the exposé of the shortcomings in the Azerbaidzhan Communist Party which appeared in March 1970. At the highest levels of economic management, the role of the Party is well expressed by the First Secretary of the Azerbaidzhan Party:

> The Azerbaidzhan Communist Party Central Committee will hold those Communists who are Ministers, Deputy Ministers, and executives of republic departments and organizations, as well as officials in the apparatus of the Central Committee and the Council of Ministers, strictly responsible for the state of affairs in their respective branches of the national economy and for improving the style of production management, in an effort to see to it that these officials justify by their deeds the great trust that has been placed in them by the Party and the people.[32]

Even at lower levels, where the work is actually done, the influence of rank-and-file party members is supposed to spur production and vastly improve morale. But we read, in the same account of rampant mischief in the Azerbaidzhan CP, that such great expectations are not always realized:

> One out of every six workers in the Shirvan Oil Field Administrations . . . is a Party member; however, the Party committee and the leadership of the oil field administration have not been able to use these forces for the fulfillment of the state plan. . . . It should be especially emphasized that thirteen of the lagging brigades are headed by Party members. But not one of them has been called to account by the Party organization.[33]

These special functions of the CPSU are intimately connected to its self-defined role as the vanguard of communism, a role which separates the CPSU from the legitimate functions of the British parties. In a sense, the CPSU does everything the British parties do, but it does much more. Its incessant de-

[32] G. A. Aliyev, *Bakinskii rabochii*, March 22, 1970 [*CDSP* XXII, no. 12, p. 3].
[33] *Ibid.*

mand to control, and thereby to systematize, all areas of the "spiritual and material" life of Soviet society has resulted in the establishment of a quasi-governmental (or perhaps better, a supra-governmental) structure within the Party—a situation which has no analog in British practice.

This discussion of party organization has indicated that both British and Soviet parties conform to Robert Michels's famous "iron law of oligarchy": that the nature of party organization inherently leads to oligarchy.[34] However, this view can only be accepted within a definition of oligarchy which includes the high probability that the "oligarchs" *of necessity* are continuously responsive to the needs of lower-ranking party members.

The most important force supporting the leadership against potential dissent or rebellion from within the Party is the functional definition of the Party as a fighting organization. The parties picture themselves as in constant battle, and the Party members are often as strongly motivated to defeat the enemy as they are to achieve any positive goals of the Party.[35] The British parties primarily see themselves as in battle with each other, in which case the enemy is clearly defined. But they may also do battle (especially when in power) with negative aspects of the environment, such as rampant inflation, shortage of housing, or a deficit in the balance of payments. In such cases, the enemy is more abstract and consequently the party rank-and-file is more difficult to organize. In either case, however, the sense of struggle heightens the feeling of party loyalty, which generally increases the power of the party leadership over the membership.

In the Soviet case, the "enemy" is always the relatively abstract set of goals which the Party has established for the country. Because the Party wants and needs to mobilize the entire population in the struggle to achieve these targets, the rhetoric is usually quite militant: "Party members went in the first ranks of fighters during the years of the Civil War, the Second World War, and the building of Socialism; now they unfailingly take on themselves the role of skirmishers in all areas of the building of communism."[36] Occasionally the Party may attempt to vivify the sense of struggle by raising the spectre of a foreign enemy, but in recent times this has been restricted to campaigns against the influence of "alien ideologies," and "decadent bour-

---

[34] See Robert Michels, *Political Parties: A Sociological Study of the Oligarchical Tendencies of Modern Democracy* (New York: The Free Press, 1962).

[35] Michels also described "the modern democratic party as a fighting party, dominated by militarist ideas and methods," but in his analysis the main consideration was that parties had to "conform to the laws of tactics," primarily the need for "facility of mobilization." As he put it: "In the daily struggle, nothing but a certain degree of caesarism will ensure the rapid transmission and the precise execution of orders." This may explain the need for unity of command at the upper levels of the party to some degree, but it hardly serves as an explanation of the tendency toward conformity at the lower levels, where there is precious little participation in such "military" maneuvers. *Ibid.*, pp. 78–79.

[36] *Izvestiia*, December 23, 1969.

geois culture." This is, of course, once again a struggle against an abstraction and thus difficult to sustain with enthusiasm.

POLITICAL FUNCTIONS OF THE PARTIES

The fundamental differences between the CPSU and the British parties that have been described lie in the additional *social* and *economic* roles assumed by the Soviet party. In terms of *political* functions, however, the parties have much more in common. In both societies the party acts as a legitimate link between the masses and the political leadership. The party in this respect acts as an institution which creates a bond of loyalty and common feeling between the leadership and the masses of citizens. Of course, this bond may be very fragile in the case of many citizens, but even when most frail, the party label or party image is usually the channel through which the citizen relates to politics. Another aspect of this function is the role of the parties in mobilizing mass society for periodic political activity. For most people this activity is confined to the act of voting in elections, but even this would be less likely to occur without the constant mobilizing efforts of the parties.

Perhaps more important than this activity is the function of the parties in mobilizing mass public opinion. The issues confronting a modern mass society are often complex, requiring an expertise and experience beyond the ken of the ordinary citizen. Even in the age of the mass media, many citizens may actually be ignorant of numerous problems of greater or lesser magnitude besetting society. In this regard, parties can be seen as simplifying devices, providing points of view, attitudes presumably based on expertise, if not superior wisdom. They thus perform an indispensable function for the political system. By crystallizing and mobilizing opinion, they provide a useful input to the political system. They provide functional participation for citizens who might otherwise sink into apathy or anomic activity born of frustration. This point was made by A. L. Lowell many years ago, when he characterized parties as

> agencies whereby public attention is brought to a focus on certain questions that must be decided. They have become instruments for carrying on popular government by concentrating opinion. Their function is to make the candidates and issues known to the public and to draw people together in large masses, so that they can speak with a united voice, instead of uttering an unintelligible babel of discordant cries.[37]

Modern experience seems to indicate that even without complex issues before the public, the tendency of citizens is to be indifferent to politics.[38]

---

[37] A. Lawrence Lowell, *Public Opinion and Popular Government* (New York: Longmans, Green, 1926), p. 66.

[38] See Seymour Martin Lipset, *Political Man: The Social Bases of Politics* (New York: Doubleday, 1960), pp. 180–219.

The citizen, in Britain as well as the Soviet Union, is primarily concerned with matters that visibly affect his personal existence. For many citizens, political activity begins only when some part of the citizen's private life is challenged or visibly threatened by a political issue.

This retreat into "privatism"—which can mean an emphasis on occupational, professional interests or an emphasis on personal acquisitiveness—has long been noted as a typical reaction of Soviet citizens to the lack of real opportunities to play a meaningful role in politics. It is, in this case, a clear example of escape from the frustration of political impotence—at least this is the most plausible explanation. Such frustrations are undoubtedly heightened by the peculiar nature of the Soviet system which, on the one hand, encourages citizens to take part in activities that are related to politics and, on the other, renders such participation irrelevant to the real concerns of the population. Since the activity encouraged by the Soviet regime is, in effect, an attempt to co-opt the citizen, to make him part of the system through meaningless activity (such as counting ballots), the tendency of many citizens to shirk such symbolically supportive "make-work" may represent a variety of political dissent.

In any case, the "frustration-avoidance" explanation of popular political apathy is relevant to the British case as well, for in the given conditions of a modern mass industrial society is imbedded the simple fact that most citizens cannot play a direct part in political decisions or policies which may vitally affect their interests. The scale and complexity of such a society inherently reduce the role of the citizen—for the most part—to that of a bemused, sometimes bewildered, and occasionally beleaguered onlooker. It is, therefore, an extremely important functional characteristic of political parties that they draw citizens into the system in ways that may provide some form of personal gratification, perhaps a psychic substitute for having real political "clout," or a feeling of affect toward the political system as a compensation for having no political effect. The party provides an identifiable and understandable point of contact with the political system, a vague but persistent image, and a generalized point of view. Those who find politics confusing and frustrating may attach themselves more or less permanently to these attributes of the party as a way out of the dilemma.[39]

In addition to their role in mobilizing the mass public, the British and Soviet parties perform an important role in providing the framework for the emergence of a coherent leadership team. The leadership team in both countries is drawn from a single party, and this party connection provides for all the leaders a background of many years' continuous association in politics.

---

[39] This explanation is certainly not new, having been approximately stated by Graham Wallas in his classic *Human Nature in Politics* in 1908. See 3rd ed. (New York: F. S. Crofts, 1921), p. 103. A more recent explanation of this kind, and empirical data from the American case, appears in Angus Campbell et al., *The American Voter* (New York: John Wiley, 1960), pp. 128 ff.

The ability to work together, the long experience of each other's frailties and peculiarities, the slow and sometimes painful development of an approximate pecking order of authority within the group, and finally the common understanding of the entire group that the interests of each one of them is most surely advanced by their steadfast unity, despite all the forces of rivalries and ambitions which constantly threaten to break them asunder—all this is the product of party associations, for in both countries the way to political leadership is through the party.

In the Soviet Union, as already described, the ladder to political leadership has many rungs of administration in party work; in Great Britain the ladder is primarily one which leads directly from the floor of the House of Commons to the Cabinet Room at 10 Downing Street. While this difference in career ladders may suggest that different kinds of talents are raised up and anointed in the two systems (see Chapter V), the point here is that the party provides an appropriate framework of relationships for potential leaders in both.

Another point to be made here (and elaborated in Chapter V), is that the system of elevation in the hierarchy of the party is essentially one of co-optation: higher ranking leaders reach down and pull up lower ranking leaders for absorption at the higher level. This presumably requires some degree of agreement within the higher ranks, an agreement which is most likely obtained on the basis of the potential colleague's conformity to the standards of the existing group. The procedure of recruitment to political leadership through the party thus greatly increases the probability that the leadership will be cohesive, and better able to handle the tensions and conflicts that must arise within it in the very process of leading.

The party as an organization thus provides a coherent leadership and a relatively loyal and coherent follower-ship, and acts as a link between them. In both countries—to update Bagehot's colorful phrase—it is the party which has become the "efficient secret" of legitimacy for the political system, for it has become the "buckle which binds" the masses to the leadership, permitting the system to be legitimized by concepts of democracy while permitting the leadership to be only indirectly and imperfectly limited by popular will.

Citizens of both countries may identify with the parties and develop loyalties to them—loyalties so fixed they may be passed from generation to generation—but the parties do not thereby gain the legitimacy required to make binding rules for society. The only institution which can legitimately make rules for society is the state, acting through its organizations for administrative rule-making, legislative rule-making, and judicial rule-making. The party may be, and occasionally is, the guiding spirit, the enunciator of principles behind the rules, but the party cannot legitimately enact these rules— even in the Soviet Union.

In Great Britain, where partisan preferences of judges and administrators would be considered illegitimate to the extent that they affected official functions, there is a strong tradition of judicial and administrative neutrality between the parties. This distinction between party and state is important (although not consistently maintained in the Soviet Union) because it permits a rather uneasy and distinctly dialectical blending of two contrary legitimizing doctrines. The state is viewed as an instrument of the whole people, working in its behalf without distinction or discrimination. The party is only a segment of the population, led by an exclusive, co-optive, self-selecting elite. Yet, in symbiotic balance, each requires the other for its very existence. The party in power legitimizes its control of authoritative organs of the state by the doctrine that the people support the ruling party, because it puts forward programs which are based on the people's true interests.

A ruling party in these countries cannot afford to give the appearance of working for its own membership rather than the interests of the whole people, which is why, for example, the Labour Party in office has been less friendly to its trade union supporters than has the Labour Party in opposition. In order to maintain legitimacy, the party in power must be transformed into an instrument of popular will, *in strictly theoretical terms*, so that it can in fact retain its elitist, hierarchical structure within the confines of the "democratic" state. The most important (or powerful) positions in the state structure are distributed without exception to leaders of the ruling party, the decision being made by the party leader (and thus Prime Minister) in the British case, and by the Politburo and Secretaries of the Central Committee in the CPSU.

Nothing in this is conspiratorial, nor should one assume a necessary evil in it. In both countries, the state structure has achieved a high degree of consensus on its legitimacy. People apparently accept the necessity of open domination of the government by a single party in return for coherence of policy and strength and consistency of leadership. The party in power does not always deliver its part of this tacit political contract, but it is difficult to imagine any better performance in the absence of a single dominant party in government. The alternation of parties in British government may help it to achieve the requisite strength, as the tired, "used up" team is replaced by a fresh new bunch from time to time. In the one-party Soviet system, there is no mechanism for sweeping out the less vigorous leaders, who simply fade away in their years of decline.[40]

PARTY CONVERGENCE AND PARTY COMPETITION

The high degree of consensus of British society has over the years brought the two major parties ever closer together in their goals, tactics, policy positions,

---

[40]This seems to be the tendency in recent years for all Soviet leaders save the General-Secretary of the CPSU. Other leaders, such as Voroshilov or Mikoyan, have been eased out of decisive positions as the aging process has taken its toll.

and even philosophy. In the late 1920's, the leader of the Labour Party could write that the Party, "unlike other parties, is not concerned with patching the rents in a bad system, but with transforming Capitalism into Socialism."[41] Today, having had two experiences in the art and responsibility of governing, the Labour Party has turned away from its earlier goal of a fundamental transformation of society, and has been engrossed in "patching the rents" of the mixed-economy welfare state with which it has become identified. The Conservative Party, having been terrified by Labour ideologists of the 1930's such as Harold Laski, who predicted the overthrow of Capitalism (the very dearest thing to the Conservatives), has now accepted the basic premises of the welfare state, and in some ways has been more dynamic than the Labour Party in advocating change.

There are several possible explanations for this convergence of the British parties around the center point of British politics. One argument that is often advanced is that the two-party system in a consensual society tends toward such centripetal motion because each party is competing for a majority of popular opinion at the center. Thus, in competing for the same votes, they are forced to make the same appeals, or quiet the same fears. (In a moment of self-critical reflection, the Conservative Party Chairman was reported to have said: "Our party's preoccupation with the so-called middle ground of politics has led us too often to fail to present to the nation our themes in a sufficiently distinctive form."[42]) The existence of only two dominant parties in Great Britain has been variously attributed to a natural tendency of society to divide into two alternatives, a peculiarly British attitude toward politics, the working of the British electoral system (which certainly disadvantages third parties such as the Liberal Party), and finally as an example of the good Lord's benevolence to the British people—of which there are admittedly many examples.[43]

Another explanation of the convergence of British parties is that the emphasis on attaining power by achieving a majority in the House of Commons forces the parties to accommodate a wide range of interest groups, and that the aggregation of so many interests tends to make party programs diffuse, contradictory, overly cautious, and quite similar to each other. This sameness is noted by Samuel Beer, who writes:

> Each party when seeking power must bid for the votes of many of the same consumers' groups and when in power must bargain with much the same set of producers' groups. These are the hard realities of getting

[41] A statement by Ramsay MacDonald in 1928, as quoted by Samuel H. Beer in *British Politics in the Collectivist Age* (New York: Alfred A. Knopf, 1966), p. 136.

[42] Edward Du Cann, as quoted in *The Times* (London), September 9, 1968.

[43] "When, in after-dinner speeches, or in text-books, or even in this book, we lift our eyes to heaven and give thanks (as we should) for the providential gift of an official Opposition, we should also recall that God helps only those who help themselves . . ." Henry Fairlie, *The Life of Politics* (London: Methuen, 1968), p. 199.

elected and of governing. Together they have worked to promote a convergence of party program, greatly lessening the ideological distance between Socialist and Conservative.[44]

This view of the parties' convergence, based on the aggregation of wide-ranging interests, assumes a society that is at once consensual in basic values and yet divided into a plethora of interest groups whose immediate objectives are contradictory. By accommodating these contrary interests, the parties' programs become muddled. To quote one supporter of this view:

> To win, [the parties] must seek to mirror in some degree the whole country; they must contain minorities of their opponents' majorities. They must be ecumenical. To preserve the unity that is imperative, differences have to be tolerated. The breadth of their support and their fear of alienating the narrow segment which makes the difference between victory and defeat inhibits them from risking offence. They may integrate opinion almost out of existence. By the time all the compromises have been made, ambiguity is rampant.[45]

A third explanation concerns the predilection of Britishers to reduce the intensity of any conflict by assuming an over-all harmony of interests, and then reducing immediate issues to a common view by bargaining and compromise, combined with unemotional practicality. The critique that can be coupled with this view is that "the absence of conflict causes weakness. The essence of the British political system is that it is more important to travel peacefully than to arrive."[46] On the other hand, one can take the more approving view of the British political scientist, David Butler, that while British parties "are not very different from each other," still the British "should be thankful that their parties have such similar policies and such untrammelled oligarchies."[47] The basis for this satisfaction with the happy state of British politics is summed up in Lord Balfour's comment that "our whole political machinery presupposes a people so fundamentally at one that they can safely afford to bicker."[48] Thus, according to this view, the unity of British society leads the parties toward ever more intimate togetherness, but neither the cause nor the effect should be despised—on the contrary, they should be the envy of other countries where deep divisions split the populace into hostile camps.

Yet another explanation of the parties' convergence is derived from the shared experience of the major British parties of governmental power, both

[44] Samuel H. Beer, "The Comparative Method and the Study of British Politics," *Comparative Politics* I, no. 1 (October 1968), p. 27.

[45] Ian Gilmour, *The Body Politic* (London: Hutchinson, 1969), p. 61.

[46] *Ibid.*, p. 14.

[47] David Butler, "American Myths About British Parties," in Andrew J. Milnor ed., *Comparative Political Parties: Selected Readings* (New York: Thomas Y. Crowell, 1969), pp. 283, 286.

[48] *Ibid.*

its sweet pleasures and its bitter disappointments. Both parties know the limitations of political power, the inertia of a vast governmental machine, the intractable obstinacy of problems which refuse to go away and refuse to be solved. Thus the experience of power breeds responsibility, and the responsibility of power breeds caution, if not timidity. By severely limiting their programs to "the art of the possible," the parties simply tinker with different details of the established system.

Finally, it can be argued that the reason for the convergence of the British parties is the middle-class origin of their leaders. According to this argument, the Labour Party has lost its socialism and working-class virtue by being captured by middle-class intellectuals and professionals, who are more adept at political communication, more knowledgeable about the issues, more fitting objects of lower-class deference, etc. Those Labour leaders who still believe in the older, working-class-based program of the Labour Party can be rather bitter about the change in the party's center of gravity:

> It is all very well to have the consensus of the middle class but unless you can maintain the support of your old traditional supporters, then you are in grave difficulty. . . . There's almost a death wish on the part of some constituency parties, that the ordinary fellow who's smelt the bottom of the pit, who has spent dirty nights in marshalling-yards, somehow is not equipped to deal with the problems of politics as the academic is.[49]

From the opposite pole, the Conservative Party has been gradually transformed from a vehicle for the old establishment Toryism to a party of the new Conservatism of business expertise and management efficiency and middle-class values. It has, in fact, scored its greatest success in projecting an image of itself as the party of skilled managers, most likely to bring prosperity to Britain. (It has campaigned in recent elections under such slogans as "Life's better with the Conservatives" and "Conservatives give you a better standard of living.")

Thus, according to this hypothesis, the two parties come together not so much on the middle ground of politics, as on the middle-class bias of politics in Britain. (This is the predictable view of Soviet writers, who see both parties as representing the interests of the ruling bourgeoisie.[50])

While all of these hypotheses have some merit, they are all more suggestive than conclusive. Yet running through all these arguments is a common thread: the parties, in competing for sufficient votes to win governmental

---

[49] From an interview with Ray Gunter, who had resigned from the Labour Government. *The Listener*, July 11, 1968.

[50] A Soviet analysis of the 1970 British election campaign stated: "The programs with which the English Labourites and Conservatives stand for election are on all important questions the same in principle (although there are small nuances of difference). This is true of both British foreign and domestic policy. Therefore, the English, who usually prefer one of the two parties (such is the strength of tradition and inertia), have, in practical terms, no choice." Vladimir Ermakov, in *Pravda*, June 7, 1970.

power, have made adjustments which are calculated to enhance electoral success. This judgment of political gain is in conformity with the party's legitimate functions, for it assures the party's continuing sensitivity to the tides of opinion and changing material conditions. When Hugh Gaitskell, after successive Labour defeats, attempted to turn the Party from its traditional doctrinaire appeals to a new image, he used precisely this sort of argument:

> Above all our object must be to broaden our base, to be in touch always with ordinary people, to avoid becoming small cliques of isolated doctrine-ridden fanatics out of touch with the main stream of social life in our time. We should be missionaries, not monks, a mass party not a conspiratorial group.[51]

Given a common political environment, electoral calculations such as these have tended to decrease the distance between the parties, with the Liberal Party being squeezed almost out of existence within the crushing embrace of the two giants. This is not a new phenomenon in British history— at the turn of the century, Ostrogorski provided much the same sort of description of the Conservative and Liberal parties:

> An important phenomenon is appearing: the political parties are more and more losing their distinctive characteristics. . . . No longer representing clearly defined opposing principles, no longer having a monopoly, the one of progress, the other of reaction, the one of solicitude for the masses, the other of aristocratic or capitalist privilege, the parties as such tend to become simple aggregates, drawn together, by the attractive force of a leader, for the conquest or the preservation of power.[52]

The amount of basic agreement between the two parties is quite remarkable. There are no substantial differences in principle concerning foreign policy, the welfare state, the extent of nationalization of the economy, the relationship between church and state, or the internal organization of the state. Differences between the parties do arise on specific legislation, particularly if it affects the two distinct client groups of the parties: labor and management; and one can differentiate subtle differences of view toward the political process which seem to characterize the parties in general.[53] Nevertheless, such distinctions seem to play a slight and discernibly decreasing part in the behavior of the two British parties. Things have indeed been turned about when the Labour Party, once the advocate of thoroughgoing trans-

---

[51] *Report of the Fifty-Eighth Annual Conference of the Labour Party* (London: The Labour Party, 1960), p. 107.

[52] M. Ostrogorski, *Democracy and the Organization of Political Parties* (Chicago: Quadrangle Books, 1964), p. 331. The original edition was published in 1902.

[53] See Samuel Beer's excellent discussion of these differing philosophies in *British Politics in the Collectivist Age*, Chapter III.

formation of capitalism into socialism, can aptly be described by *The Economist* as "a good guardian of a stable and cohesive society."[54]

Behind the convergence of British parties lies the consensus of British society. It is, to a great extent, a self-satisfied consensus, and thus one which is likely to resist calls for sudden or substantial change. To some extent, this conservative consensus may be a symptom of success of the system in sufficiently providing the needs of the population—sufficient, that is, to give these groups an interest in preserving much of the status quo. Indeed, this process may be taking place in many relatively developed industrial societies.[55]

In terms of policy, a system based on widespread consensus has both its good and bad side. As Robert Dahl notes: "High-consensus polities are able to give relatively rational consideration to small changes but they are prone to ignore the possible advantages of radical changes in the status quo."[56] When the matter concerns small changes, the careful observer can usually detect a *marginal differentiation* between the policies of the two parties. This marginal differentiation is sufficient to enable one to speak of nuances or differing emphases in policies, but when the matter concerns radical change, the major parties are equally likely to shun quantum leaps, and in this they are supported by the overwhelming consensus of British society.

It is precisely these characteristics which bring the British party system close in effect to the Soviet system. A system in which two hierarchical parties formulate marginally differentiated policies, based on an established consensus in society, bears some resemblance to a system in which one party, hierarchically organized, but consisting of marginally differentiable interest groups, formulates policies based on an established consensus that has been largely structured by the Party itself.[57] In both cases, the existence of a consensus establishes limits beyond which no party will want to tread, because they are limits on the range of solutions that the party and society would accept as legitimate. The consensus is ultimately one of judgments on the limits of legitimate action to which the parties and the populace subscribe.

---

[54] *The Economist*, May 30, 1970, p. 17.

[55] According to Andrew J. Milnor: "Within each of the major democracies throughout the developed world there has been emerging over the past two decades a pattern of social and economic organization that has created increased internal agreement on policy goals. The decline of old arguments and the rise of new social groups with a high degree of agreement on national purpose had led to the possibility of a new kind of political life: the politics, not of reconciliation of absolutely divergent views, but of the technical pursuit of relatively accepted goals." Milnor, *Comparative Political Parties*, pp. 365–66.

[56] Robert A. Dahl, "Epilogue," in Dahl, ed., *Political Oppositions in Western Democracies* (New Haven: Yale University Press, 1966), p. 392.

[57] The policy-making implications of the party systems will be discussed in Chapter V.

The existence of a competitive two-party system does, however, provide some important benefits. It does provide public discussion and information on the marginal differences between the major parties—which in a high-consensus society may be the only relevant differences. The Soviet system tends to camouflage, if not entirely cover up the marginal differences which are the substance of its politics. Open discussion undoubtedly serves to bring more views into the arena and enhances the probability that reasonable and effective conclusions will be reached. Secondly, it may be argued that the existence of electoral competition between parties forces the parties to be more responsive to public opinion, at least once every four or five years. Although the British parties have been generally responsive to long-term popular pressures, they have both been far from craven instruments of those pressures—as is evidenced by their common stand, against popular opinion, in favor of British entry into the European Common Market.

As previously discussed, neither the British parties nor the Soviet party view their role as merely registering the fancies of the mass public. They rather see themselves as reflecting the best interests of the population, even, occasionally, against its will. Of course, the Soviet party has greater leeway in enforcing its own view of the public interest, for the absence of an opposition prevents any group from capitalizing on the unpopularity of party policy.

A more substantial advantage inherent in the two-party system is the possibility, and in fact inevitability, of replacing the top political leadership when its ideas and energies have been drained by a period of years in power. Indeed, the relative longevity of Soviet leadership can be viewed as a primary problem and deficiency of the system. Any leadership group, no matter how talented and fortunate, will accumulate mistakes that must be rectified, as well as past successes which must be adjusted to changing conditions. A relatively permanent leadership, however, becomes personally identified with past decisions and commitments which weigh heavily against its continued flexibility in meeting the changes of a modern industrial society. Furthermore, the continued experience of power may lead to complacency, if not euphoria, as the leadership tends to place the best possible interpretation on its past performance.

In the Soviet case, past mistakes can be blamed on lower officials, who are always available in incredibly large numbers as convenient scapegoats. The top leadership cannot be criticized by any other group in the system, and as a result of a developing interest in mutual security at the top, there may be very little criticism from within. The British leadership, on the other hand, is perpetually saved from the dangers of euphoria, and made painfully aware of its deficiencies, by the incessant, sharply pointed criticism of the opposing party.

Finally, the existence of two parties permits one of the leadership teams the luxury of an extended period in opposition for reflection on the long-term problems of the system, the unmet needs of the population, the missed opportunities of the past, and the waiting opportunities of the future—time to reflect on the larger picture of politics without the burdens of governmental responsibility or day-to-day administration. The regular recurrence of a period in opposition—no matter how painful it may seem to the party faithful on the morning after an unsuccessful election—may be as important to the party and as functional to the political system as the alternating periods in power. Thus Harold Wilson's remark to the recently defeated Parliamentary Labour Party in June 1970: "This Parliament provides an opportunity for the party to refresh its thinking, ideals and policies. We must prepare to be in government again."[58]

Despite this potential advantage, it must be added that British parties in opposition are subject to the same inexorable constraints of a conservative societal consensus as when in power. Great changes will most likely be eschewed because they will not help the party's chances of returning to power. A period of opposition is more likely to produce a realistic set of short-term programs to meet problems that arose in the previous administration, and a new set of party leaders, as the opposition party cleans out the dead and dying wood from its upper ranks in preparation for a new assault on the summit of power. Here again, the effect of a high-consensus society is to de-emphasize policy differences and re-emphasize personality differences. The question in Britain is usually less which policy is best, than which set of men is best—best equipped to carry through the policies roughly defined by the consensus view of Britain's major problems. Thus, while the British two-party system usually does not offer significant policy choices for citizens, it does offer a choice of leadership teams with somewhat different sets of priorities in setting public policy. This may not be everything that theories of democracy require, but it does provide a legitimate procedure for the renewal of leadership and succession to political power.

In contrast, one of the most grave problems of the Soviet system is the absence of a legitimate procedure for the removal of political leaders who have demonstrated, beyond any doubt, the desirability of their speedy retirement. In contrast to the British system:

1. the leaders are chosen and replaced without any involvement of the population;
2. the leaders are changed individually rather than in alternate teams;
3. removal of a leader before dotage and senility requires hostile action of his colleagues;
4. the procedures for replacement of leaders are shrouded by secrecy; thus uncertainty about the procedures continues and the legitimacy of the leaders is consequently diminished.

[58]*The New York Times*, June 30, 1970.

As discussed earlier, a sense of legitimacy about a political office can only be established if the procedure by which men achieve that office is accepted as legitimate. This condition holds for the British Cabinet, for it results indirectly from the electoral process. It does not hold, however, for any member of the Politburo, and because of this, the role of the Politburo in politics is almost entirely ignored in the Soviet press, and primary legitimacy is officially attached instead to the Party as a whole. This discrepancy between legitimacy and reality creates a "credibility gap" for the Soviet leadership, a gap that can only superficially be papered over by the continuous flow of newsprint extolling the monolithic and democratic Party.

In both the British and Soviet political systems, the party provides political leadership and raises men to the pinnacle of the political system by a process that is private and privileged. In the Soviet Union, the privacy is maintained right to the top in the Politburo. In Great Britain, at the penultimate step, the public is called in to make a choice. From this difference comes the British success in legitimizing *elitist* political leadership in a state system legitimized by *democratic* theories. And from this difference comes the Soviet difficulty in legitimizing elitist leadership in a state system that proclaims itself "the most democratic in the world."

The differences in style and method of leadership in these two countries can at least be partially explained by the existence of competitive parties in Britain, and the lack of such parties in the Soviet Union. Despite the differences that flow from this distinction, however, the party in both countries performs an essentially similar function: it links the leadership to a mass following and provides a basis in legitimacy for the relationship between the leaders and their many followers.

Representative
Assemblies

*History shows abundantly that men in society long not
only for success, prosperity and the implementation of
their wishes, collectively and individually, but also for
legitimacy in government and institutions. Parliament
provides this legitimacy and were respect for it to be
diminished, the parliamentary idea on which many of
our liberties and our society of tolerance depend might
be in danger.*

Ronald Butt,
The Power of Parliament

Within rather different interpretations of the terms, both
the Soviet and British governments rest their case for
legitimacy on the principle that "the people rule" and
that this popular rule is expressed through *representative
organs of government.* As we have already noted, the
party systems are an expression of a basically contrary,
elitist concept of the system. The parties become means
by which the mass of the population can be organized
behind a leadership group, can develop affective ties of
loyalty to the leadership, and thus become allegiant subjects of the system theoretically founded on their sovereignty. This paradoxical situation is resolved—or partially resolved—by the concept of representation of the
people. The primary organs of government through
which this concept is expressed are the Supreme Soviet
of the U.S.S.R. and the British House of Commons.[1]

[1] The House of Lords is of less interest in this regard because
it is not based on any discernible principle of popular representation and has, therefore, suffered a severe crisis of legitimacy, and
consequent loss of power, in this century.

It would be difficult to find two more apparently unlikely subjects for comparison than these two institutions of popular government. The present House of Commons has emerged from an almost continuous sequence of epic struggles with a succession of kings, with Cromwell, and with the aristocratic principle embodied in the House of Lords. With the advent of the industrialized society and new theories of governmental legitimacy, it reached its zenith of powers in the nineteenth century, at a time when Russia was still struggling to free itself from autocratic tsarist rule and a semi-feudal, fully primitive agrarian system.

The U.S.S.R. Supreme Soviet dates back, in its present form, only to 1936, and there is no historical precedent for it whatsoever before 1905. It thus has not even seventy years of history behind it, a great poverty of tradition beside the seven centuries of British parliamentary history. Its history is not only short—it is undistinguished. Born in the midst of the great and terrible Stalin purges, it seemed at first a cruel jest. As we shall see, it was conceived as a parliament in some ways similar to the British structural model, with the chief difference being that it was intended not only to represent the people, but to provide a public demonstration of the presumed unity of the people on every issue. It ably performed this rite whenever called upon, and survived the vicissitudes of Stalin's reign without many scars or any notable accomplishments. Such discussions as were held at its infrequent and irregularly scheduled meetings were perfunctory, apparently stage-managed by a heavy-handed director. In its first three decades of existence, it was called into session only 45 times—despite the constitutional requirement that it meet at least semiannually— and "decided" a total of only 169 matters put on its agenda.[2] Despite this relative inactivity, or more likely because of it, the Supreme Soviet survived Stalin, and became available to the post-Stalin leadership as a potential vehicle for the enhanced legitimacy it needed. Since Stalin, and especially since Khrushchev (who was opposed to enlarging the role of the soviets), the Supreme Soviet has made a modest—but in terms of past history, impressive—comeback as an institution with more than purely symbolic functions.

In comparing the formal constitutional framework within which the Supreme Soviet and British Parliament operate, it should be kept in mind that neither actually operates completely in accordance with the formal relationships established for it. In both cases, the constitutional requirements may

---

[2] R. I. Kulik, A. I. Luk'ianov, B. P. Tokmakov, *Vysshii organ narodnoi vlasti* (Moscow: Gosiurizdat, 1966), p. 15. According to another source, the Supreme Soviet passed 564 "acts" during this period, but 265 of these were simply confirmations of previously announced decrees and many others were awards of honors and medals. See V. I. Vasil'ev and F. I. Kalinchev (eds.), *Verkhovnyi sovet SSSR*, (Moscow: Izdatel'stvo "Izvestiia," 1967), p. 37.

serve certain symbolic functions related to the need for regime legitimacy, rather than serve as rules defining relationships and processes of government in actual practice, although the Supreme Soviet does seem more engrossed with symbolic legitimizing functions than the British Parliament.

In order to achieve maximum possible clarity in this comparison, some aspects of the constitutional basis of these two representative bodies must be discussed before proceeding to an analysis of their present functions in the political structure.

ORGANIZATION OF THE PEOPLE'S REPRESENTATIVES

In formal terms, the constitutional organization of the Soviet political system is surprisingly similar to the British. Both are parliamentary systems, in which the unity (rather than the separation) of power is stressed. At the head of the Soviet Government stands the Council of Ministers, formally equivalent to the British Cabinet. According to the Soviet Constitution, the Council of Ministers is "the highest executive and administrative organ" of the Soviet Government, and true to parliamentary form, it is "appointed" by the legislature, the Supreme Soviet. Although there is no specific constitutional requirement to do so, the ministers are all chosen from the membership of the Supreme Soviet, thus preserving another fundamental requisite of the parliamentary form: that members of the executive be drawn from the legislature.

In practice, the composition of the Council of Ministers is submitted for the characteristically unanimous approval of each newly elected Supreme Soviet. The list has been drawn up elsewhere (no doubt in the Politburo of the CPSU), and there is no discussion of it in the Supreme Soviet before approval. Changes in the personnel of the Council of Ministers during the long intervals between sessions of the Supreme Soviet are approved by the Presidium of the Supreme Soviet "on the recommendation of the Chairman of the Council of Ministers" (Art. 49), who is equivalent to the Prime Minister. Such changes are ratified, again without debate, at the next regular session of the full Supreme Soviet. While the original list of ministers presented every four years to each new Supreme Soviet contains only Supreme Soviet deputies, replacements and additions to the Council of Ministers during the interim before the next elections are not necessarily members of the Supreme Soviet.[3] One might say that an attempt is made to conform to the niceties of parliamentary form, but when such adherence becomes too inconvenient, the

[3] For example, of the four new ministers in the construction industry appointed in February, 1967 (*Pravda*, February 22, 1967), only two (A. M. Tokarev and S. D. Khitrov) were members of the Supreme Soviet. Both probably had been made members in recognition of their important posts as *obkom* (party province committee) first secretaries.

niceties are overlooked. First deputy and lower-ranking junior ministers are rarely members of the Supreme Soviet, and then no doubt only coincidentally.

British constitutional practice, which created the parliamentary model, also adheres more closely to it. Senior ministers, whether in the Cabinet or out (in the larger group known as the Government) are always members of one of the houses of Parliament. A seat in the Parliament must be found, one way or another, for any appointee who has not had the benefit of such high honor.

If the position is important, a seat must be found (with few exceptions) in the House of Commons, by making the prospective cabinet member stand for election to a vacant seat in a by-election. It is also possible (since 1958) to create a Life Peerage in the House of Lords for those who will not or cannot be enticed into an election, but this technique has not been used very often and would in any case be inappropriate for a few important Cabinet posts, since there is a strong and growing sentiment against removing important ministers from the scene of the major debates in the Commons.

The constitutional question of which ministers *must* sit in the Commons is not entirely clear. Here, as elsewhere, the British constitution is in a state of flux, and no precise determination of its present position can be made. By long-established precedent, the Chancellor of the Exchequer must sit in the Commons, and the Lord Chancellor (a member of the Cabinet) must sit as presiding officer in the Lords. Since 1923, when Lord Curzon was passed over for the prime-ministership in favor of the commoner, Stanley Baldwin, it has been established that the Prime Minister must sit in the House of Commons, symbolizing his direct responsibility to the people's representatives. This requirement does not seem to hold for other Cabinet posts, with the possible exception of the Foreign Secretary (officially the Secretary of State for Foreign Affairs).

When Lord Home (later Prime Minister as Sir Alec Douglas-Home) was appointed Foreign Secretary in the Macmillan government in 1960, the Labour opposition made a strong protest that this was a violation of constitutional principle, since the Foreign Secretary would, by virtue of his peerage, be unable to sit in the House of Commons. As Hugh Gaitskell, then leader of the Labour opposition, put it: "Foreign affairs concern the lives and destinies of all of us today. They are not a subject about which it is the prerogative or privilege of a few people to argue."[4]

Gaitskell's "few people," of course, were those who sit in the House of Lords, a body of men without any legitimized representative function. Since the modern British constitution is centered on the legitimizing concept of

[4] 627 *H. C. Debates* 1974 (July 28, 1960)

governmental responsibility to the people, either directly through elections or indirectly through representation in the Commons, the presence of a minister in the House of Lords does not seem to conform to current standards of political legitimacy. Symbolically, it removes a governmental function (performed by a particular ministry) from responsibility to the people. It is in terms of this symbolism that we must understand Gaitskell's remark (made in the course of the same adjournment debate) that "the Foreign Secretary should be in the House of Commons because, in representing our democracy abroad, his prestige must rest on his position at the heart of our democracy at home, in this Chamber."[5]

In practical terms, however, the effects of placing a head of a ministry in the Lords do not seem particularly significant. In this case, a junior minister (or Cabinet member without portfolio) is appointed to represent the department in Commons debates and to bear the burden of defending department policy. Even those ministers who sit in Commons often delegate responsibility for debates to their juniors, because of the press of administrative matters. If the matter is one of Government responsibility, which is often the case, other members of the Cabinet, including the Prime Minister, can be brought in to defend policies in the Commons, while the noble Lord in charge of the department debates—in more polite and restrained terms—with his noble foes in "the other place." For example, when Lord Halifax was briefly made Foreign Secretary in 1938, the Prime Minister, Neville Chamberlain, undertook to represent the Government in all matters of foreign policy in the House of Commons,[6] and in the case of Lord Home in 1960, Macmillan appointed the Lord Privy Seal (who was then Edward Heath, a member of the Cabinet without specific departmental responsibilities) as "deputy to the Foreign Secretary over the whole field of Foreign Office business."[7] During ordinary times, therefore, the practical consequences of placing a ministry in the hands of a peer do not seem worthy of much anxiety.

It is true, however, that on those rare occasions when the personal responsibility of a minister is at question, his enforced absence from the Commons could create difficulties, and there is the practical problem, pointed out by Sir Ivor Jennings, that "the conduct of Government business in the House of Commons is such an onerous task that the absence of an important minister places a considerable burden on the rest."[8] There are additional considerations which dictate that the majority of ministers will be drawn from the membership of the House of Commons. In choosing the members of his

[5]*Ibid.*

[6]332 *H. C. Debates*, 5 S., 747 (February 28, 1938).

[7]627 *H. C. Debates* 1999 (July 28, 1960).

[8]Sir Ivor Jennings, *Cabinet Government*, 3rd. ed. (Cambridge, England: Cambridge University Press, 1961), p. 60.

Cabinet, any Prime Minister will want to find men who have achieved some degree of eminence within the party, and some degree of public prominence. If he does not, he will be open to criticism from the Opposition and to grumbling from within his own party.[9] Most of those who have achieved importance in the party have done so through a career in the House of Commons, which is the center of the contemporary political stage, and not in the House of Lords, which is off to the side. The Prime Minister's choices, which in large measure are predetermined by the political standing of his colleagues, must follow political necessities.[10]

Modern practice, therefore, has been to include a preponderance of MPs in the Cabinet, with the tendency accentuated during Labour Governments and reduced during Conservative Governments.[11] The principle that the Government be drawn from the Parliament is preserved, with only the usual British toleration for temporary lapses from principle. Gladstone, Ramsay MacDonald, and General Smuts all held Cabinet positions for a period of months without being members of Parliament, and in recent times Mr. Patrick Gordon-Walker was Foreign Secretary for slightly more than three months without having a seat in the House of Commons.

The Gordon-Walker case is useful for illustrating the limits of British toleration for violations of constitutional practice, and for distinguishing between this rather sensible flexibility and the usual Soviet approach of ignoring constitutional principles which get in the way. Despite the narrow Labour victory in the elections of October 1964, Mr. Gordon-Walker, who had been the MP from Smethwick for almost twenty years, lost his seat to the Conservative candidate. In spite of this setback to his career, he was appointed Foreign Secretary in the new Labour Government the very next day. By January, the sitting member for Leyton had been persuaded to move to "the other place" (the House of Lords, not Heaven—although the two are apparently sometimes confused and may, indeed, resemble each other). Leyton was considered a "safe" constituency because it had just returned a Labour plurality of over three thousand votes, and the assumption was that the new

---

[9]When the relatively unknown Lord Home was appointed Foreign Secretary, Gaitskell asked in derision: "Is it really very difficult to find somebody qualified by experience and ability to hold this position who at the same time is a supporter of the Prime Minister's policy? Can he defend this appointment on the grounds that it is exceptional because he really cannot find anybody else for the job?" See 627 *H. C. Debates* 1977 (July 28, 1960).

[10]See Chapter IV for more details on the selection procedure. It should be mentioned here that three ministers in addition to the Lord Chancellor must be appointed from the House of Lords in each Government, according to the Ministers of the Crown Act, 1937.

[11]For example, in the MacMillan Government of 1960, four peers were designated members of the 19-member Cabinet; the Wilson Government of 1965 contained only two peers in a Cabinet of 23 members.

Foreign Secretary would take his seat in the Commons on January 22nd, directly after the results of the by-election had been certified. This assumption that only a temporary delay was involved, that the outcome was a certainty, seemed to satisfy constitutional scruples on both sides of the aisle in Commons. Just two weeks before the elections, *The Times* reported: "They are holding what is meant to be a one-horse race here. . . . The purpose is to provide the Foreign Secretary with a parliamentary seat. The result of the by-election is in no material doubt." This expectation carried right through to the day of the election (January 21), when *The Times* reported that "some erosion of the Labour vote seems certain," but was far short of predicting the actual result—which was a defeat for the Foreign Secretary by a scant 205 votes. Since the Labour Party had gone on record, during the debate on Lord Home's appointment, as opposed to the designation of a Foreign Secretary from the House of Lords, there was no possibility of creating a peerage for Gordon-Walker, and he was forced to resign.[12]

Several points emerge from the experience of Gordon-Walker and Lord Home as Foreign Secretaries:

1. the principle is well-established and absolute that members of the Government must be drawn from the Parliament;
2. temporary departures from this rule are permissible as long as there is some assurance that the principle will be re-established in a definite and reasonably short time;
3. it is possible for ministers, except the Prime Minister and Chancellor of the Exchequer, to be drawn from the House of Lords, but the Labour Party's constitutional objections to the appointment of a peer as Foreign Secretary make it rather unlikely that even a Conservative Government will make such an appointment in the future. In this case, the constitutional requirements for the office of Foreign Secretary are in process of transition toward a new definition that is not yet determined, and this evolutionary process is quite typical of British constitutional development as a whole.

It should be pointed out that Lord Home was able to become Prime Minister by disclaiming his peerage under special terms of the Peerage Act, 1963. However, this possibility is not open to future peers who apply for membership in the House of Lords or hold a peerage for more than 12 months. Thus, those who have created a distinguished record in the Lords must remain there to the bitter end.

Both Soviet and British Parliaments are bicameral, but beyond the simple presence of two houses in each case, there are considerable differences in

---

[12]Even after Gordon-Walker's defeat, however, *The Times* (January 22, 1965) suggested the possibility that Harold Wilson would become his own Foreign Secretary until "a really safe seat was found" for Gordon-Walker.

both reality and theory. The distinction between the two Councils of the Supreme Soviet is one of a difference in the basis of representation; the distinction between the two British Houses is that one of them is not representative at all—nor is it intended to be.

Of 1,018 members of the House of Lords in 1965, 883 were hereditary peers, and 100 were life peers appointed by the government under the Life Peerages Act (1958). There were also 9 Law Lords (who discharge the Lords' judicial function as the ultimate appellate court of the realm) and 26 clerics of the established Anglican Church. None are elected, none can be said to represent any particular group or locality in society except as an indirect outcome of their background and voluntary desire to do so. They are all members of a broadly defined "elite," with careers spanning the range from manufacturing to the military. Life peers, of which there were 119 in 1966, were drawn mainly from political careers, 51 being former M.P.'s and another 16 being former party workers. Educators accounted for another 19 and there were 9 company directors. Most of the life peers and a number of hereditary peers form a nucleus of expertise upon which the House of Lords draws heavily in its role as an auxiliary unit of the Commons, relieving the Commons of a portion of a very heavy work-load. The functions of the House of Lords spring directly from the rather peculiar composition of its membership. Less than one-fifth of its members attend sessions on any given day, and about 150 members regularly devote themselves to the work of the House.[13] This small group forms a core of "elder statesmen," generally combining considerable experience and expertise in various walks of public life with a degree of relative detachment from party warfare—a combination which makes them particularly useful to the system. Because of its expertise, the House of Lords can help to remove deficiencies in bills through detailed examination in committee, and it can conveniently add amendments accepted in principle by the Government during the Commons debate, if the bill has been rushed through the Commons before reaching the Lords. Because of its relative detachment from partisan and electoral considerations, it can provide, through debate, a forum for independent and often cogent analysis of public issues, particularly issues which the Commons prefers to avoid, or must avoid because of time pressure. The House of Lords also has a special role in tackling delicate issues of public and private morality which politicians prefer to bypass. As J. R. Vincent puts it: "The House of Lords is . . . by consent, and by default, the government department . . . principally concerned with modifications of moral tradition, and for effecting and interpreting the general will or general complaisance (or general self-mistrust) of powerful men on

---

[13] In the session of 1965–66, only 163 peers attended more than half the sittings of the House. Peter Bromhead and Donald Shell, "The Lords and Their House," *Parliamentary Affairs* XX, no. 4 (Autumn 1967), p. 338.

questions such as the Abortion Bill."[14] The noble Lords need not fear the wrath of an offended local electorate or constituency party organization, and they can, therefore, afford to tread fearlessly on timeless totems and taboos. It is this possibility, and not the literary quality and high intelligence which sometimes (although certainly not always) characterizes House of Lords debates, that makes the Lords a valuable chamber. On a number of issues such as abortion, capital punishment, homosexuality, and divorce, the Lords have sometimes (again not always) been less conservative than the Commons.

The Lords' function as a legislative revising chamber, however, is open to serious criticisms. The introduction of non-controversial bills in the House of Lords may be a real convenience and may help to spread the work-load of the Commons over the sessional year, but it can hardly be seen as a real saving of Commons time. As S. A. Walkland mentions: "In the Session 1951-52, the House of Commons spent eight times as long on the committee and Report stages of Lords' Bills than the Lords had done."[15] On the basis of this and other data supplied by Peter Bromhead,[16] he concludes that "it does not seem to be the case that the Commons is willing to rely implicitly on the Lords' handling of legislative detail."[17] Examination of Lords' amendments to Government bills by J. R. Vincent reveals that they steadily declined in quantity from 996 in the session of 1946-47 to 203 in the session of 1964-65.[18] More important than this is the finding that most amendments amount to minor changes in wording rather than matters of substance. As Vincent puts it, most amendments accepted by Government and incorporated in bills in the House of Lords "are not the work of lynx-eyed elder statesmen ruthlessly scrutinising the work of the parliamentary draftsmen. They are the work of the draftsmen and officials, dotting the i's and crossing the t's of their work with rare pendantry and refinement."[19]

On the other hand, some of those who are critical of the present composition of the House of Lords, such as Bernard Crick, find the work of the Lords useful, and in fact indispensable to the efficient working of Parliament, pre-

[14] J. R. Vincent, "The House of Lords," *Parliamentary Affairs* XIX, no. 4 (Autumn 1966), p. 484.

[15] S. A. Walkland, *The Legislative Process in Great Britain* (London: Allen and Unwin, 1968), p. 85.

[16] Peter Bromhead, *The House of Lords and Contemporary Politics* (London: Routledge and Kegan Paul, 1958).

[17] Walkland, *Legislative Process in Great Britain*, p. 84.

[18] J. R. Vincent, "Legislation in the House of Lords: A Correction and Reconsideration," *Parliamentary Affairs* XX, no. 2 (Spring 1967), p. 178. Further data for the session 1966-67, supplied by P. G. Henderson, show an increase to 736 amendments but this was for 70 bills during a period of 18 months, as opposed to only 45 bills in a normal session in 1964-65. See his "Legislation in the House of Lords," *Parliamentary Affairs* XXI, no. 2 (Spring 1968), p. 177.

[19] Vincent, "The House of Lords," p. 483.

cisely because the Lords normally stick to details which must be ironed out, despite the "pedantry." As Crick puts it: "Someone must do this work whatever are the objections to the present constitution of the Lords. The work they do is, on the whole, well done."[20]

Normally, the House of Lords steers clear of political controversy by debating matters without forcing them to a vote or by arranging sufficient abstentions to permit Government measures to pass even though the majority of members present oppose the bill. When amendments tacked on by the Lords are not accepted by the House of Commons (actually the Government, which controls the Commons), the Lords usually acquiesce and accept defeat with aristocratic grace and philosophical detachment. This seeming indifference to the fate of their own decisions flows from the peers' recognition that present definitions of their legitimacy exclude a more active political role.

This assessment highlights the important connection between the composition of the House of Lords and its present functions. As a nonrepresentational body, it cannot *legitimately* obstruct Government measures or meddle in matters of high partisan controversy without inviting wrathful reprisals. Those like Crick, who accept the necessity of the Lords' functions, tolerate the Lords only as long as it shows good behavior and directs its energies toward "dotting the i's and crossing the t's" of technical legislation. When it rises in defiance, as most recently in the Rhodesian sanctions vote of 1968, it must expect punishment for being unruly.[21] The British system has a high tolerance for political anachronisms, but has little patience with anachronisms which obstruct the orderly flow of Government business.

A frequently voiced objection to the present composition of the Lords is its bias in favor of the Conservative Party. This party, the traditional defender of privilege and hierarchy in society, has had a consistent majority in the Lords during this century. Both major parties have apparently recognized the desirability of redressing the party balance by appointing predominantly Labour-leaning life peers,[22] but the bias in the House of Lords remains per-

---

[20] Bernard Crick, *The Reform of Parliament* (Garden City, N.Y.: Doubleday Anchor Books, 1965), p. 117.

[21] The House of Lords on this occasion rejected a Statutory Instrument (executive order) implementing sanctions directed against Rhodesia, even though the order had been previously approved by the House of Commons. There was no recent precedent for such an action, although it was undoubtedly constitutional in a strictly legal sense. It was this act, added to some earlier defiance by the Lords (such as the Burmah Oil Co. vote and law reform vote in 1965) which caused the Labour Government to break off interparty discussions on Lords reform, and introduce its own "comprehensive and radical legislation" (Prime Minister Wilson's phrase) a few months later. Said Wilson irately: "This House cannot accept what has happened and cannot but treat it as a denial of democracy and a total frustration of the spirit of our Constitution." 766 *H. C. Debates* 1315 (June 20, 1968).

[22] By 1966 there were 41 peers who had previously been party workers or M.P.'s for the Labour Party and only 23 life peers with similar careers in the Conservative Party.

sistently Conservative.[23] The Bryce Conference, over forty years ago, defined one of the Lords' functions as "the interposition of so much delay (and no more) in the passing of a Bill into law as may be needed to enable the opinion of the nation to be adequately expressed upon it."[24] The continuous Conservative majority in the House of Lords, however, has meant that the House has been strangely quiet and peaceful during the years of Conservative Government, exercising its constitutional function of "so much delay (and no more)" only during those periods when the Labour Party (or Liberal Party in earlier times) has been in power. This potential or actual use of the Lords as a political arm of the Conservative Party has created a climate of opinion unfavorable to any vigorous pursuit of the constitutional prerogatives still possessed by the House. The present partisan bias of the House is considered tolerable only so long as the House limits itself to nonpartisan chores. When the House of Lords takes actions against a Labour Government bill, it is not viewed primarily as a constitutional conflict between the two houses of Parliament, but rather as an inappropriate and unfair intervention of a Conservative Party minority (in the House of Commons) in the prerogatives of the Government. Thus Harold Wilson reacted to the Lords' rejection of sanctions imposed against Rhodesia by calling it "a deliberate and calculated decision of the Conservative Party," emphasizing the role of the Conservative leadership in engineering the vote. Spurred by the Rhodesian sanctions vote, the Wilson Government proposed a sweeping reform of the House of Lords.[25] Although these proposals of the Wilson Government were dropped, there is general agreement between the parties that the present composition and powers of the House of Lords should be changed. Whether they will be changed in the foreseeable future is quite another matter.

The Soviet parliamentary structure has nothing even approximating the House of Lords, whose very spirit is antithetical to the professed egalitarianism and proletarianism of the Soviet system. The two Councils, or houses, of the Supreme Soviet are co-equal in powers—or the lack of them—and almost equal in size: at present the Council of the Union has 767 members and the

---

[23] In 1968, according to Labour Government figures, the Conservatives had an edge of 125 to 95 over Labour (with 19 Liberals and 52 who were unaffiliated) amongst those who attended more than one-third of the time ("the working House"). However, if we add those who attended occasionally, but less than one-third of the sessions—including some of the so-called "backwoodsmen" who can defeat the government by swamping the normally circumspect regular membership—we find the Conservative majority over Labour jumps to 201 members. Figures from Cmnd. 3799 (November 1968), "House of Lords Reform," p. 5.

[24] Cd. 9038 (1918), "Conference on the Reform of the Second Chamber," p. 4.

[25] Cmnd. 3799, p. 28. This proposal, eventually embodied in Parliament (No. 2) Bill of 1968, was debated in Committee of the Whole House for several months but was finally dropped by the Wilson Government because of time pressure and the urgent necessity of dealing with labor legislation.

Council of Nationalities has 750. There is no particular distinction between the functions of the two Councils, which meet simultaneously, either in joint session (to hear important speeches) or in separate chambers, but only for a few days each year.

The Soviet parliamentary structure is derived from the multinational character of the Soviet Union. In fact, the entire federal structure of the state is derived from the existence of many nationalities, and from the special importance that the "nationality question" has had in Bolshevik thought from the time of Lenin to the present. The Bolshevik slogan, to cover this question, enunciated by Stalin, is that the culture of these groups should be "national in form, and socialist in content," a marvelously dialectical formulation according to which, for example, the identical "socialist" message from the leadership in Moscow is translated into the various languages of the country and published in local, native-language newspapers. In parliamentary terms, the "national form" of the system is embodied in the existence of the Council of Nationalities. This Council is drawn from the various administrative subdivisions of the U.S.S.R. federal structure—subdivisions which are all based on the ethnic composition of the population. The major subdivisions, the fifteen union republics, are each composed of a major ethnic group living within the Soviet Union. In addition to the dominant Slavic peoples—the Great Russians, Ukrainians, and Belorussians—the following peoples have been given union republic status: Uzbek, Kazakh, Turkmen, Tadzhik, Moldavian, Georgian, Azerbaidzhanian, Armenian, Estonian, Lithuanian, Latvian, and Kirgiz. Each union republic returns thirty-two deputies to the Council of Nationalities.

The next smaller administrative and national subdivision of the federal structure is the autonomous republic, of which there are twenty. Each of these republics is contained within the borders of a union republic, sixteen of them being within the huge Russian Republic. Each autonomous republic returns eleven deputies to the Council of Nationalities, and in addition there are smaller autonomous regions, each of which elects five deputies. One could go further in detailing the administrative structure of the system, but suffice to say that there are approximately 110 nationality groups in the Soviet Union and the presence of each is in some way reflected in the organization of the state.

If composition had any meaning, the Council of Nationalities would be the "nationality equalizer" in the Supreme Soviet, since the approximately 117 million people of the Russian Republic (including many ethnic non-Russians) are represented by the same number of deputies as the 1.2 million Estonians.[26] It was this theoretical consideration which no doubt appealed to Stalin and the framers of the Soviet constitution and which is the raison

---

[26] Data are from the 1959 census, as in *Itogi vsesoiuznoi perepisi naseleniia 1959 goda* (Moscow, 1962), p. 18.

d'être of the Council of Nationalities. However, it has no practical importance. The Council of Nationalities does not differ in its political effect from the Council of the Union, which is elected simply and without reference to nationalities, on the basis of one deputy per 300,000 electors. There is a widely known Marxian belief that nationality differences fade away and eventually vanish under Communism, and the Soviet system tends to reflect such preconceptions. The net result is that the two Councils of the Supreme Soviet, while they differ in method of election, are identical twins in functions and composition.

Both the British Parliament and the Supreme Soviet have the same requirement for the passage of legislation: it must pass both houses in identical form; but in the British system this ancient requirement has been reduced (by the Parliament Acts of 1911 and 1949) in the case where the House of Lords rejects legislation from the House of Commons. In this case, bills can become law after a delay of one year (one month for "money bills") without the approval of the Lords. On the other hand, in order to handle the inconceivable contingency that a disagreement would occur between the Council of Nationalities and the Council of the Union, the Soviet Constitution provides for a "Conciliation Commission" to be formed from both chambers to iron out differences.[27] As previously mentioned, the necessity for this commission has yet to arise.

The general relationship between the two chambers in the Soviet and British systems can be summarized as follows:

1. The composition of the House of Lords as a largely hereditary body with an inherent party bias greatly weakens its legitimacy as a body with political decision-making powers. Its composition as a body of experts, however, enhances its legitimacy as a subordinate, revisory chamber, concerned with tidying up legislative details, while its composition as a group of distinguished "elder statesmen" enhances its legitimacy as a forum for relatively non-partisan discussion of important moral issues.

2. The functional differentiation and inequality of the two British Houses springs from the difference in the legitimacy of their composition, rather than from conscious consideration of the efficient performance of the functions of Parliament.

3. Even though the two Councils of the Supreme Soviet are elected on a different basis of representation, there is no functional differentiation or inequality between them. This is in accord with the fact that in

---

[27]In fact, Article 47 of the Constitution carries the fantasy even further, stating that "if the Conciliation Commission fails to arrive at an agreement or if its decision fails to satisfy one of the Chambers, the question is considered for a second time by the Chambers. Failing agreement between the two Chambers, the Presidium of the Supreme Soviet of the U.S.S.R. dissolves the Supreme Soviet of the U.S.S.R. and orders new elections."

Soviet theory both methods of election (one supposedly reflecting national origins, the other, the unifying influence of the Soviet state system) are equally legitimate.

All of these points involve a fundamental connection between the method of selecting members and the composition of the representative assemblies, on the one hand, and the function given to or held by the assemblies on the other. The connecting link is legitimacy, the feeling of the people in the system that the composition of the representative assembly is such that it ought, by right, to discharge certain functions of the state. This is the theoretical foundation against which the actual activities of these bodies are judged, and perhaps found wanting. The relationship between legitimacy and function is neither fixed nor precise. When the House of Lords rejects a Government measure, it raises questions of legitimacy, but the answers from different participants in the system will be various. All the answers, however, will reflect individual interpretations of the legitimacy of the action, *given the present composition of the House.* In a similar way, many criticisms of the present work of the House of Commons (which we shall discuss later) are based on the consideration that the Commons, because of its composition, should be performing certain functions, which in fact it does not.

The composition of a representative assembly depends upon the procedures of nomination and the values of the nominators. The resulting selections are based upon a consensus concerning the legitimate *functions* of the assembly, for the selectors normally attempt to find representatives who are thought to be appropriate for the requirements of the job. This relationship between composition and legitimate functions is particularly well-illustrated by the case of the Supreme Soviet, whose membership accurately reflects its specific and limited role in the political system. Since this relationship involves the composition of the representative assemblies, the method by which members are chosen must be examined more closely.

ELECTIONS

We have already discussed in Chapter I the importance of representation in establishing the legitimacy of the British and Soviet regimes. Both regimes derive their legitimacy from the proposition that they serve the real interests of the population. The parties create, or at least advocate, policies that ostensibly serve these interests, but the final test of this claim is that representatives of the people, acting for the people by their consent, approve these policies and thus convert them into binding rules for the population (laws).

There are two possible claims that can be made for representative assemblies as legitimizing institutions. One is that they act as the people would if given the opportunity; the other is that they act as the people would if the people really understood their best interests. The first claim is based on a democratic ideal. The people are seen as fully capable of their self-management and the representative is seen as a delegate whose chief virtue is that he is just like the people he represents and that he maintains close contact with them. The second claim is elitist in essence and implies that the people are not always (or perhaps rarely) able to judge the merits of policy themselves and that the representative is more intelligent, more knowledgeable, or wiser than the people, but shares their interests and serves them.

The second approach has long history in Britain. In 1774, Edmund Burke declared to his electors in Bristol: "Your representative owes you, not his industry only, but his judgment; and he betrays, instead of serving you, if he sacrifices it to your opinion."[28] A century later, J. S. Mill wrote: "It is so important that the electors should choose as their representatives wiser men than themselves, and should consent to be governed by that superior wisdom."[29] These attitudes were the natural outgrowth of a society which was, as Walter Bagehot noted a century ago, a "deferential society" in which "the numerous unwiser part wishes to be ruled by the less numerous wiser part."[30] Even today, Richard Rose writes that "instead of resenting the assumed superiority of a relative few, many Englishmen defer to those they regard as legitimately superior."[31] Despite this strong strain of elitism, it seems universally recognized that the British expect their representatives to act in their *true, best* interests, even when the public appears to be leaning in another direcron. It is, in other words, elitism in pursuit of a democratic objective.

This is perhaps the dominant attitude in Britain toward the role of the representative, although one often meets a somewhat contrary theme which justifies a larger role for the Parliament (vis-à-vis the Government) because it is close to the people and "knows the mood of the country." This sensitivity of the Parliament to an always vaguely defined public opinion would seem to imply that Parliament's special purpose is to register public reaction to policy, rather than act with relative independence of judgment, as suggested by Burke.[32]

In Soviet political theory, the first approach to representation is taken consistently: representation is doing what the people would do, and doing it with absolute fidelity. One reason for this clear position is that the Party has been invested with all the elitist pretensions of the entire political structure,

[28] Edmund Burke, "Speech to the Electors of Bristol" (November 3, 1774) in *The Works of Edmund Burke*, I (New York: George Dearborn, 1837), p. 221.

[29] J. S. Mill, *Representative Government* (London: Everyman Library, 1910), p. 319.

[30] Walter Bagehot, *The English Constitution* (New York: Cornell University Press, 1963), p. 247.

[31] Richard Rose, *Politics in England* (Boston: Little, Brown and Co., 1964), p. 40.

[32] For a thorough discussion of British attitudes toward representation, both past and present, see A. H. Birch, *Representative and Responsible Government* (London: Allen and Unwin, 1964).

so that the people, through their representatives, need only approve and admire the Party's work. Another reason is the egalitarianism which is stressed by the regime as a principle of legitimacy and which denies that representatives are "special people." According to one Soviet text: "The U.S.S.R. Supreme Soviet is a comprehensive assemblage of workers' representatives, called upon *to express the will of the people*, and to guarantee their fundamental interests."[33] Since the representatives are assumed to act just as the people would, and since this assumption is based on the claim that there is no basis for social conflict in the Soviet Union, the Supreme Soviet is viewed by Soviet writers as an instrument of direct democracy. This not only legitimizes its own existence, but legitimizes the laws which it unanimously passes from time to time. One Soviet author carries this argument to the extreme of declaring that all organizations of the Soviet state derive their powers from the Supreme Soviet.

> The direct nature of the expression of the Soviet peoples' will in acts of the Supreme Soviet is the result of the fact that in the Soviet socialist state all power belongs to the people through the soviets. . . . The organ in whose hands are concentrated the supreme power of the U.S.S.R. is the U.S.S.R. Supreme Soviet. All other organs of the state either directly or indirectly receive their powers from the U.S.S.R. Supreme Soviet.[34]

The same author makes the essential connection between the legitimacy of the Supreme Soviet and the legitimacy of its laws by stating that "the higher standing of laws of the U.S.S.R. in comparison with all other activities of organs of the Soviet government is derived from the fact that the Supreme Soviet receives its authority to exercise state power directly from the people, and that *the people's will is directly expressed in its laws.*"[35] This, of course, supplies the necessary reason for obeying the law: the people simply conform to "their own" will. Thus the Supreme Soviet supplies legitimacy, and therefore authority, for laws. While this may be a matter of considerable indifference to some Soviet citizens, for those whose affective ties to the regime are predicated on such symbolically democratic notions, the Supreme Soviet performs a significant function. This function may be more expressive than substantive, but it is important nevertheless.

The format of election in each country nicely expresses the legitimized functions which the elections are expected to perform. In Great Britain, the competition is between two or three pre-selected candidates who are chosen

---

[33]*Spravochnik: Nash narodnyi parlament* (Moscow: Izd-vo politicheskoi literatury, 1966), p. 6. Emphasis added.

[34]A. V. Mitskevich, *Akty vysschikh organov sovetskogo gosudarstva* (Moscow: Izd-vo "Iuridicheskaia literatura," 1967), p. 60.

[35]*Ibid.*, p. 63. Emphasis added.

on the basis of their apparent superiority rather than typicality. The stated objective is to produce men of high quality representing different party organizations (and thus alternative potential governments) and presumably different policy alternatives and points of view. The purpose of the election is thus to select:

1. men of high capabilities in the work of government;
2. a cohesive group of leaders who can form a unified governmental team; and
3. a program or set of policy objectives defined by the party as the goal of its future activities if it becomes the Government.

A Soviet election, by contrast, is not intended to present alternatives or choices to the electorate. As already mentioned, the legitimacy of the Communist Party is embodied in the proposition that it can and does use "scientific Marxism-Leninism" to determine correct policies for the Soviet government. Naturally, to provide a choice of policies is to suggest that the Party has been unable to determine beforehand the single best policy; and this would further imply that the Party cannot fulfill the functional requirements of its elitist principle of legitimacy. Instead of this, the election is used as a demonstration of the reality of two central legitimizing propositions of the Soviet political system:

1. The policies chosen by the Party are supported by the people because the policies are scientifically correct.
2. The Government is a "people's government" because it is chosen by the people.

This type of election is an affirmation rather than a selection. The name of a single candidate, representing the officially approved "people's bloc of party and non-party members," appears on the ballot. The voter need only drop the ballot in the box for his vote to be cast, or he can vote against the approved candidate by scratching out his name before depositing the ballot.

In both systems, the names which finally appear on the ballot are the result of a selection procedure that is closed to the public. This fundamental fact is of tremendous significance, for it means that a very important stage of the electoral process in both countries is a private, secretive procedure. In practically all cases in the Soviet Union, the nomination stage determines who will be elected. Although—and perhaps because—this stage is secret, it is the only competitive stage of the electoral process, i.e., the only stage in which genuine alternatives are considered.

In Great Britain, the nomination stage determines, in effect, who will be elected in at least about two-fifths of the cases. In the General Election of 1964, the nomination procedure yielded 1,757 candidates (including 134 independents and nominees of minor parties). Taking a very generous definition of a serious contest as one in which the second running candidate came within 20 percent of the winner's vote, we find that in 1964 there were only 370 (including 22 three-way races). In 260 constituencies there was no serious contender for the seat—and this occurred in one of Britain's closest elections of recent times, yielding a Labour majority of only four seats.[36] In such virtually uncontested constituencies, the nomination stage is clearly more important than the election itself. Even in more closely fought constituencies, the nomination stage emerges as a crucial, and in many cases, decisive stage in the electoral process.[37]

All this considered, the question of who nominates candidates is of crucial importance. It seems quite clear that in the vast majority of cases the local constituency organizations of the national parties exercise virtual autonomy in choosing their candidates. Austin Ranney's thorough study of candidate selection in the three major British parties concludes that in each case:

> ... the national organization's actual influence over candidate selection is substantially weaker than their formal supervisory powers allow. . . . Rarely are they able to persuade a particular local association to adopt a particular individual, and in most instances any obvious effort to do so is likely to kill his chances altogether. . . . Thus we may conclude that . . . the great majority of the choices have been made in "law" and in fact by the constituency organizations.[38]

It may be true that local Conservative associations have somewhat more autonomy than Constituency Labour Parties (CLPs), but even in the Labour Party, Ranney could find very few occasions when the central apparatus (Transport House) successfully opposed the choice of a CLP.[39]

There is not a great deal of information available on the social background of members or leaders of constituency organizations in either party. Jean Blondel, summarizing the impressions of several studies of individual constituencies, states that both Conservative and Labour organizations are largely middle-class affairs. He writes of the typical Conservative association:

---

[36] Figures compiled from data in B. R. Mitchell and Klaus Boehm, *British Parliamentary Election Results, 1950-1964* (Cambridge: Cambridge University Press, 1966).

[37] Thus Max Nicholson's comment about British elections: "The brutal fact remains that the sovereign electorate are supposed to choose between two or three semi-finalists already selected out of a much larger number by a local party committee, which may well have eliminated, before they are consulted, the very men the voters would have preferred." *The System: The Misgovernment of Modern Britain* (London: Hodder and Stoughton, 1967), p. 161.

[38] Austin Ranney, *Pathways to Parliament: Candidate Selection in Britain* (Madison: University of Wisconsin Press, 1965), pp. 272-73. The same conclusion has been reached by Michael Rush in his study *The Selection of Parliamentary Candidates* (London: Nelson, 1969), pp. 279-83.

[39] *Ibid.*, p. 193.

These social organizations have a definite middle-class atmosphere. Whoever comes and acquires the tastes and values of these middle-class clubs is certainly welcome: the associations are not closed societies. On the other hand, those who do not have these tastes and values are barred, not by any conscious decision taken against them, but simply because these individuals are unlikely to feel at home in a society which behaves in a manner which is somewhat foreign to them.[40]

This characterization of middle-class predominance is supported by Professor Ranney's impressions.[41]

A small but judiciously chosen sample of CLP leaders has recently been investigated by Edward Janosik.[42] His findings indicate that CLP leaders are drawn from a wide spectrum of occupational backgrounds, although about half (49 percent) could be classified as roughly middle-class (including Janosik's categories of "professional," "business," and "white-collar").[43] A more revealing result which emerges from this study is that the vast majority of CLP leaders are actively involved in politics as a major part of their life.[44] In a quite obvious sense, these people are truly "activists," distinguished from the relatively apathetic electorate and party membership not so much by their background as by their consuming interest and involvement in the day-to-day work of politics. Whether they seek such involvement because of the psychic rewards they derive from it, or whether they are thrust into these positions because of their demonstrated leadership abilities in other fields, they do seem separated from the public at large precisely and fundamentally because they give themselves to their party to a much greater degree than the vast majority would countenance.

The same sort of pattern appears if we analyze how nominations are made in the Soviet Union. Nominations are not made by local constituency organizations, but by a range of "public organizations" officially sanctioned by the state, such as cooperative farms, youth organizations and cultural societies. In

[40] Jean Blondel, *Voters, Parties, and Leaders: The Social Fabric of British Politics* (Baltimore: Penguin Books, 1963), pp. 99–100.

[41] Ranney describes the "most visible types" in a typical Conservative association as including "middle-class women, small tradesmen, junior company executives, white-collar workers and retired military officers, with a sprinkling of the aristocracy and their offspring." By comparison, the Labour activists "include substantially higher proportions of unskilled and semi-skilled workers and schoolteachers, and fewer small merchants, scions of the aristocracy, and middle-class housewives." *Pathways to Parliament*, pp. 70, 178–79.

[42] Edward G. Janosik, *Constituency Labour Parties in Britain* (London: Pall Mall Press, 1968).

[43] *Ibid.*, p. 17.

[44] Janosik found that 72 percent of CLP leaders in strong Labour constituencies and 64 percent in marginal constituencies held two or more additional party or public offices. *Ibid.*, p. 16.

most localities, however, the trade union organization, working closely with the local organization of the CPSU, is responsible for nominating candidates. The records of the best workers are reviewed from the files and a choice is then made by the party leaders in consultation with the trade union officials.

Here again the choice is made by local activists, although in the Soviet Union the position of activists is more clearly professional or occupational than in Great Britain. Nevertheless, in both cases it seems correct to say that the activist is not chosen so much as he chooses himself. He proves himself and his devotion to the cause of the party by giving himself up to the numerous petty chores of party organization, by remaining loyal to the party leadership, by building personal relationships with the other party activists. In other words, the party activists push open a door which is at least slightly ajar to everyone but which most people pass by without touching. Still, while the door may be theoretically open, many people may pass it by because of the certain or supposed knowledge that they wouldn't "fit in" with the group inside.

No comprehensive study of the social background of local party activists has been published in the Soviet Union. However, it is probably not much of an error to use party membership figures as a whole to describe them. From such data, it would appear that the local party activists in the Soviet Union are a closer approximation to a cross-section of the entire population than one would expect to find in Great Britain. Specifically, it would appear that there is a higher proportion of working-class activists in the Soviet Union than in Great Britain, even if we consider only the British Labour Party. Official figures show that, as of the beginning of 1968, working-class members comprised 52.2 percent of the CPSU.[45] Even after allowance is made for the well-known Soviet eagerness to inflate such statistics, and the probability that activists are somewhat more "elitist" in attitudes than the party rank-and-file is taken into account, the high probability remains that Soviet activists are more typical of the population in their background and training than British activists. However, working-class origins and even continued blue-collar status do not necessarily ensure identification with, or sympathy for, prevailing working-class attitudes. Those who assume minor leadership roles within the Soviet working class (shop foremen, trade-union leaders, etc.) probably identify more closely with regime values and are probably more supportive of regime policies than average workers are.

The most important point that can be made about the nomination procedures in both countries, however, is that the nominees and the nominators resemble each other rather closely. In the Soviet Union, they both come from the cream skimmed off the top of the working class—about 45 percent are party members—plus an over-representation of professionals and "specialists"

[45] *Partiinaia zhizn'*, No. 7 (April) 1968. [*CDSP* XX, no. 16, p. 11.]

(primarily engineers and managers). In Great Britain, it's the middle-class and high-status professions which supply the large proportion of both groups. Nominators and their nominees have the same background and life experience and one is entitled to suspect that they share many political values. It is not surprising that the nominators have high regard for the probity and ability of the nominees: it is, no doubt, the same pleasant sort of feeling they experience when standing in front of a mirror.

This high degree of similarity should not be taken as evidence of some conspiracy by self-conscious elites to perpetuate their domination of political life. One of the elements of power is the ability to transmit some portion of it to others. Some such transmission of power is inevitable in any political system and it is probably to be expected that the receivers will resemble the transmitters in all cases where regime stability is reasonably high.

Although it seems that the nominators and the nominees share certain sociological characteristics—perhaps it would be better to use the term "life-style"—it cannot so easily be concluded that they share the same points of view. There is some evidence in the British case that party activists have about the same distribution of views on issues as elected MPs of their party,[46] and as mentioned previously, the portrayal of the typical activist as an extremist seems clearly false. While it seems likely that nominators and nominees in the Soviet Union share basic political beliefs and opinions on political issues, there is absolutely no empirical evidence either way.

The nomination of candidates is followed in both countries by a campaign. In both countries propaganda is generated by the parties and disseminated through the mass media. The major effort and emphasis of the parties is on positive propaganda, i.e., information or views which display the past accomplishments of the party and its candidates in the most favorable light. Some attention is also given to negative propaganda, which in the Soviet Union means acknowledgment of past shortcomings in work coupled with pledges of improvement, and in Great Britain means an emphasis on the deficiencies and past shortcomings of the opposing party and its candidates.

What sort of messages are transmitted to the electorate during the campaign? In neither country can it be said that detailed and well-reasoned arguments are presented to the public, the emphasis being rather on simple (often simplistic) statements, slogans, catch phrases and the like. But that is where the similarity ends. Soviet campaign propaganda never touches on major issues of national policy. The entire policy content of this propaganda is restricted to local issues, such as the promise to construct more local service establishments. Aside from this, the propaganda pictures voting as a demon-

---

[46] See Richard Rose, "The Political Ideas of English Party Activists," *American Political Science Review* LVI, no. 2 (June 1962), pp. 360–71; also Janosik, *Constituency Labour Parties*, pp. 26–61.

stration of support for the regime as a whole and its avowed purpose of "building communism." British campaign propaganda does deal with major political issues, although again rarely in concrete and dispassionate presentations which would help to elucidate the problems involved.

Richard Rose's study of campaign propaganda in Great Britain[47] reveals that the parties' approach to the public has become very much like the approach of a producer trying to sell his product to consumers. Campaign publicity for both parties has been managed by people with experience in commercial advertising; "market research" is conducted and sample political advertisements are tested by polling techniques to determine their effectiveness with "scientific" rigor. The Conservative Party has actually preferred to hire an outside agency, while the Labour Party has relied on its own internal publicity group, but the "selling" attitude has characterized the recent campaigns of both parties. Simple slogans have been preferred over full and reasoned arguments. Complicated issues are reduced to catchwords and conundrums. As Lord Woolton, the Conservative architect of his party's postwar "new look" in public relations, once candidly remarked: "The most difficult task that we set ourselves to perform at the Central Office was to translate these political arguments into simple forms that were likely to be useful and convincing."[48]

Richard Rose reports that when market research during the 1964 campaign revealed that Harold Wilson's personality was one of Labour's strongest selling points, the Labour publicity group prepared advertisements which "featured a larger photograph of Wilson. The amount of prose attributed to the party leader was reduced to about 125 words per advertisement, one-third the amount in the earlier layouts. In short, the face rather than the statements of Wilson was increasingly thought more important."[49]

In both countries, it would seem that the political leadership has employed propaganda that is designed to appeal to reflexive identifications rather than reflective thinking. In both countries, the party in power emphasizes past accomplishments, with prosperity or improvement in living standards high on the list of priority themes.

The similarity of political propaganda in the two countries is greater during election campaigns than at any other time, and the reason may well be the similarity of the mass audiences. In neither country is the citizenry attuned to detailed, comprehensive discussion of governmental affairs. The public is apparently not interested in such details, and the media do not report

[47]Richard Rose, *Influencing Voters: A Study in Campaign Rationality* (London: Faber and Faber, 1967).

[48]*Ibid.*, p. 35.

[49]*Ibid.*, p. 82.

them. In some respects, the citizenry is unable to cope with the substance of many issues which require specialized knowledge for an adequate understanding. During normal times, this detailed information is provided to expert audiences through lower-circulation, specialized media. Yet at election time, the legitimacy of the political system requires that the citizenry participate by giving its approval to a group of law-affirming representatives. A high rate of participation in elections (which actually amounts to about 80 percent in Great Britain and over 99 percent in the Soviet Union) is required to achieve maximum legitimacy; and to draw the maximum number of people, propaganda usually seeks the lowest common denominator.

Having pointed to the large element of similarity in the two cases, it is essential to turn toward the differences. In Great Britain, an election is a competitive process among 2½ parties, while the competitive element is entirely absent in the Soviet Union. This difference has an interesting effect on campaign propaganda. Contrary to usual notions contrasting the two systems, the British parties are much more likely to approach the electorate in the pristine white cloak of infallibility than is the Soviet Communist Party. Because the British parties are competing, each party will use part of its propaganda to reveal deficiencies in the other. Since each party is being attacked for its real or imagined faults, it cannot afford to provide additional grist for its opponents' mill. As Ian Gilmour has put it: "Under the conditions of modern party politics admission of error is a more serious matter than error itself."[50]

The CPSU, on the other hand, has put itself in the thoroughly delightful position of facing the electorate without opposition. It need not worry about opponents' attacks, and views the election as an opportunity to provide "an accounting" of its past stewardship to the public. It knows that some dissatisfactions exist and it wants to be the channel of all negative, as well as positive, political sentiments in the nation. Campaign speeches are thus in the nature of balance sheets on past performance. Although the balance is always very favorable, there is generally some mention of the debit side of the ledger. For example, Leonid Brezhnev's campaign speech in 1966 contained the following admission:

> Everyone knows that the growing requirements and needs of the population have not been fully satisfied because in the past our light industry and food industry did not receive sufficient resources for their development. This problem found no proper solution for many years. There were both objective and subjective reasons for this, but we shall not discuss them here. We have opportunities for correcting the disparity that has evolved. This task has become urgent and immediate. . . . Our people have

[50]Ian Gilmour, *The Body Politic* (London: Hutchinson, 1969), p. 165.

a right to look forward to a broader assortment and higher quality of manufactured and food products.[51]

While Soviet election propaganda may over-emphasize the positive, the competitive process in Britain may produce a considerable quantity of misinformation, as the parties desperately search for ways of attracting additional votes. Although campaign standards are usually higher, a descent to the level of the electorate's fears and prejudices is not unknown in Great Britain. In the Soviet Union, a campaign speech is much more likely to be dull than demagogic. The outcome is known in advance and there is no need for panegyrics. The style of Soviet campaign oratory is very much like that of a corporation's annual report to its stockholders.

Perhaps the most obvious characteristic of the Soviet electoral system is that it is designed to provide a legitimate and *strong* government. It is almost as obvious that the British system has the same effect, although not by design. The British electoral system of single-member constituencies (with a plurality sufficient for victory) usually produces large parliamentary majorities, even when the popular vote is very close. The average shift of votes (the "swing" vote) between the parties at elections since 1945 has not exceeded 3.1 percent, but the number of seats in Commons has oscillated from a Conservative majority of 100 seats in 1959 to a Labour majority of 97 seats in 1966. Unless the popular vote is very evenly distributed between the parties, one party will have a clear working majority in the House of Commons, and will thus form a government that cannot be defeated by a Commons vote for a period of almost five years.[52] David Butler's analysis of the effect of the British electoral system led him to the conclusion that:

A swing of 1 percent in votes is likely to cause about 18 seats to change hands—making a difference of 36 in a parliamentary division. A 2 percent swing is, therefore, more than enough to make the difference between a comfortable majority for one party and a comfortable majority for the other. Only if the division of votes happens to be within 1 percent of the critical point is there serious danger of indecisive results.[53]

The British system, then, exaggerates the differences between the parties' popular votes and usually provides a government with the backing of a clear majority in the Commons. This occurs even though the presence of the Liberal Party and other, minor parties has the effect of denying the winning

[51]*Pravda*, June 11, 1966. [*CDSP* XVIII, no. 23, p. 15.]

[52]This does not mean that such a government can afford to ignore the "feeling of the House," and particularly the opinions of its own back-bench members in the House.

[53]David Butler, *The Electoral System in Britain Since 1918*, 2nd. ed. (Oxford: Oxford University Press, 1963), p. 202.

party a majority of the total votes cast. (For example, the large Conservative majority of 100 seats in 1959 was obtained with 49.6 percent of the popular vote.) A British government, even one with a large majority in Commons, normally receives the votes of only about 40 percent of the total registered electorate, including nonvoters. The emergence from this system of a clear parliamentary majority can be viewed as a great benefit to the cause of stable government, since a more accurate system of translating votes into seats in such an evenly divided country could produce a succession of weak minority or coalition governments. On the other hand, the system may be seen as producing majorities that are too large for effective parliamentary opposition to operate. Both points are summed up by David Butler's remark that "one of the main virtues of the British electoral system is that it produces clear parliamentary majorities; one of its main weaknesses is that it produces excessive parliamentary majorities."[54]

In any given British election, a certain number of seats can be considered "safe" for one party or another. In these constituencies, there is a high probability that one party will win the election, and this prediction can be made with relative assurance because it is known that most Britishers consistently and even habitually support a single party, and cannot be budged by the blandishments of the other side. As R. L. Leonard has observed, "the majority of voters form their voting habits during their youth and do not deviate thereafter."[55] A survey taken in 1960 by Mark Abrams showed that 71 percent of respondents with Conservative fathers were voting Conservative, and 61 percent of those with Labour fathers were voting Labour.[56] Allegiance to a party can apparently survive undamaged even when the voter disagrees with the party's policy.[57] Party loyalties, for whatever reasons, seem to be quite strong. A survey taken by the *Daily Mail* just before the 1966 elections showed that 40 percent cared "very much" and 32 percent cared "quite a lot" which party won the election, and 74 percent indicated that they supported a party "very strongly" or "quite strongly."[58]

Over-all, the picture emerges of a large number of strongly partisan and consistently loyal voters, but for these voters "it is the general impression or

[54] *Ibid.*

[55] R. L. Leonard, *Elections in Britain* (London: Van Nostrand, 1968), p. 139.

[56] *Ibid.*

[57] See R. S. Milne and H. C. Mackenzie, *Marginal Seat, 1955: A Study of Voting Behaviour in the Constituency of Bristol North East at the General Election of 1955* (London: The Hansard Society, 1958), p. 119. The Conservatives were actually more consistent than the Labour voters, since in addition to the 38 percent expressing "very pro-Conservative" views on the four issues, there were 43.5 percent classified as "moderately pro-Conservative."

[58] See Peter G. J. Pulzer, *Political Representation and Elections: Parties and Voting in Great Britain* (New York: Frederick A. Praeger, 1967), p. 115.

'image' presented by the parties, not a detailed assessment of their approach to each issue, which seems to be most influential in winning or keeping votes."[59] For this majority of British voters, the act of voting has the same meaning as it apparently does for most Soviet voters: it becomes an act of faith in a party by a loyal supporter. For these voters, the party has achieved affective legitimacy and has become the object of the voter's allegiance. These voters are not in a state of "perpetual choice," coolly considering party positions on their merits and making rational calculations of relative advantages. For these voters, the distinction between Soviet and British elections is lost, because the competitive nature of British elections is lost on them.

According to Jorgen Rasmussen's definition and calculation of safe seats, there were 465 (combined total) in the election of 1959 and 429 in the election of 1964.[60] That left only 146 constituencies in 1959 and 179 in 1964 where genuine contests were to take place, so-called "marginal seats." These marginal constituencies differ from the others only in that the habitual voters on both sides are evenly divided, giving the undecided minority, or the "floating voter," the opportunity to decide the issue.

If the floating voter could be characterized as the ideal, well-informed, rational decision-maker, it could be said that the outcome of a British election hinges on the actions of the "best" voters, but it would appear that the floaters are on average no better informed than those firmly anchored to party loyalties—in fact, the data indicate that the floaters may on average be more ignorant than the average voter. As Jean Blondel has put it: "Floating voters may play a crucial part in the British system of government, but they do not seem to be aware of their responsibilities. They do not seem to be drawn from the most politically conscious section of the community. The reasons for their change of allegiance are often trivial. They seem to be less committed not because of a genuine independence of mind but more out of apathy."[61] If the outcome of a British election, therefore, hinges on the actions of the floating voter, and particularly the floating voter in the marginal constituency, it would appear that the outcome is determined by those least equipped to render rational, knowledgeable choices.

Available data indicate that the entire British electorate, floaters and loyalists together, is woefully uninformed about politics. A survey taken in Greenwich showed that one-third of the respondents did not know the party to which their M.P. belonged, and one-quarter of the respondents did not

[59] Graeme C. Moodie, *The Government of Great Britain*, 2nd ed., (New York: Thomas Y. Crowell, 1964), p. 62.

[60] Jorgen Rasmussen, "Implications of Safe Seats for British Democracy," in Richard Rose, ed., *Policy-Making in Britain: A Reader in Government* (London: Macmillan, 1969), pp. 38, 43.

[61] Jean Blondel, *Voters, Parties and Leaders: The Social Fabric of British Politics* (Baltimore: Penguin Books, 1963), p. 72.

know the name of their M.P.[62] Another poll taken just before a general election, when political information was presumably at its height, asked the respondents to name nine party leaders, three from each major party. Only 5 percent could name as many as seven party leaders. Only 30 percent could name five or more party leaders and 20 percent could not name any party leaders.[63] Along with rather low levels of political knowledge, the British electorate seems to be only moderately interested in political matters. A study made by Mark Abrams produced the finding that 52 percent of the respondents answered that they were "very interested" or "interested" in political matters, while 48 percent indicated that they were "not really interested" or "not at all interested" in politics.[64]

Since the electorate is apparently not very well informed and since it evinces only a moderate interest in political matters, it seems quite fortunate for the political system that these electors vote according to well-fixed party images rather than according to rapidly changing reactions to individual party policies. Blondel has carried his argument further in asserting: "There is nothing inherently wrong in the fact that electors associate the parties with images and not with policies. . . . In the long run, these images are modified and influenced . . . by the policies and record of the parties. Moreover, if party support was entirely rational and solely based on policies, representative government would become unworkable. The parties would never be able to count on some loyal support in cases of blunders and difficulties; nor would they ever be able to rally their supporters and thereby educate public opinion."[65]

While electoral behavior—and particularly the "swing of the pendulum" which from time to time shifts power from one leadership team to another— cannot be explained in terms of considered responses to party programs and election appeals, it does seem that those voters who can be budged from steadfast loyalty to a particular party do so on such grounds as the following:

1. a general feeling that the existing government is unable to cope with domestic problems;
2. significant personal dissatisfaction with living conditions, real earning power, etc., which the voter may relate to inadequacies of government;
3. a particularly newsworthy scandal or *cause célèbre* which reflects badly on the existing government's (or opposition's) efficiency or conformity to prevailing standards of morality;

[62] Moodie, *Government of Great Britain*, p. 67.

[63] Mark Abrams, "Social Trends and Electoral Behaviour," in Richard Rose, ed., *Studies in British Politics* (New York, St. Martin's Press, 1966), p. 135.

[64] *Ibid.*

[65] Blondel, *Voters, Parties, and Leaders*, p. 83.

4. a change in leadership of either party, particularly the party leader;
5. open disunity in one of the parties which makes it doubtful that the party can function effectively as a strong government team.

The overall picture, then, is not very encouraging, if one has in mind theories of democracy which posit ideal images of electors. Furthermore, this picture of the British electorate seems roughly equivalent to the picture we can draw from our scant information about the Soviet electorate. Even without opinion poll data we can assert with a fair degree of certainty that the Soviet voter is not very excited about election campaigns, nor is he particularly well-informed or interested in political matters. Both Soviet and British voters live in a mass society relatively removed and isolated from the high levels of the political structure. Their lack of detailed and sustained interest in politics is quite understandable and natural under the circumstances. To some extent their apathy may be a measure of their contentment with the system and particularly with the system's distribution of goods and services. Lack of sustained interest in politics is not necessarily a measure of alienation; in fact, some evidence would lead to the contrary conclusion. The cross-national survey reported by Gabriel Almond and Sidney Verba indicated that the British as a whole are quite proud of their political institutions and are second only to Americans in this respect.[66] Nor can one assume that the lack of interest shown by Soviet citizens toward election campaigns is a symptom of a general alienation from the values of the political system. In Great Britain the outcome of elections is often uncertain. Thus elections have at least the inherent interest of a sporting event. In the Soviet Union, on the other hand, the uncertainty and drama end at the moment when the nominations are announced.

Even though voting as an individual act may in many cases appear quite similar in Great Britain and the Soviet Union, elections as a whole in Great Britain perform one very significant function for the political system which is lacking in the Soviet Union. The total result of votes—based on ignorance, prejudice, and foolishness as well as intelligence, careful study, and rationality—is that, from time to time and with fair regularity, the government in Great Britain changes. One team of leaders, having exercised power for sufficient years to demonstrate their capacities, is swept away and another team of leaders, whose program is probably largely unknown even to many of those who voted for them, is brought to power. Whatever deficiencies may be found in the mechanism of British elections, it can certainly be said that it brings about a regular alternation of parties and a regular renewal of personalities who assume the major responsibilities of political leadership. Peter Pulzer has stated the matter quite well:

---

[66] See Gabriel Almond and Sidney Verba, *The Civic Culture: Political Attitudes and Democracy in Five Nations* (Boston: Little, Brown and Co., 1965), Ch. 4.

It is as a device for controlling political leaders that elections fulfill their most important function; it is by their effectiveness in doing so that their utility in British politics must in the last resort be judged. If they are effective, then the whole political culture is thereby transformed. Power, as a result, comes to be regarded as a trust, not as a right, and the politicians' tenure of office as probationary, not permanent. The party struggle becomes a non-violent way of resolving a type of conflict which exists in all except the most primitive societies—the rivalry between different interests for state power. Elections become a non-violent way of solving a difficulty common to all political systems—how to organize the succession from one group of men holding authority to another. For this reason, any electoral choice is better than none, even if the policy differences between the parties are trivial or their attitudes on major issues overlap. It is still worth-while to be able to choose between contestants of whom one is younger, or abler, or more honest than the other; indeed, it may be very important to be able to do so.[67]

It is this renewal function, this bringing of new blood, new energy, and perhaps even new talent to the test of political leadership that British elections perform so well for the political system. It is this function which the Soviet system of elections fails to perform at all. Yet, of course, the Soviet system has no less need of refreshing the vigor of its leadership. In fact, the Soviet system has even greater need for such refreshment since its pattern of recruitment to political leadership is so much more confined and rigid.[68]

By forcing leadership teams to alternate, by preventing one team from becoming entrenched in power, British elections have a great effect on the character and style of leadership in Britain. Elections create and legitimate not only a government team, but also an opposition team. From these groups arises the endless confrontation of the proposer and the opposer, and the style of politics that by nature attacks problems by looking at "both sides" of the issue. The government team has been, and most assuredly will someday be again, the opposition. From its remembrance of things past and its expectations of things to come, it is aware of its limits, and of its accountability for all that it does and fails to do. The opposition has been and will be the government, and from the former experience it—or at least its senior members—have some awareness of the limitations of governmental power, and the assurance that it will be expected to deliver its present promises at some time in the future. By being drawn so close to government and the certainty of sharing power, the opposition becomes "responsible," although it is also possible that, by being drawn too close, the opposition may fail after a time to offer a real alternative. The certainty of criticism by the opposition may

[67]Pulzer, *Political Representation*, p. 147.

[68]The Soviet regime partly meets this need, however, through the continual "poor performance purges" of all ranks of leadership.

make the government too timid and may prevent it from adopting imaginative but risky policies. As David Vital has noted: "Where the Executive is aware that its policy is likely to be opposed it may tend to be marginally more cautious, more circumspect in its choice of verbal formulae to explain its actions, chary of arousing the kind of opposition that would reflect upon its leadership as a whole or, more seriously, hamper its work in the truly sensitive and politically critical domains of social and economic policy."[69]

British elections, then, serve to "turn the rascals out" on occasion, while in the Soviet Union the rascals easily survive elections with no difficulty to themselves, but at the expense of the political system's need for periodic invigoration of its leadership. Beyond this the British system can be seen as one aspect of the general legitimization of political opposition, as an outgrowth of the generally accepted feeling that contention, conflict, and competition amongst groups in the political process is a healthy thing for society. The Soviet system which denies the necessity for conflict and which, in theory if not in fact, works towards a society free of social conflict has adopted a system of elections that symbolizes its adherence to the monolithic, harmonious model of society.

In both cases, however, the institution of elections can be seen as a legitimizing device, as a vivid demonstration of the legitimacy principle that "the people rule." The representatives who emerge from this process are in some symbolic sense the people's choice and they can, therefore, make some claim that their subsequent actions as representatives within the structure of government are legitimate, because elections conform to the generally accepted principles of legitimacy underlying the regime. The holding of elections serves to mobilize support for the regime itself. In addition, the elections serve as a means of bringing forward complaints about past performance, a means of generating feedback which is needed by the political leadership. In the Soviet Union this feedback is in the form of complaints about primarily local conditions and requests for remedial action. In Great Britain this feedback is more likely to come in the form of the electorate's rejection of the party leadership team in power and the substitution of the opposing party. In both systems, therefore, elections perform useful and needed functions for the political system beyond the legitimizing of political power.

Yet in neither system can the objective observer ascribe to elections the functions which the regime's legitimacy principles give them. The electorate does not "choose" its representatives, except in a purely symbolic sense. Nomination of candidates is essentially a private matter of a relatively small group of political elites. Elections, for most voters, are demonstrations of

[69] David Vital, *The Making of British Foreign Policy* (London: Allen and Unwin, 1968), p. 81.

fixed loyalties. Richard Rose and Harve Mossawir put the matter extremely well when they wrote:

> For individuals, the chief functions of voting are emotional or allegiance-maintaining. Only a limited fraction of the electorate seems able or willing to act so that their votes can consciously have for them the function of choosing governors or influencing government policy. ... In democratic and non-democratic societies alike, voting is a norm. When this norm is internalized by an individual and/or supported by strong social pressures, a majority of individuals will vote, even if lacking in partisanship, anticipating a one-sided result, expressing not much interest in the campaign, having no concern about the election outcome, and a low sense of political efficacy. For such individuals, voting may provide a mild gratification, or simply dissipate tension arising from failing to act according to established norms.[70]

COMPOSITION OF MEMBERSHIP

In the Soviet Union and Great Britain, the membership of the representative assembly is composed of people whose attributes reflect the standards imposed by society. The representatives are, by and large, achievement elites rather than ascriptive elites. They are, or are supposed to be, highly capable. They are more likely to be articulate and ambitious and to have assumed leadership roles in their past activities. Their achievement, as measured by education, occupational status, and annual income is likely to be higher than the average for society.

Each society clearly has its own set of ideal standards against which it measures the attributes of potential representatives, and there is in each case some variation and flexibility in the application of these standards. If one examines the present composition of the House of Commons and the Supreme Soviet, it is immediately apparent that there are indeed several different types of individuals representing different backgrounds in their society. Clearly there is no single ideal type in either of these societies, and just as clearly, no elector, or very few electors, consciously and specifically set up a set of standards against which they measure the candidates. Each society, however, has its values, and individuals brought up in these societies learn these values and translate these values in their attitudes in politics as well as other areas of their lives.

As already mentioned, in neither Great Britain nor the Soviet Union are the candidates presented by the parties at elections really typical of the entire population. Obviously the Soviet voter has no choice in this respect (as well

---

[70]Richard Rose and Harve Mossawir, "Voting and Elections: A Functional Analysis," *Political Studies* XV, no. 2 (June 1967), p. 192–93.

as others), but the British voter has hardly any more opportunity to select candidates on the basis of their qualifications. Because of the nomination procedure, British candidates are likely to resemble each other in most respects. As Austin Ranney has written: "In social status, personality, and outlook the parliamentary candidates of all three British parties . . . resemble each other more closely than they resemble their respective supporters. They may not constitute a ruling class in the traditional sense, but they are certainly a political elite."[71]

Voting for British candidates on the basis of their personal qualifications may not be very sensible. The candidate, if elected, will be subject to party discipline in his future activities as representative. For this reason, the candidates' merits may be less important than the policies of their party and the quality of its leadership. Furthermore, even during election campaigns it is very difficult for the average voter to obtain any knowledge or even impressions of the personality and qualifications of the candidates in his own constituency. British ballot papers until 1970 listed the names of the candidates without their party affiliation, and since the candidates' names have such low salience for the voters, it was "fairly common for an absent-minded voter to check with his party's teller on his way into the polling station the name of the person for whom he should vote."[72] In a survey taken by Rose and Mossawir, 68 percent of those questioned felt that "voters should vote for the party they think best" rather than "for the men they think best without regard to party."[73] The evidence points clearly toward the conclusion reached by Peter G. Richards, who writes: "The role of the individual candidate in an election campaign is of little importance. . . . Where the political scene is dominated by two parties, the essential choice facing the electors is which of these parties they wish to see in office."[74]

Of course, the average Soviet voter is likely to know even less about the qualifications of his single candidate for the Supreme Soviet. The party affiliation of the Soviet candidate has little significance. In recent elections for the U.S.S.R. Supreme Soviet, approximately 75 percent of the candidates were members of the Communist Party. The rest are listed simply as "non-party," but they, no less than the party members, can be depended upon to support party policy in all particulars. Party members do indeed play a larger role in the subsequent work of the Supreme Soviet, but this fact has no significance for the voter. The most important piece of information about the candidate for the voter is conveyed by the ballot paper: the mere presence of the

[71] Ranney, *Pathways to Parliament*, p. 279.

[72] Leonard, *Elections in Britain*, p. 112.

[73] Rose and Mossawir, "Voting and Elections," p. 191.

[74] Peter G. Richards, *Honourable Members: A Study of the British Backbencher* (London: Faber and Faber, 1959), p. 37.

candidate's name on the ballot signifies that he is officially approved by the regime.

As already mentioned, the Soviet view of representation is summed up by the typical statement that "in the U.S.S.R. Supreme Soviet, the social and national structure of our society is reflected literally as in a mirror."[75] Despite this, the data indicate that the composition of the U.S.S.R. Supreme Soviet diverges markedly from the characteristics of the entire population. Using the data of Roger A. Clarke,[76] it appears that full-time workers in government, the Communist Party, the Komsomol, trade unions and other social organizations are more than 80 times over-represented in the Supreme Soviet in comparison to their weight in the entire population. Writers and publicists are approximately 20 times over-represented and, in general, all categories of "brain workers" are over-represented in the Supreme Soviet. On the other hand, manual workers such as collective farmers and industrial workers are under-represented by almost half. Still, one does find in the 1966 Supreme Soviet 141 collective farmers and 243 representatives who were regularly employed as industrial workers.

Although the British concepts of representation do not usually include the mirror-image model, the present composition of the House of Commons is sometimes criticized by Britishers as being too elitist. Data for the 1966 House of Commons show that there is an even greater disparity between British representatives and the British population than we noted for the Soviet case. Based on data given by Butler and King, 44 percent of M.P.'s in the 1966 House of Commons were employed as professionals and an additional 17 percent were normally occupied as directors or executives in business; only 17 percent in all were listed as manual workers and this group came almost entirely from the Labour Party.[77] Thus "brain workers" form 83 percent of the membership of the House of Commons, while in the Soviet Union "brain workers" form 62 percent of the composition of the Supreme Soviet.

Unless one is gravely afflicted with excessive naiveté, these figures should be neither surprising nor distressing. Neither the system by which representatives are recruited nor the activities of representatives once elected would lead one to suspect that manual workers would or should be prominent amongst their numbers. The selection process winnows out those who could not be presented to the electorate as superior to the ordinary average man, and in neither country has the electorate ever raised a clamor that the candidates are

[75] M. Georgadze, *Izvestiia*, October 1, 1967.

[76] Roger A. Clarke, "The Composition of the U.S.S.R. Supreme Soviet, 1958–66," *Soviet Studies* XIX, no. 1 (July 1967), p. 55.

[77] David Butler and Anthony King, *The British General Election of 1966* (London: Macmillan, 1966), p. 208.

too good, too skilled, or too educated. In both countries, the representative is supposed to represent the best qualities of the people, not their usual frailties. The representative who comes from a common background is assumed to understand the aspirations and interests of common people, but no one expects either his talents or accomplishments to be common.

In both countries one detects a quality of widespread deference in attitudes toward the political structure. This has been particularly noted in Great Britain, where approximately one-third of the working class regularly votes for the Conservative Party. Recent studies of the British working-class Conservative have distinguished between the deferential voter on the one hand and the "pragmatist" or "secular" voter on the other hand.[78] Even the pragmatists and seculars, however, evaluate candidates on the basis of their presumed superiority. Even those who vote for the Labour Party acknowledge that the Conservatives are more capable by virtue of their superior education and upbringing. As a measure of the deference of the British working class, Eric Nordlinger found that 49 percent of the workers in his sample regarded themselves as "politically impotent, or nearly so," but nevertheless *approved* of this situation. As Nordlinger notes: "It is this cultural edifice which constitutes a singularly important support for the system's hierarchical structure of authority, the independence of the government from the non-elite, and the elite's private decision-making style."[79] McKenzie and Silver have reported that 54.3 percent of their sample felt that they had no influence over government. As one respondent in this study remarked: "Simple reason is that the ordinary working-class person has no say at all in anything."[80]

In the Soviet Union deference is mainly directed toward the top Party leaders, for whom nomination as members of the Supreme Soviet must surely be less than exciting. If one eliminates from consideration the important political figures who sit in the Supreme Soviet, it appears that the other deputies are chosen as models of behavior and achievement on a more mundane work-a-day level of activity. In the 1966 Supreme Soviet, 38 percent of the deputies held official positions in the Party, state, Komsomol, trades unions, and armed forces, while another 11 percent were economic managers in agriculture or industry. Occupations normally grouped under the heading of "intelligentsia" amounted to 13 percent, and the remaining 38 percent were agricultural and industrial workers.

[78] David Butler and Donald Stokes, *Political Change in Britain: Forces Shaping Electoral Choice* (New York: St. Martin's Press, 1969).

[79] Eric Nordlinger, *The Working Class Tories: Authority, Deference and Stable Democracy* (Berkeley: University of California Press, 1967), p. 102.

[80] Robert McKenzie and Allan Silver, *Angels in Marble: Working Class Conservatives in Urban England* (Chicago: University of Chicago Press, 1968), pp. 124–25. Over-all percentage computed from Table 4.7.

Izvestiia once gave the following recipe for the perfect soviet deputy:

What sort of person do we wish to have as our deputy? What are the most important qualities demanded of him as a state official? Some say: deputies must only be those who do outstanding work, those we call "advanced workers." Another opinion: he must be a man made wise by the experience of life, worthy of the respect of the voters in his district, having experience in state activities. A third group considers: what sort of work he does is not of primary importance; experience and the respect of others will come with time; we want a deputy to know how to "get to the bottom of the problem," to organize people, and put things in order. All three points of view, obviously, are well justified.[81]

Thus in both systems representatives tend to be portrayed as people of uncommon ability, even when they have common backgrounds.

In both systems, although for somewhat different reasons, a high (and probably unwarranted) value is placed on formal education. It is therefore natural that representatives, in both cases, reflect this value by above-average achievement in formal education. In the House of Commons elected in 1966, 58.2 percent of the members had a university education.[82] Not very far behind is the Supreme Soviet of the same year, in which 50.2 percent of the deputies had a higher education.[83] At the other end of the education scale, 5.6 percent of the M.P.'s and 5.9 percent of the Soviet deputies had only an elementary education. In regard to education, neither body can claim to be a mirror of the nation. It is estimated that less than five percent of the British population has a completed university education, while less than seven percent of the Soviet population has a higher, incomplete higher, or specialized secondary education, according to the last census.[84] Perhaps more revealing than this, in the British case, is the fact that 44.1 percent of M.P.'s attended one of the handful of exclusive private preparatory schools (so-called "public schools"). Furthermore, 57 percent of Conservative M.P.'s and 23 percent of Labour M.P.'s had been to Oxford or Cambridge University. Education in Great Britain thus plays a social as well as purely pedagogical role and acts as a selective mechanism for entry into the higher levels of the political system. Attendance at one of the exclusive public schools is largely restricted to families of considerable means, and this is also true, although to a considerably lesser extent, of Oxford and Cambridge. Thus the higher requirements for formal education, which seem to be imposed informally by those who se-

[81]*Izvestiia*, January 14, 1969.

[82]Butler and King, *British General Election*, p. 108.

[83]*Verkhovnyi sovet...*, p. 79.

[84]Frank Stacey, *The Government of Modern Britain* (Oxford: Clarendon Press, 1968), p. 65; *Itogi vsesoiuznoi perepisi...*, p. 111.

lect candidates, act as an impassable barrier to most lower-class recruits. If it were not for the 130 Labour M.P.'s sponsored by the trade unions—the group which supplies almost the entire working-class contingent in Commons—the formal educational achievement figures for M.P.'s would be even higher.[85]

There is no exactly parallel situation in the Soviet Union. Although there are several more prestigious universities, generally the older and larger ones in Moscow, Leningrad, Kharkov, Kiev, and Kazan, none of these universities can claim the special status as an avenue of recruitment to political leadership which the Oxbridge universities occupy in Great Britain. In fact, it is rare that a graduate of an academically elite school like Moscow or Leningrad University achieves high political office. Although educational requirements may be more diverse and of a more vocational, technical, or specialized nature in the Soviet Union, it seems clear that the criteria for political leadership increasingly involve higher education of some sort.

The age distribution of Supreme Soviet deputies and British M.P.'s reveals that membership in either body is primarily a middle-aged occupation. In 1966, 61 percent of M.P.'s were between the ages of 40 and 59, while 53 percent of Soviet deputies were between the ages of 41 and 60. The bias in both systems is toward men of more experience, and more settled, if not more conservative, views. Furthermore, this bias toward middle age reveals that, generally, entry to the representative assembly is achieved after one has spent some years in pursuing a nonpolitical career. The general pattern, although there are exceptions, is that the representative not be a "professional politician," but that he make his mark in some other walk of life, and then enter politics. Even though the reality often belies the sentiment expressed, both British and Soviet writers on the subject have traditionally abhorred the image of the professional politician as representative. For example, the Select Committee on Members' Expenses of the House of Commons reported that "few would support the idea of a House of Commons composed principally of full-time politicians in the sense of men and women cut off from any practical share in the work of the nation."[86] In a quite similar vein, a Soviet writer comments: "Soviet deputies are not transformed into professional parliamentarians. Having become deputies, they all continue to work in various

[85] See Douglas Houghton, "Trade Union M.P.'s in the British House of Commons," *The Parliamentarian* IL, no. 4 (October 1968).

[86] H. C. 72 (1954), p. xxvii, as quoted in Jennings, *Cabinet Government*, p. 45. This sentiment is echoed by Ronald Butt, who writes: "There would be some loss to the community if M.P.'s generally became so professionalised that they were less representative of the ordinary citizen and instead became counter-bureaucrats." (*The Power of Parliament* [London: Constable, 1967], p. 440.) Yet it would be difficult to imagine a group significantly "less representative of the ordinary citizen" than the present House— if one thinks of representation as replicating the characteristics of the represented.

sectors of the economy and cultural life, remaining in the very midst of the masses."[87]

The business of representation involves quite different life-styles in the two countries. One obvious difference here is that the House of Commons is likely to be in session for about eight months of the year, while the Supreme Soviet is unlikely to be in session for more than one week in any given year. Such work as is accomplished at sessions of the Supreme Soviet—and for most deputies it amounts to very little—is obviously only an incidental activity in the life of the deputy.

The life of the average M.P. must appear by comparison to be all hustle and bustle. According to one popular guide: "Parliament is no longer a recreation for gentlemen of leisure. It is a busy work shop."[88] Whatever meaning may be attached to the work of the M.P., it is apparent that a great deal of his time is consumed in parliamentary business.

Another basic difference between the systems in this regard is that the soviets are viewed as not only mechanisms for educating the public, but also as a means by which the deputies themselves are politically educated. Under this concept, efforts are made to include large numbers of Soviet citizens as deputies at various lower levels of the network of local soviets. In addition, a system of rotation has been used to maximize the exposure of the above-average citizen to the work of the soviets. Over two million citizens are deputies at the various levels of the system at any one time. Typically, more than half the membership of a soviet is replaced at each election (50.6 percent of all deputies in 1969). This means that in the past decade over six million citizens have been deputies at one level or another. Considering particularly those deputies who serve only one term, deputization is simply one additional technique in the over-all program of the regime to strengthen the popular support for, and identification with, the regime's goals by co-opting a large body of local leaders as minor officials of the regime. In a very important sense, the soviet deputy represents the regime to the population as well as representing the population to the regime. His activity in his home district is largely directed toward instilling support for the regime amongst the citizenry. He is, in a sense, recruited as a regime propagandist. The political education of deputies is apparently considered one of the major functions of the soviets:

> The furthest development of the soviets as functioning groups means in particular that their role as "schools of management" for millions of workers must grow. Periodic renewal of the membership of representative

[87]I. I. Kuznetsov, *Zakonodatel'naia i ispolnitel'naia deiatel'nost' vysshikh organov vlasti* (Moscow: Izd-vo "Iuridicheskaia literatura," 1965), p. 174.

[88]Charles D. Bateman, *Your Parliament* (Oxford: Pergamon Press, 1968), p. 52.

organs of power is the direct solution of this task. It guarantees a continuous flow of new vitality into the soviet, permitting an improvement in its work, enlivening and strengthening its ties with the workers.[89]

Ever since the time of Burke, the British Parliament has been considered a useful instrument for educating the public in politics, but in the British view the representatives are the teachers, not the taught. However, the House of Commons is a necessary stepping stone on the way to a career in national politics. There is no other channel for entry into such a career, and no other way of gaining the necessary experience. Thus, while the House of Commons is a proving ground for future national leaders, the Supreme Soviet is a nesting place for present national leaders and a political finishing school for model workers and junior executives in the Soviet economic system.

---

[89] Kuznetsov, *Zakonodatel'naia . . . deiatel'nost'* p. 175.

Parallel
Functions of
the Assemblies

In Europe, the legislature has, to a great extent, become the intermediary body between the citizens and the administration, with greater legitimacy and tighter institutional structure than the pressure groups or the parties, but not necessarily more useful or more efficient in the eyes of the citizens. . . . Everywhere the original model of a parliamentary regime is to some extent in the process of disappearing.

Alfred Grosser,
"The Evolution of European Parliaments"

The political function of representative assemblies today is not so much the initiation of legislation as the carrying on of popular education and propaganda and the integration and coordination of conflicting interests and viewpoints.

Carl J. Friedrich,
Constitutional Government and Democracy

Look at the faces of any crowd pouring out of a morning train on the way to work—some stupid, some harassed, some predatory, some vacuous, some trivial—and reflect that with them rests the determination of our destiny; however ardent a democrat you may be, you will be driven to ask yourself what provision our system makes for affording leadership, knowledge and understanding to these listless masters of our fate.

Ramsay Muir,
How Britain Is Governed

87

Having briefly described what the representative assemblies are, we must now examine what they do. In this chapter, we shall concentrate on those activities which lie outside the domain of policy-making, which is the subject of the next chapter. While the policy-making roles of the two assemblies are quite different, their remaining activities are surprisingly similar because in the visible aspect of their work, in their style and atmosphere, they appear so totally set apart.

These visible differences reflect differing concepts of legitimate political activity in society. The most important difference in legitimizing doctrines is that conflict within the political system is accepted in the British political culture, while its very existence is denied in the Soviet Union. Each representative assembly reflects the values of its political system in this respect, and provides mechanisms for the public display of its own particular political virtues. The British Parliament is well-designed to display political conflict and in some respects its internal procedures almost seem to heighten the conflict that exists or even create the semblance of conflict where no fundamental difference of view exists between the two sides. The Supreme Soviet, on the other hand, is designed to display the unity of a society supposedly without antagonistic classes, where scientific Marxism-Leninism provides a ready solution to the vexing and perplexing problems that beset all mass industrial societies. The word which is usually used to describe the British parliamentary style is *debate.* The Supreme Soviet style can best be characterized by the words *report* and *discussion*, the latter meaning mainly amplification and support of government reports.

The differences in style are important indications of the underlying disparity in fundamental political values. In the same way, the similarity in style points up the necessity of both regimes to legitimate the procedures which, in turn, legitimize the laws of the system. In both systems the procedures are arranged so that the government can gain approval of its program without delay. This activity takes precedence over all others. In both systems, the representatives are given an opportunity to change some aspects of the government's legislation, but these changes amount to very minor adjustments (particularly in the Soviet case). In both systems, the procedures of the assembly are such as to reflect the fundamental consensus amongst the members. Even the procedures of House of Commons debate require a civility and indirection which reduce emotional intensity and contribute to the good fellowship and club-like atmosphere often noted of the House. The members of both assemblies believe in, and espouse the values of, their political system, and agree on the legitimacy of the existing political institutions. In addition, there are no groups in either assembly which are outside this consensus and which attempt to obstruct the procedures of the assembly to force radical change.

The amount of conflict in House of Commons debates should not be exaggerated. A careful look at *Hansard's (Parliamentary Debates)* reveals that most debates consist of carefully considered low-key comments on pending business, comments which often reflect essentially personal views and which have demonstrably insignificant effect on the outcome. The major thrusts in the debate are delivered by the important members of the two major parties—the ministers of the government and the potential ministers of a future government. Although—and perhaps because—this stylized conflict is important to the British political system, it may have to be forced and prodded into an unwilling existence from time to time. As Henry Fairlie points out:

> Conflict—permanent and if need be, artificial—is part of the life of politics in a free society. By the procedures and habits of the House, the permanence of this conflict is ensured, and its sometimes necessary artificiality prescribed. Perhaps the highest tribute that can be paid to the House of Commons is that, over any issue which takes its fancy, it can give a dramatic exhibition of derring-do, both sides competing in implausible but satisfying heroics, and at the end of the day admit it was all about very little.[1]

While there is no equivalent debate in the Supreme Soviet, it should be pointed out that within the procedure of that oft-maligned body there is room for the appearance of minuscule differences and for criticism of past government activity.

The normal Soviet inclination is to mute public displays of disagreement, for open disagreement amongst the leaders would imply uncertainty as to the single "scientific"—and therefore, correct—solution to each problem. Criticism is directed to the implementation of policy by lower level officials and to specific instances of maladministration. It does not strike at the basis for major policy or delve into the activity or motives of high officials.

The formal procedure in the Supreme Soviet provides a rudimentary form of "debate." After each report by a government minister, a "co-report" (*sodoklad*) is presented by the chairman of a corresponding Supreme Soviet committee, in which some mild and indirect criticisms are made, along with mild and indirect recommendations for remedial changes. There is no rebuttal—and, in fact, there is virtually no further reference to the criticisms that are made in the co-reports. Still, the very existence of this criticism is an indication that the regime is aware that the role of the representative, in legitimizing theory, involves something more than listening to, and providing applause for, official speeches—and the usual attendance at banquets and command performances of the Bol'shoi Opera.

The following excerpts from Supreme Soviet discussions are reproduced in order to give an indication of the kind of "disagreement" which arises in open sessions.

> Project estimates are prepared behind schedule and with major defects by the State Union of Institutes for Planning Metallurgical Plants, and by

[1] Henry Fairlie, *The Life of Politics* (London: Methuen, 1968), p. 198.

the Ukrainian organization "Gipromez," its affiliates and several other institutes. . . .

The Budget Committee considers that ministries and departments which are at present in charge of planning and scientific research organizations, must take measures guaranteeing an increase in the quality of project planning and insuring the distribution of technical documents to the construction sites. . . .

The Budget Committee considers that the Councils of Ministers of the union republics and the ministries and departments of the U.S.S.R. must carry out concrete measures to raise the quality and assortment of products, and together with material incentives for good quality production must increase responsibility [i.e. penalties] for manufacture of products of sub-standard quality. . . .[2]

The State Planning Commission established a new schedule for starting production and shipment of 50 thousand refrigerators at the beginning of 1966. But the State Committee for Material-Technical Supply of the U.S.S.R. Council of Ministers, in its letter of November 30, under the signature of its vice-chairman, Comrade Mil'nikov, informed us that the equipment needed for painting parts of the refrigerator in an electrostatic field will be delivered from Hungary only in the third quarter of 1966. It turns out, then, that the plan for production of refrigerators in 1966 has become quite unrealistic. Mistakes such as this, of course, do not mobilize the collective of the factory in the struggle for fulfillment of the state plan, but on the contrary, introduce disorganization.[3]

As can be seen from these quite typical examples, the give-and-take, the thrust-and-parry of debate is missing from the Supreme Soviet discussions. It is understood by everyone present at the session that the criticized agencies, practices, or officials are worthy of censure. They have probably already been criticized in less public ways. They do not appear with rebuttals, nor do they appear with confessions or explanations. The confrontation of opposites, which is the essence of debate, is thus entirely missing from the sessions of the Supreme Soviet. Unity is preserved at the expense of vitality.

Another typical and consistent activity of the Supreme Soviet has been to change the government's annual budget by some very small amount. This is generally done as the result of recommendations by the Budget Committees of the Supreme Soviet. (For example, revenue and expenditure for 1966 were each increased by 120.6 million rubles, an amount which represents 0.11 percent of the revenue then projected for that year.) This change is supposed to demonstrate the important role played by deputies in making decisions. There is little doubt that the amount of the budgetary adjustment is arranged

[2]Co-report by I. V. Kapitonov, Chairman, Budget Committee of the Council of the Union, December 7, 1965, in *Zasedaniia verkhovnogo soveta SSSR, 6 soziva, 7 sessia, stenograficheskii otchet* (Moscow: Izdanie Verkhovnogo Soveta SSSR, 1966), p. 64.

[3]Speech by S. A. Movseian, *ibid.*, p. 290.

beforehand by the government, since there is no open debate on the amount or direction of the change. Thus the whole procedure has the verisimilitude of an amateur theatrical performance.

For the most part, open sessions of the Supreme Soviet are rather dreary affairs. Its most important moments are spent listening to first-ranking leaders making long speeches. Its lesser moments are spent listening to lower-ranking officials making shorter speeches. According to a Western reporter's recent observations of a session:

> Some of the deputies listened attentively. Some read *Pravda* . . . Many, by chatting among themselves, created a buzz when speakers on the rostrum drew a breath, or yielded to their successors. A few deputies appeared to be asleep.[4]

The mere presence of an opposition does not ensure that the sessions of the House of Commons are always more exciting than the scene in the Supreme Soviet. Most of the time, House of Commons sessions are poorly attended, the chamber appearing nearly empty. There are times when the House provides a vivid contrast, when the big guns on both sides of the aisle wheel into position over a major policy issue, but these are exceptional times, certainly not the normal occurrence. In fact, most sessions of the House achieve very little more controversy than can be found in sessions of the Supreme Soviet. Oftentimes, the matter under discussion is not particularly controversial or is quite technical, in which case the discussion is likely to be over details and quite cordial. In many cases, it would seem that the M.P.'s are bemused by the technical difficulties of the legislation, and therefore avoid addressing themselves to the substance of the bill, substituting irrelevancies and idiosyncratic views.[5]

Another factor which reduces the heat of controversy is the already-mentioned club-like atmosphere of the House, reinforced by the similar social and educational backgrounds of M.P.'s. But even without this, and considering M.P.'s of quite dissimilar origins, the occupational role of Member of Parliament carries with it a set of common activities, inter-personal relation-

---

[4] James F. Clarity, *The New York Times*, December 18, 1969.

[5] For example—and there are all too many of this sort—during a debate on import quotas for apples, Mr. Jasper More included the following remarks in his contribution to debate: "There has been one misconception running through all those speeches—that is, that apples should be bought by the housewife. That is fundamentally wrong. Apples should never be bought by the housewife. They should always be bought by the husband. Apples should not be judged by their appearance. The right way to judge apples is by their grade and species. . . . I would like to hear it seriously suggested to those hotels which get public funds that on every hotel breakfast table there should be the different types of English apple which every Englishman should eat at least once each breakfast-time, if only to keep the doctor away, and similarly with British Railways and all other publicly supported enterprises of that kind." *H. C. Parliamentary Debates (Weekly Hansard)*, vol. 791, no. 10 (November 10, 1969), cols. 142–43.

ships, and role-conforming attitudes that draw M.P.'s together, regardless of their assumptions upon entering the House. Ronald Butt has remarked that "discontent on the part of the new Member is commonplace ... [but] ... the enthusiasm for parliamentary reform tended to die down as Members have found appropriate niches of activity and interest at Westminster."[6]

Debates in the House of Commons are characterized by short personal contributions of back-bench members, preceded and concluded by longer, more detailed comments by front-bench ministers and members of the opposition. Because time is usually short and front-bench speakers take so much of it, there is little time left for backbenchers, particularly on important matters where more members wish to participate. In addition, many members raise "constituency points" (i.e., matters of concern to their own constituency but not of general interest), and this reduces the available time for general debate.[7] When a backbencher manages "to catch the Speaker's eye" (i.e., gain the Speaker's recognition and thus have the floor for a speech), he faces a situation described humorously by A. P. Herbert as the "torture chamber":

> The backbencher, clutching his notes, is like a lonely man standing up in the middle of a public meeting. His audience is all round him, some in front, some behind, some above him, some below—and a great many high up in galleries in a building not highly meritorious for "acoustics." An interruption, a sneer, an ironical laugh may hit him from any quarter. . . . More, unless he is very good, or fairly important—and even if he is—his audience is moving and changing all the time. Members, good friends, it may be . . . march out as he approaches his principal, or only, joke. The Minister whom he hopes to convert, or intends to shatter with a deadly jest, is relieved by another Minister and goes out for a cup of tea, just before the unanswerable argument or the crushing quip is reached. . . . There is movement everywhere. It is like making a speech in a beehive.[8]

The difficulties of delivering a speech are compounded by the difficulties of publicizing it. Very few daily newspapers report the vicissitudes of parliamentary life. Even the few high-quality (and therefore low-circulation) newspapers pay scant attention to the contributions of back-bench M.P.'s But in this the newspapers have simply and correctly reacted to the well-known fact that the vast majority of the public is not interested in what transpires at Westminster Palace, and most particularly is not interested in the speeches of obscure back-bench members. The public, in turn, is quite simply reacting to

---

[6] Ronald Butt, *The Power of Parliament* (London: Constable, 1967), pp. 182–84.

[7] See A. H. Hanson and H. V. Wiseman, *Parliament at Work: A Case-Book of Parliamentary Procedure* (London: Stevens, 1962), p. 114.

[8] A. P. Herbert, *Independent Member* (London: Methuen, 1950), pp. 46–47.

the fact that only very exceptionally does anything occur on the floor of the House which is politically significant.

In the Soviet Union, the sessions of the Supreme Soviet are covered in full by all but the most specialized or local newspapers. Of course, this is a matter of government policy rather than public demand. Indeed, the Supreme Soviet receives better press coverage than the House of Commons. However, it is highly unlikely that these full reports are read with any sustained interest by the Soviet population. In both the Soviet Union and Great Britain, the public intuitively reacts to a central fact of national political life: that *the primary function of open and full sessions of the representative assembly is to present and publicize views held by politically significant persons.*

Some publicity outside the chamber is gained for these views, but there is no attempt to persuade or dissuade other members inside the assembly through parliamentary oratory. Other members are not likely to be swayed by speeches, particularly by the modest efforts made in these assemblies, and in any case, the views of the members do not necessarily coincide with the way that they vote; for the party leaderships determine the vote before the debate begins. The gentle and exhausting art of persuasion may be used by a representative, but it is more effective in the government official's office than on the floor of the assembly.

The speeches are not for the other members of the assembly, but primarily for the public outside the chambers. This view is openly endorsed by the Soviet regime, in pointing to the "public education" function of the Supreme Soviet. It is not so warmly and universally embraced by British writers, although the eminent parliamentary scholar, Sir Ivor Jennings, has written that "a private member's speech usually has one of two objectives, to indicate his ability to his party leaders, or to obtain publicity outside."[9]

Here we have a curious paradox: the representatives are speaking over the heads of their colleagues to the masses outside, but very, very few people— inside or outside—are listening. A particularly brilliant speech in the House of Commons—alas, there has not been one as yet in the Supreme Soviet—may win acclaim and heightened prestige for the speaker, may even mobilize existing opinions in the House and sway just a few, but even in the most brilliant and rare case, very few opinions and even fewer votes are affected. As for the

[9]Sir Ivor Jennings, *Parliament*, 2nd ed. (Cambridge: Cambridge University Press, 1957), p. 163. Bernard Crick has also adopted this point of view in his *The Reform of Parliament* (Garden City, N.Y.: Doubleday Anchor Books, 1965), p. 27, where he writes: "Parliament is to be seen as a forum of publicity. . . . Its real functions are those of alerting and informing the public on matters relevant to the decision which way (or whether) to vote." On the other side, Sir Austen Chamberlain stated (in 1931) that "there is nothing so untrue as to say that votes are not changed by speeches." Jennings, *Parliament*, p. 161.

public, all empirical evidence points to the inescapable conclusion that its attention is directed only sporadically to the forensic efforts of its representatives.

Why, then, do they go on, filling the unread pages of *Hansard's* and the *Stenograficheskie otchety*? If there is to be any answer at all, beyond the normally expected amounts of human folly and egotism, it must lie in the primary function of these assemblies as the chief legitimizing organizations for the government. One of the most important functions of the representative in both countries is to act as a link between the citizen and the government, to make its restrictions and rules palatable to the citizen. The government, to use Samuel Beer's suggestive term, "must continuously mobilize consent," and the legislature is given a large role in achieving this consent. In Beer's terms, this consent is particularly crucial in contemporary Britain:

> The Welfare State and the managed economy bring many benefits, but also, inevitably, they impose many new and complex coercions—often in the very process of conferring benefits. A great deal is expected of the citizen in the form of new necessities that oblige him to conform in his behavior to the complex requirements of economic and social policy. On the one hand, the burdens that Government imposes on citizens are very demanding and, on the other hand, the reasons for these impositions are often highly complex and technical. To win both the mind and the heart of citizen to an acceptance of these coercions is a major necessity, but a severe problem. . . . The democratic process, focused by the legislature upon periodic elections, can do a great deal to meet this problem.[10]

For the very same reasons and to an even greater degree, the Soviet government must continuously mobilize consent. Its impositions are even more complex and omnipresent, for it acknowledges no limits on its legitimate sphere of activity in organizing society. The coercions it imposes over citizens are even more demanding, for it has established a particular model of the ideal citizen and recognizes no restraints in its drive to make everyone conform to it.

However, the main problem for both governments is not the public reaction to "coercions"—for few citizens view them as such—but rather the psychological distance between the national government and the individual in the modern mass society. It is the indifferent rather than the alienated man-in-the-street whom one meets most often in these societies.

While the mere presence and formal operation of these representative assemblies is a large factor in building system legitimacy, they have not been very effective in mobilizing consent for particular measures. Ian Gilmour has

---

[10] Samuel H. Beer, "The British Legislature and the Problem of Mobilizing Consent," in Bernard Crick, ed., *Essays on Reform, 1967: A Centenary Tribute*, (London: Oxford University Press, 1967), p. 98.

written that the defect in the present procedure of Parliament is "that the government is so successful in gaining the consent of those inside the House that it has been losing some of its ability to gain the consent of those outside it."[11] The consent of the representative assembly is assured by the dominance of the government or, put another way, the party in power. This dominance greatly reduces the importance of open sessions of the representative assembly, for the ultimate results of its "deliberations" are well known in advance. This almost total predictability of outcome makes the assemblies less interesting and explains the usual indifference of the public. Still, although neither assembly performs very well in mobilizing *consent* for specific legislation, they do *legitimize* legislation and give it authority.

Although full sessions of these assemblies are not particularly effective in reaching the *masses*, they do serve as a *means of political communication amongst politically important people*. The debate in Parliament enables the government to assess the feelings of both its supporters and its opponents, and may cause it to alter its future strategy. The discussion in the Supreme Soviet is, on the other hand, a means primarily of one-way communication from the government center to lower-ranking administrators whose responsibilities entail the implementation of government policies. The full sessions may, therefore, have a long-term informational utility which is not reflected in the immediate outcomes or votes of the assemblies.

The information flow among representatives and members of government (who are also representatives) is not confined to the open sessions of the assembly. Informal meetings, discussions, and consultations occur in the halls, antechambers, and offices around the assembly chamber. This is a regular and well-documented occurrence in Westminster Palace. Even chance meetings have occasionally had significant results. There is no documentation for the Soviet case, but it seems likely that the comparatively rare and short sessions of the Supreme Soviet afford an unusual opportunity for locally-based political leaders to share experiences, iron out difficulties, and consult with the leadership at the center—an opportunity which they are not likely to overlook.

Despite this possibility of lateral information flow among deputies, the Supreme Soviet clearly does not compare with the House of Commons as a focal point for political communication. The brevity of sessions and the strong possibility that the more important deputies will have other, better channels of communication available to them, make the Supreme Soviet less important than the House of Commons in this respect. In addition, M.P.'s serve an important function in gathering local opinion—or at least what passes for local opinion from the mouths of locally powerful persons—and transmitting it to the center by various informal means. This function is far less

[11] Ian Gilmour, *The Body Politic* (London: Hutchinson, 1969), p. 279.

likely to be performed by a deputy to the U.S.S.R. Supreme Soviet. The M.P.'s ability to speak for local opinion is directly linked to his clear advantage over the ordinary deputy in influencing policies (as will be discussed in Chapter V).

Another technique for gaining information, long hallowed by the procedure of the House of Commons, is Question Time, in which M.P.'s ask previously submitted questions of Ministers of the Government, who appear before the House in a regular rotational schedule. These questions, particularly those set down for oral answers, may be more than mere requests for information—they may be attempts to shine the "searchlight of publicity" on administrative problems or mistakes which the Government would much prefer to sweep under the rug. In the hands of opposition M.P.'s, this weapon may be used in an attempt to embarrass the Government or to correct an error or injustice, or simply to reveal a wasteful or anomalous administrative procedure that has escaped the Government's attention. It presumably has a salutary effect on administrators, for, as H. J. Laski wrote some years ago, "men who have to answer day by day for their decisions will try so to act that they can give a good account of themselves."[12]

Nevertheless, the effect of Question Time is not as great as its most ardent supporters apparently believe. It can be a device for gaining information, especially about details (and especially in those questions put down for written answers), but the echoes of most questions do not reach the world outside the Chamber, for lack of publicity or interest in them. The tremendous growth in the administrative machinery of government has also increased the difficulty of shining a searchlight on it systematically, especially through the haphazard device of relying on M.P.'s, without staff assistance of any kind, to uncover flaws and bring them to light. As one British writer comments: "The public service has become too extensive for the searchlight to cast anything more than a diffused light which becomes intense only if it happens to fall upon a more flagrant mistake or abuse."[13] Questions all too often waste the time of the House and try the patience of civil servants (who must prepare the Minister's answer), without achieving anything of substance. Most Ministers know—or quickly learn—how to turn questions aside with bland assurances, noncommittal or uninformative replies, or sharp ripostes which add insult to the questioner's frustration. (For example, Prime Minister Wilson's reply to a supplementary questioner that "the hon. and learned Gentleman can always be relied upon to denigrate any subject which he

[12] Harold J. Laski, *Parliamentary Government in England* (London: Allen and Unwin, 1938), p. 152.

[13] Nevil Johnson, "Parliamentary Questions and the Conduct of Administration," *Public Administration*, vol. 39 (Summer 1961), p. 143.

touches . . . "[14]) Questions involving individual abuses can occasionally achieve spectacular results, but "immediately the Question strays on to wider issues involving more general policy matters and issues of political concern, then little, if anything, of practical significance can be achieved."[15] But even in the realm of details and individual abuses, it would seem that correspondence from the M.P. to the ministry concerned is of more consequence than questions asked on the floor of the House—at least this is a conclusion of the comprehensive study conducted by Chester and Bowring.[16] What, then, is the justification for taking four hours of Parliament's time each week for questions? Despite its deficiencies and limitations, most observers find something useful in Question Time, even when they are highly critical of other parliamentary activity. For all its shortcomings, Question Time can be credited with the following accomplishments:

1. It provides information for M.P.'s.
2. More rarely, it provides information for the public.
3. It reinforces Ministerial responsibility before Parliament.
4. It has (possibly) a positive effect on the efficiency, honesty, and compassion of administrators.
5. It provides a channel of activity for backbenchers, whose role in other respects has diminished.
6. It makes the Government more responsive to Parliamentary opinion, and more particularly to opposition criticism.

It may not do any of these things very well or very often, but if it does them at all, it is probably worth the four hours per week spent on it.

The legitimization and information functions of the Soviet and British assemblies are also carried out individually by the representatives in their localities. In both systems it is considered an important function of the representative to maintain close contact with his constituents. They are supposed to gauge the general morale of the public and ascertain the opinions of more politically salient groups in the community. In addition, they are supposed to act as ombudsmen, as channels for citizens' grievances against maladministration or pettifogging bureaucracy, and as sympathetic and effective agents of the system for correcting these injustices. In Great Britain, the average M.P. conducts "surgeries" in his constituency on weekends, taking complaints and acting as the citizen's advocate where appropriate. This function has been institutionalized, for "the fact is, as any Member's post bag confirms, that whenever they come up against the folly, or tyranny of lesser

[14] 769 *H. C. Debates*, col. 269.

[15] Johnson, "Parliamentary Questions," p. 143.

[16] See D. N. Chester and Nona Bowring, *Questions in Parliament* (Oxford: Clarendon Press, 1962), p. 284.

or greater officials, ordinary people are still apt to turn to their sitting Member, acting in the confident belief that he will be readily available to them."[17] M.P.'s can also be found ceaselessly orating before local groups and organizations, and appearing at all sorts of local festivals and feasts.

Soviet deputies are also expected to carry out extensive "educational" work in their localities. Since the Supreme Soviet deputy either represents 300,000 people or is elected at large from one of the fifteen union republics or other large administrative units of the U.S.S.R., he cannot be expected to maintain the same degree of personal contact on an individual basis with his constituents as the M.P. Nevertheless, his activities, on a somewhat larger scale, are apparently quite impressive, particularly considering that he retains his ordinary occupation. The Soviet deputy carries out three activities associated with this function: he makes speeches at public meetings, takes complaints from individuals, and collects so-called "mandates" from public meetings. The content of his speeches is quite different from that of the British M.P. The deputy's speeches are attempts to inform, and to elicit support from, the population for policies already adopted. The point is made abundantly clear by one Soviet writer who states:

> The most important obligation of deputies is to explain decisions adopted by the Supreme Soviet and to organize the masses for carrying them out. All other activities in the electoral district are essentially subordinated to this task. As a rule, after each session of the Supreme Soviet, deputies conduct meetings with their electors in which they inform the voters about the decisions that have been taken. . . . As a result of meetings with deputies, the voters often, on their own initiative, respond to the decision of the Supreme Soviet by accepting responsibility for fulfilling their part of the plan for the national economy on time.[18]

This activity can apparently be quite a burden for the Supreme Soviet deputy, one of whom received favorable mention for personally receiving about twelve thousand voters, and holding about two hundred public meetings, at which forty thousand voters attended, over a period of ten years.[19] The taking of complaints about local or personal grievances is probably more closely associated with the work of deputies to local soviets, who are closer to such matters.[20]

[17] Fairlie, *Life of Politics*, p. 25. This function has not been significantly lessened by the introduction of a central ombudsman, the Parliamentary Commissioner, in 1967. The Parliamentary Commissioner can only investigate complaints sent by citizens through their M.P.'s, thus essentially preserving (and perhaps strengthening) the M.P.'s role in this regard.

[18] I. I. Kuznetsov, *Zakonodatel'naia i ispolnitel'naia deiatel'nost' vysshikh organov vlasti* (Moscow: Izd-vo "Iuridicheskaia literatura," 1965), p. 178.

[19] *Ibid.*, p. 178.

[20] A rough indication of this work load is given by a Soviet survey of local deputies which showed that these deputies were approached by more than 13 percent of their

In both systems, then, the representative can legitimately act as an ombudsman, as a channel of corrective feedback to the administrative system in individual cases. As for the propaganda or information function: the representative who belongs to the party in power will not normally attack the policy of the Government (in either country) when addressing his constituents, although he may privately have his doubts and reservations. Since the legitimacy of the representative is based on his close contact with those he represents, the state provides free transportation to representatives for travel back to, and around, the areas they represent. In addition, both M.P.'s and deputies receive many letters from constituents and the state provides free postal privileges to facilitate this means of communication.

In acting as ombudsmen and system legitimizers in their localities, the British and Soviet representatives perform the same functions for their systems, but they do so in different styles appropriate to the political cultures of their societies. The Soviet deputy will appear more blatantly like a cheerleader for government policy than even a solidly pro-government M.P., but this is expected of him by his constituents no less than by his superiors. The style of these messages is more or less dictated by such expectations, but the underlying message is supportive and legitimizing for the regime in both cases.

A further activity of the Soviet deputy is to collect "mandates" from public meetings, and to forward them to the soviet. The purpose and form of these mandates are explained by one Soviet writer as follows:

> Voters' mandates are one of the institutions of direct democracy. . . . The mandates, i.e., proposals made by voters, are collectively adopted at meetings of voters. The purpose of the mandates is to outline the concrete tasks of the Deputies and the Soviets for a specific period. . . . If an elected representative of the people fails to fulfill his mandate, and hence does not do the bidding of the voters, the latter have the right to deprive him of his authority.[21]

There is, of course, no direct equivalent in the British system for these mandates, but since the mandates are in general rather modest proposals for local improvements, they are usually presented to local and republic soviets rather

---

constitutents in one year. See V. A. Pertsik, *Sovetskoe gosudarstvo i pravo*, no. 7 (July) 1967 [*CDSP* XIX, no. 33, p. 5.] Another poll of deputies to local soviets showed that although 69 percent felt they had enough time to perform their official duties, some mentioned that it was necessary "to put off taking a vacation" or that "the family suffers some loss." Only 24 percent were able to satisfy their constituents' "legitimate requests," and 49 percent said they got all necessary help from the executive committee of the local soviet. See the article, "O chem rasskazala anketa," *Sovety deputatov trudaishchikhsia*, no. 10 (October), 1966.

[21] V. F. Kotok, *Izvestiia*, August 21, 1968 [*CDSP*, XX, 34, p. 25.] For a fuller discussion of the subject by the same author, see *Nakazy izbiratelei v sotsialisticheskom gosudarstve* (Moscow: Izd-vo "Nauka," 1967).

than to the U.S.S.R. Supreme Soviet. Furthermore, as the same writer had to admit: "It frequently happened that individual proposals could not be realized for objective reasons—because of the absence of material possibilities, for example."[22]

In essence, the legitimizing functions of the Soviet and British representatives, both at home and in full sessions of the assemblies, are virtually identical. The representative represents the system to the people as much as he represents the people to the system. In neither assembly does one find representatives who oppose the existing institutions of government. Even in Great Britain, where the once feared "radical Socialists" form a large contingent in Parliament, there are no anti-system representatives. The immediate cause of this unanimous support for the existing system in both countries is the nomination procedure, which assures that the major parties will bring forward as candidates only those who adhere to the values of the party—a major component of which is support for the system.

The underlying cause, however, and the reason why this nomination procedure attracts very little opposition is that both political systems are supported by wide popular agreement on their fundamental legitimacy. Thus the representatives do "represent" the prevailing values of the people. This high degree of consensus is an indication of a very successful process of political socialization in these countries; it is both a result of, and a contributor to, the high degree of political stability of these regimes.

Thus the role of the representative acting between the system and the people can be seen as another factor contributing to stability. The effectiveness of this role in practice, however, is limited, because the representative is not seen by the public as affecting important outcomes, and the representative's role in bolstering system legitimacy is somewhat redundant, since this legitimacy is already firmly established. These are the primary reasons why, as we have mentioned, not many people listen when the representative speaks.

It can be seen from the preceding analysis that the two representative assemblies are not as different in their normal functions as is commonly supposed. In their day-to-day activities they differ more in their superficial aspects than in matters of substance. If one seeks to discover a fundamental difference between them, one finds that it does not reside in the area of constitutional powers or in the routine exercise of those powers, but instead lies in the "extraneous" fact that the party systems differ and that *the influence of party organization changes the whole context of parliamentary activity.* In seeking to explain this difference, Sir Ivor Jennings has written: "The real difference between Britain and the dictatorship countries is that with us there is not one faction seeking to maintain itself in power by per-

[22] *Ibid.*, p. 26.

suasion, fraud or force, but at least two factions each trying to achieve and maintain power by persuasion."[23] Sir Ivor is not quite correct in this case. The real difference is not between a monolithic leadership in the Soviet Union exemplified by its unanimous Supreme Soviet, and a British leadership split in two or three or more factions contending for power. In fact, the essential difference here is that the contention of opposing factions is legitimized in Great Britain, and being legitimized is capable of open and continuous organization. The major factions have become parties in Britain, a process that began in the eighteenth century. In the Soviet Union, open conflict is not legitimate, but conflict cannot thereby be eliminated. In the U.S.S.R. there is not "just one faction seeking to maintain itself in power," as Jennings mistakenly asserts, but many factions, shifting, overlapping, temporary and, most important of all, *illegitimate*. Factions are, in essence, illegitimate groupings, called into existence by conflict within organizations with a high consensus value on unity. Factions thus form within parties, and where there is only one party, factions are the only possible means of organizing political leadership in conflicted situations.

The open and full sessions of the assemblies, therefore, differ in that the conflict between the illegitimate Soviet factions can play no part, while the open and legitimate conflict of British parties is the very essence of parliamentary debate. On occasion this debate can provide information on alternative views and policies, which, while not heard or understood by many, can be of value to the small portion of the population which is politically informed and politically efficacious.

As for the "powers" of the assemblies, in the theory of constitutional texts or unwritten but widely and deeply held beliefs, the assemblies are plenipotentiary and, in fact, the source of all state power. In practice, in normal routine activity, neither assembly exercises even a small portion of this theoretical power.

Nevertheless, the real power of the British Parliament lies in its rarely exercised but genuine potential for using its constitutional power. This potential is rarely used primarily because it is so effective unused. In other words, the House of Commons exercises an *inhibitory power*, measured not by the attacks of Parliament on the executive, but by the prior self-limitation of leaders, based on their predictions or instinctual assumptions about the likely reactions of Parliament to proposed measures. Thus an effective British leader is one who is continuously attuned to the state of opinion in Parliament, and who plots his future course of action with this opinion in mind. It is this which former Prime Minister Harold Wilson had in mind when he stated: "I don't think it is true . . . that they [backbench M.P.'s] have got less power, or

[23] Jennings, *Parliament*, p. 528.

less influence in policy-making than ever before. They have got more power than ever, in my experience."[24]

In apparent contrast, the leadership of the Soviet Communist Party does not have to give any consideration to the opinions of the vast majority of the members of the U.S.S.R. Supreme Soviet. But it is not true that Soviet policy can be made by its leadership in a vacuum. Surely, here too, leaders must be cognizant of and responsive to opinions of those with less political power. Included in that group of influential people must be a sizeable minority of the Supreme Soviet, whose permanent occupation is political in nature. If we include in this group only those who have full-time jobs in the party or state administration, we find that they form 33.5 percent of the Supreme Soviet membership (1966). The government policy must appeal to these people, not because they are deputies in the Supreme Soviet, but because they are the bureaucrats, the administrators, upon whose enthusiasm and efforts the success of any government policy will depend. It is probably not true to the same extent, but true nevertheless, that these *important* Soviet deputies have some inhibitory power in the decisions made by the Soviet leadership. Since the top leaders will want a policy that is workable, they cannot afford to ignore the expert advice of the practitioners and specialists below them in the hierarchy. Since the leaders will also prefer a policy—if possible—that will be enthusiastically supported and welcomed by lower ranks, it is to their advantage to hear the opinions of the lower ranks. They never do this in public, for the value of monolithic unity is too important as a legitimizing principle, but they apparently do this to some extent behind the scenes.

While the Soviet leadership may find its own interests served by responding to inputs from important political figures who happen to be members of the Supreme Soviet, it does not respond to them because of their Supreme Soviet membership, but because of their other roles in the political system—and this is an essential element in the great difference in influence between members of the Supreme Soviet and members of the House of Commons. M.P.'s are influential because they are Members of Parliament; Supreme Soviet deputies can only be influential if they are something else as well—preferably members of the party-state apparatus.

The inhibitory power of the House of Commons over the leadership is the power to withhold support from the Government on that incredible, never-to-be-reached day when the Government stands so clearly aside from the consensus that even its own backbench deserts it. The power is based on a situation that never occurs, but it never occurs primarily because the power exists. The real cutting edge of this parliamentary power is the day-to-day influence of M.P.'s, individually or in groups, on a score of lesser matters

---

[24]Interview with Prime Minister Harold Wilson, *The Listener*, April 6 and April 13, 1967.

where the threat of exercising inhibitory power is never raised. It is quite possible to argue that this influence of M.P.'s is not very great, or not great enough, but it is not realistic to argue that this influence does not exist at all.

LEGISLATIVE ACTIVITIES

Neither representative assembly functions primarily as a legislature. L. S. Amery has written about the British Parliament that its "main task . . . is still what it was when first summoned, not to legislate or govern, but to secure full discussion and ventilation of all matters, . . . as the condition of giving its assent to Bills, whether introduced by Government or by private members, or its support to the executive action of Ministers."[25] The limited legislative activities of both the British Parliament and the Supreme Soviet can be compared with a list of activities that would be performed by a theoretical fully-empowered legislature. Such a list would at least include the following:
1. initiation of legislation;
2. examination of legislation (in full session and committees);
3. revision and alteration of legislation;
4. delay and/or postponement, when felt to be necessary;
5. acceptance or rejection of legislation.

There can be no doubts that both the British and Soviet representative assemblies fall far short of the functions that one would expect a legislature to perform. Neither assembly at present initiates major legislation. The draft legislation is almost without exception drawn up by the Government. Both assemblies retain the function of examination of legislation, both in full session and in committees, a matter to which we shall return shortly. Both assemblies have some minor, severely restricted functions of revision and alteration of legislation. The House of Commons has more scope in performing this function than does the Supreme Soviet, and in the rare but nevertheless significant case of highly controversial legislation, the House can effect modifications.

The fourth function, delay or postponement, is not possible in either case if the government is determined and committed to rapid implementation of the measure. Normally, neither assembly imposes any significant delay, but it is true that the opposition party in the House of Commons can attempt to apply brakes to the legislative process when it senses that the Government is on weak ground. In this case the Government, which controls the agenda and a majority of votes, can call up its full arsenal of parliamentary weapons, such as the "guillotine" (a debate-limiting procedure which forces votes after allotted time periods have elapsed). Of course, the House of Lords can still stall

[25] L. S. Amery, "The Nature of British Parliamentary Government," in Lord Campion, et al., eds., *Parliament: A Survey* (London: Allen and Unwin, 1952), p. 44.

legislation for up to one year, but this power is gradually shrinking through disuse. Even this limited, rarely tried, and even more rarely successful power of delay separates the British Parliament from the Supreme Soviet, whose sole function in this regard is to *expedite* government measures. This alacrity is quite consonant with Soviet theories of legitimacy, which state that government policy is always optimal primarily because it is inspired by the Communist Party. Once this assumption is made, delay could only be equated with *disloyalty* to the interests of the people and the Party. This, of course, could not be tolerated, for as one Soviet writer has said: "The soviets of workers' deputies exercise the power of the people in our country and are the true and active helpers of the Communist Party, the reliable exponents of [the Party's] policies. All activities of the soviets are infused with Communist Party spirit."[26] To avoid the possibility of even procedural delays, the Presidium of the Supreme Soviet is empowered to issue decrees, having the force of law, during the approximately half-year periods between sessions of the full Supreme Soviet.

On the other hand, the delaying function can be seen in a positive light if one has in mind controversial issues, and if one assumes that government may be prone to hasty and ill-considered legislation, unless there is sufficient time for calm and reasoned counsel to prevail. This was the view of the Conservative Party leaders in 1948, when they wrote: "It is an essential constitutional safeguard to ensure that, in the event of serious controversy between the two Houses of Parliament on a measure on which the view of the electorate is doubtful, such a measure shall not pass into law until sufficient time has elapsed to enable the electorate to be properly informed of the issues involved and for public opinion to crystallize and express itself."[27] In the Soviet system, of course, it is assumed that public opinion has "crystallized" in unswerving support for government measures before they appear on the agenda of the Supreme Soviet, thus making delay unnecessary.

The acceptance or rejection function is performed by both assemblies—by accepting without exceptions virtually all government measures presented to them. In the Soviet Union this is a very simple matter, the acceptance being shown by a steadfastly unanimous show of hands. In fact, over the Supreme Soviet's entire history since 1936, not a single work-hardened hand has been raised in opposition to anything the government has proposed to it.

This function is performed in a slightly more complex way in Great Britain, as a result of the interplay of government and opposition. Divisions of the House of Commons—so called because the M.P.'s file into the chamber through two separate entrances to record their vote—are generally along party

[26]M. Krakhmalev, *Izvestiia*, November 1, 1969.

[27]"Agreed Statement on Conclusion of Conference of Party Leaders," Cmd. 7380, p. 4.

lines, with considerable abstentions on both sides. The high cohesion of both major parties means that voting across party lines is extremely rare.

There are usually many absentees at division time, since the outcome of the vote is assured by party discipline and the usual substantial majority of the Government party. On many occasions, not even half the members can be found to file through the appropriate aisle "like so many sheep." This lack of interest is the characteristically sensible reaction of M.P.'s to the fact that there are more important ways of spending their time than engaging in a purely symbolic act. Voting by representatives symbolizes acceptance of legislation by those who will be bound by it: the citizens of the system. The representatives are not expressing a choice they have made. They are just as bound by the discipline of their party whips as the majority of the electorate is bound by the rigidity of its party prejudices. Whatever effect M.P.'s or Supreme Soviet deputies may have had in determining the shape or content of legislation at some earlier stage, by the time the matter has been brought to a vote, they have no more influence, and no power to change the outcome. This is understood by the representatives and by the citizens. The actual numerical results are not significant and are not widely reported. On a few well-remembered occasions (such as the famous Tory defection from Neville Chamberlain in 1940) the size of the Government majority in the House of Commons may be significantly reduced by purposeful abstentions of Government supporters, but even in the most trying circumstances the ultimate power of party loyalty has prevented a Government defeat—something that has not happened in this century. When the majority is small, it is possible for the opposition whips to catch the Government napping, and suddenly force a vote at an unexpected moment when Government supporters have wandered away from Westminster. This can embarrass the Government, but it cannot force the Government to resign, since the vote can easily be reversed the next day.

Thus the ultimate importance of voting in Great Britain, as well as the Soviet Union, is that by this act the representative assembly performs its most important function: *legitimizing government-sponsored legislation and thus imparting authority to law.* The structure of the act implies the possibility of individual choices, but the actual function does not require that the choices be really offered to the individual representative.[28] Although the Soviet representatives go one step further to perfect unanimity, it can be said that both governments in effect have the same 1.000 batting average on votes con-

---

[28]There are exceptional cases in the House of Commons when a "free vote" with the whips off is permitted because the question is a "matter of conscience." The principle invoked here is that one should not be forced by party loyalty to violate the dictates of one's deeply felt convictions, but these questions are usually so loaded with explosive moral and emotional issues that the parties are delighted to avoid them and leave these politically risky issues to the individual M.P.'s.

cerning government proposals. And in Britain, where such things are permitted, there are very few cases indeed where government measures have been withdrawn or greatly reduced because of pressure before the vote. Where retreats occur (such as the oft-mentioned Resale Price Maintenance debacle of the Conservatives in 1964), the crucial factor is the inability of the Government to hold its own backbenchers, not the effects of Opposition's opposition. These occurrences are very rare. Normally, the only uncertainty that surrounds the roughly five hundred divisions that occur during a sessional year of the House of Commons is the number of absentees—by design or necessity—on both sides of the aisle. The pattern of voting in the House of Commons is the direct result of the presence of two highly disciplined predominant parties, just as the voting in the Supreme Soviet is the result of the dominance of a single party over the political activities of all Soviet citizens, whether or not they are elected representatives or formally party members.

COMMITTEES

The great complexity of the industrialized mass society places great burdens on the political system to coordinate and regulate the interlocking social and economic activities connected with production, distribution and consumption. To meet this challenge, the administrative structures of the regimes have grown enormously and have been increasingly differentiated into specialized sub-structures. By contrast, the representative assemblies have not evolved in ways which would permit them to adapt to the increased complexity of modern society. Neither British nor Soviet representatives are supplied with even a small staff, or office, or the most rudimentary of all requirements, a desk—a neglect which is both a cause and a symptom of their present inability to cope with the legislative function in a consistently meaningful way. As we have already seen, neither representative assembly was designed to initiate legislation, but they both have retained the function of examination and alteration of legislation when required. Open and full sessions of these assemblies clearly do not perform this function, nor are they expected to do so. Karl Bracher mentions two basic problems of parliaments in reviewing modern legislation: the problem of personnel and the problem of time. In connection with the first problem, he states that "the expansion of the state places too great demands on the abilities of the members of parliament," and that "an elected representative cannot, by the nature of the thing, be equal to the many-sided detailed problems with which society and bureaucracy confront him."[29] This view centers on an inherent structural defect of representation

[29] Karl Dietrich Bracher, "Problems of Parliamentary Democracy in Europe," *Daedalus*, vol. 93, no. 1 (Winter 1964), p. 188.

in the modern, industrial society, regardless of the general quality, level of intelligence, or specialized knowledge of the representatives.[30]

The second problem, that of time, is described by Bracher as follows:

> Overtaxed in its assignments, the parliament limits itself to topics that have an effect on the election and abandons important decisions in practice to the planning and formulating bureaucracy. Thus their roles are often exactly reversed. Law-giving is transferred to the apparatus of administration and parliament loses its authority to a quasi-dictatorship of the executive.[31]

Bracher's critique is based on the assumption, made by many others also, that the ideal parliament should be equipped to initiate and revise all legislation as a prerequisite to legitimizing it as law. There is no very convincing reason why representative assemblies must be refurbished as fully capable legislatures in order to carry out their other important—and still reasonably well done—functions of information and legitimization.

Nevertheless, Bracher's assumption seems to be the consensual view of the British and Soviet governments, for the representative assemblies have taken some modest organizational steps in recent years to alleviate, if not eliminate, the fundamental problem of insufficient time for legislative review. This has been done primarily through an increase in the number of parliamentary committees and a strengthening of their role in the legislative process.

There are three types of committee in the British Parliament. Of most ancient vintage are the Select Committees, which are, according to Bernard Crick, "simply small committees of Members appointed by the House to examine, to investigate and to make a report on a particular subject or problem on a particular occasion. They perform a kind of task for which the House itself is not suited: the examination of witnesses, the sifting of evidence, the production of a reasoned and concise report and usually proposals."[32] There are also perennial Select Committees which are in effect specialized standing committees of the House and which are empowered to oversee and investigate specific areas of governmental activity on a continu-

---

[30]The question of the quality of M.P.'s in Britain is much debated, the answer depending mainly on what one thinks an M.P. ought to be. Those who deplore the low quality of the contemporary House, such as Andrew Hill and Anthony Whichelow (pseud.), in *What's Wrong with Parliament?* (Baltimore: Penguin Books, 1964), tend to connect this with the general uselessness of Commons, which fails to attract men of greater ability. Most observers take the contrary view that the modern M.P. is the equal of, or superior to, his predecessors (for example, Butt, *The Power of Parliament*), while Henry Fairlie positively delights in the "ordinary people of ordinary talents" whom one finds in Commons, finding in them "our defence against the extraordinary people who are always wanting to do extraordinary things to us." *The Life of Politics*, p. 21.

[31]Bracher, "Problems of Parliamentary Democracy," p. 189.

[32]Bernard Crick, *The Reform of Parliament*, p. 96.

ous and permanent basis. Some of these committees (such as the Committee of Selections and the House of Commons Services Committee) deal with the internal management of the House and will not concern us here. The most important perennial Select Committees are the committees of Public Accounts, Estimates, Nationalized Industries, Statutory Instruments, Agriculture, and Science and Technology. In addition, the Select Committee of Privileges investigates possible cases of breaches of parliamentary privilege. None of these Select Committees is directly involved in the review of legislation. Primarily, their function is to examine various branches of government administration and to make recommendations, on occasion, which may eventually result in legislation. The British committees which are directly involved in legislative review are the Standing Committees, established (since 1882) to examine virtually all public bills between second and third reading stages. These committees are now organized anew for each bill that reaches committee stage. The committees have no permanent membership, and are simply designated by letters of the alphabet.[33] They have short lives but are compensated for this by a continual cycle of reincarnation, members being appointed to them at each rebirth on the basis of their interest in, and knowledge of, the subject area of the bill to be considered. According to the Standing Orders of the House, selections to these Standing Committees must be made with "regard to the qualifications of those Members nominated and to the composition of the House"—which in practice means that the Government party must have approximately the same percentage majority in each Standing Committee that it has in the House as a whole. The work load of the Standing Committees naturally fluctuates according to the legislative activity of the Government; in the relatively inactive session of 1965–66 (when the Labour Party had a small majority), the Standing Committees considered only 11 bills and held only 60 sittings in all, while in the succeeding session of 1966–67 (when Labour held a large majority), the Standing Committees considered 69 bills and held 364 sittings.[34]

Ministers or junior Ministers are likely to be in attendance at these sittings, which are held in the mornings to avoid conflicts with the sessions of the full House.[35] The details of bills are discussed here, although the pressure of time can severely restrict such perusal, and the "guillotine" can be used by

[33] There are in addition to the "A" through "H" Standing Committees several other special committees which have legislative review functions including: The Scottish Grand Committee and Welsh Grand Committee, two Scottish Standing Committees, and Second Reading Committees (for minor, non-controversial bills).

[34] House of Commons, "Standing Committees," H. C. 137 (March 10, 1966) and H. C. 677 (October 27, 1967).

[35] Experimental morning sessions (on Mondays and Wednesdays) were introduced in 1967 but were subsequently dropped because they conflicted with the work of the committees and worked a particular hardship on the relatively few stalwart M.P.'s who shouldered the heaviest burden of committee work.

the government in an emergency. It is generally agreed that the atmosphere at committee meetings is businesslike, and the discussion wholly unspectacular, but occasionally useful in tightening up loose ends of legislation, and perhaps adjusting it to meet strongly felt objections of immediately interested groups. The lack of publicity and informality of these meetings tends to blur some-what the lines of party division—at least until the vote is taken. The Govern-ment is more likely to accept with good grace some minor amendments in committee, since the relative privacy of the proceedings reduces its embarrass-ment; and its flexibility at this stage may make the bill marginally better and more acceptable to affected interests. Although party discipline tends to be looser in committee stage, the Government can ultimately marshal its major-ity to force the bill through a reluctant committee.

Generally, the standing committees can be seen as adaptive structures of the House, enabling it to fulfill a legislative function, very narrowly inter-preted. The attributes of the committees counteract the deficiencies of the House as a whole in considering legislation: the committees' small size, rela-tive privacy, increased time for more detailed discussion, and greater expertise and interest of members, combined with a more flexible procedure and a greatly decreased symbolic significance of party unity—all lead to more pro-ductive discussions in committees than are attainable in the whole House. The tendency of individual M.P.'s to act as spokesmen for various outside interest groups in the committee stage can make the standing committees into a helpful channel of communication, enhancing governmental responsiveness to the needs of functional groups.

One of the most interesting developments in the recent history of the Soviet state has been the increasing importance of the standing committees of the U.S.S.R. Supreme Soviet. Committees had been a part of the Supreme Soviet structure ever since the adoption of the Stalin Constitution in 1936, but under Stalin they had gotten a bad and well-deserved reputation, along with the Supreme Soviet as a whole. Under Khrushchev, however, the com-mitees began their evolution toward greater significance. As John N. Hazard noted: "Since 1955 the emergence of committee hearings well before the Supreme Soviet sessions . . . may be preparing the way for a change. The Communist Party under Khrushchev's secretaryship gives evidence of having decided that it is to its advantage to utilize the committee structure to seek to improve efficiency through consultation with the republic and provincial ex-perts who sit on committees."[36] Since Khrushchev's "retirement," the progress of the Standing Committees toward a more meaningful role has accelerated. It is well-known that Khrushchev favored the use of the Party over the soviets, and possibly as a reaction to this, the post-Khrushchev

---

[36] John N. Hazard, *The Soviet System of Government*, 3rd ed. (Chicago: University of Chicago Press, 1964), p. 54.

leadership has reversed this neglect since 1965 (see Table IV.1). By August, 1966, the number of Standing Committees in each council of the Supreme Soviet had grown from five to ten, and the total membership of all Standing Committees had grown from 259 deputies (out of a total of 1,443) before 1966 to 700 deputies involved in committee work in 1966 and 912 by 1970 (out of 1,517 total deputies). This growth in size has been paralleled by a growth in stature and significance. One important step in this direction was taken in the Decree on the Standing Committees, passed on October 12, 1967. The decree formalized the increase in the number of committees which had already taken place and strengthened and enlarged the role of the committees in legislative work. The purposes of the Standing Committees were established in Article 1 of that decree as "preliminary consideration of questions for introduction to the Supreme Soviet" and "active cooperation in implementing decisions of the Supreme Soviet."[37] Only the first of these activities is legislative in nature, the second being investigatory, but it is this activity which apparently consumes most of the standing committees' time. In fact, in recent years, a number of fundamental codes defining basic legal relationships have been given in draft form to the standing committees for discussion, collection of opinions, and redrafting (*razrabotka*). Such codes as those on marriage and divorce, land use, public health services, etc., have been refined through this procedure and eventually adopted. With characteristic attention to such niceties, identical committees in both Councils of the Supreme Soviet preserve the legal equality of the two houses. The committees have the right to hold meetings between full sessions of the Supreme Soviet, have the right to request a "comprehensive public discussion" of a pending piece of legislation, and have the right, according to the decree, to oblige directors of ministries and departments at all levels of the state structure "to appear at a session of the committee and present an explanation [*raz'iasnenie*] on questions being examined by the committee." In addition, the Standing Committees are entitled to deliver so-called "co-reports" (*sodoklady*) directly after the main reports of the ministers at sessions of the full Soviet. These reports, as previously mentioned, usually contain some criticism of the work of the minister and the ministry, although the general tone is complimentary.

In addition, the Supreme Soviet committees have formal rights which go beyond those of the House of Commons Standing Committees. They have "the right to demand from ministries and departments [at all levels of the state structure] and from responsible persons the presentation of documents, policy statements, accounting data and other materials. All government organs, organizations, and responsible persons are obliged to fulfill the demand of the committees and present them with the necessary documents,

---

[37] "Polozhenie o postoiannikh kommissiiakh soveta soiuza i soveta natsional'nostei, Verkhovnogo Soveta SSSR," *Izvestiia*, October 13, 1967 (extra edition, no. 243).

Table IV.1

Growth of Supreme Soviet Standing Committees, 1965–1970

Committee	Number of Deputies[1]			
	6th Convocation 1965	7th Convocation 1966	1969	8th Convocation 1970
Credentials	42	62	62	62
Planning and Budget	78	102	102	102
Legislative Proposals	62	62	62	70
Foreign Affairs	46	62	62	64
Economic[2]	31	–	–	–
Industry, Transport, and Communications[3]	–	82	82	–
Transport and Communications	–	–	–	66
Industry	–	–	–	82
Construction and Construction Materials Industry	–	62	62	62
Agriculture	–	82	82	82
Public Health and Social Welfare	–	62	62	62
Education, Science and Culture	–	62	62	70
Trade and Everyday Services[4]	–	62	62	62
Youth Affairs	–	–	62	62
Conservation	–	–	–	62
Total Deputies in Committees	259	700	762	908
Total Deputies in Supreme Soviet (at election)	1443	1517	1517	1517

[1] Total for both houses of Supreme Soviet
[2] Was established in Council of Nationalities only; now abolished
[3] Split into two separate committees at 8th Convocation
[4] Trade, Everyday Services and Local Economy after 1969

NOTE: Tabulation does not include the "Council of Elders" which in theory sets the agenda for sessions of the Supreme Soviet.

conclusions, and other materials."[38] In addition, the Standing Committees have the right to make recommendations to state organs, including the Council of Ministers of the U.S.S.R. (the government), "recommendations of the Standing Committees come under obligatory review by the state organs or organizations," and "the results of this review or [information on] measures taken must be communicated to the Standing Committee within a period of two months."[39]

Of course, one is entitled to be skeptical of such formal rights, since "Soviet legality" often inscribes such rights which cannot in practice be exercised. Nevertheless, in this case there seems to be a real attempt to institute a

[38] *Ibid.*
[39] *Ibid.*

committee system which can carry out some useful functions for the state, without posing any conceivable threat to the supreme authority of the Communist Party. This certainly was an implication of Leonid Brezhnev's speech to the twenty-third Party Congress, which initiated the movement toward strengthening the Standing Committees, and it was also the theme of Nikolai Podgornyi's follow-up speech to the Supreme Soviet in August 1966. Podgornyi stated the main reason for strengthening the committee structure:

> Practice indicates that the discussion of a constantly widening range of economic, social and cultural questions in the Standing Committees of the two chambers demands the detailed study and thorough analysis of these questions according to the various branches of the national economy . . . the increasing amount of work of the Standing Committees of the chambers . . . necessitated a considerable enlargement of the committees' membership. . . . The formation of new Standing Committees in the chambers as well as an increase in their membership will make for a considerable improvement in the discussion of the plans for the development of the national economy and the state budget. . . .[40]

Podgornyi's approach suggests that legislation can be improved by consultation with committees composed of representatives of the various economic interests in the country. The Supreme Soviet committees can, then, be a convenient forum for discussion with these interests, in a fashion broadly similar to discussions in the House of Commons Standing Committees. Podgornyi gave an example of this reasoning:

> Take, for example, the draft law on water utilization that is being worked out. . . . It incorporates a whole set of complex economic questions. The rational utilization and preservation of water resources can be ensured only by observing the interests of agriculture, industry, power production, fishing, inland shipping, etc. Therefore it would obviously be correct for the appropriate branch committees to participate in the work on this bill.[41]

While the legitimizing value of this development of the committees cannot be overlooked—Podgornyi also talked of the "further development of the democratic principles of Soviet statehood"—the practical utility of such committees in working out the details of relatively "non-political" legislation, whose main lines have already been drawn by the Party, seems to have been an important motivation.

The suspicion that these committees do more than simply listen submissively to government reports is strengthened by an examination of their membership. The chairmen of these committees are certainly not the milkmaids and collective-farm chairmen who always find some seats in the Supreme Soviet; they all are important, ranking members of the party-state apparatus.

[40] *Pravda* and *Izvestiia*, August 3, 1966. [*CDSP* XVIII, no. 31, p. 9.]
[41] *Ibid.*

For example, of the nine chairmen of the substantive Standing Committees of the Council of the Union in August, 1966 (excluding the Credentials Committee), seven were members of the Central Committee of the CPSU (including one secretary of the Central Committee and a member of the Politburo) and one was a member of the Party's Central Auditing Commission. The only chairman who did not hold a high party position was N. N. Blokhin, who is an internationally known professor of surgery and president of the U.S.S.R. Academy of Medical Sciences, and who appropriately headed the Committee on Public Health and Social Welfare. Obviously, these are not men who must sit with hands folded because of their inferior political position (and/or technical expertise) in comparison with the ministers who come before them. In fact, a number of these committee chairmen hold higher party positions than the state functionaries who appear before them. The committees, then, can act as a legitimate form of party-dominated surveillance over state activities, one of the fundamental legitimate functions of the Party. In addition, the committees seem to contain a number of personalities who are apparently climbing the ladder of political power. For example, S. D. Khitrov, who was Chairman of the Construction and Industrial Construction Materials Committee in 1966 became Minister for Rural Construction for the U.S.S.R. in 1967; Yu. V. Andropov, who was a member of the Foreign Affairs Committee, became head of the KGB (Secret Police); A. M. Tokarev, who was a member of the Construction and Industrial Construction Materials Committee became, appropriately enough, Minister of Industrial Construction of the U.S.S.R.; and K. I. Galanshin, erstwhile member of the Committee on Industry, Transportation and Communications, became U.S.S.R. Minister of the Pulp and Paper Industry in 1968. Such men clearly do not have to pay deference to the government officials who appear before them, and indeed there may be some political advantages in delivering well-prepared and carefully timed criticisms in the privacy of the committee room, criticisms which go well beyond the polite critiques that are made during open sessions of the Supreme Soviet.

As already mentioned in the preceding chapter, the usual legislative procedure in cases of laws involving basic codes is to submit draft texts for public discussion, mainly through the press and letters to government agencies. The Standing Committees seem to have taken on the function of coordinating this discussion and revising the draft for final promulgation. A good illustration of this is the case of the law on the principles of public health adopted in December 1969. N. N. Blokhin, in his report as chairman of the Public Health and Social Welfare Committee, outlined the procedure that had been followed:

> The draft Principles of Legislation . . . on Public Health were published in the press and widely discussed by the public. Many Soviet citizens and the collectives of plants and factories, collective farms and state farms, medical institutions and research institutes took an active part in this discus-

sion, as did state agencies and public organizations in all the Union republics and autonomous republics. . . . The draft was discussed in the Academy of Medicine and in medical and legal research institutes. The . . . newspapers, as well as radio and television, gave regular coverage to the discussion. More than 3,000 suggestions were received by the U.S.S.R. Supreme Soviet alone.

The materials of the discussion testify to the public's unanimous approval of this important legislative act. . . .

All letters and materials relating to the discussion of the draft have been generalized and carefully studied. Taking into consideration the proposals and comments received, *the committees have made a number of changes* in and additions to the draft, clarified the wording of certain articles, and included a number of new provisions in the draft.[42]

If Blokhin is to be taken at his word, the discretionary power to make changes based on the public discussion lies with the standing committees of the Supreme Soviet. It may be that the committees submit such changes for review by higher party organs, but the committees' role in this procedure still appears to be substantial, perhaps because the changes usually are not.

Committees have also been increasingly used to investigate shortcomings in the state administration. An example of this was the study, reported in the press, of the construction of medical institutions and enterprises by the Committee on Public Health and Social Welfare of the Council of Nationalities in 1968. According to the chairman of that committee, a preparatory group was set up "for detailed study of the problem." The group eventually wrote a report which "contained a detailed analysis of the causes of the lag in construction."[43] After the full committee heard reports by the construction ministries and by the U.S.S.R. Ministers for Public Health and the Medical Industry, the committee drew up a list of "practical recommendations . . . aimed at improving the construction of public health institutions, strengthening the material and technical base of construction and raising the level of medical services."[44] This report gives no indication of disagreements amongst members of the committee, but when the subject is the budget where important economic interests are at stake the discussion can apparently generate more heat.

In fact, there is some evidence that committee meetings in recent years have increasingly become the scenes of heated debates and strongly expressed differences of view. The legitimacy doctrine of the state only implies that there be no *open* disunity. There is still room for disagreements to be aired in private, as in fact has been done in the past in the inner and upper reaches of the party structure. Disagreement, even violent disagreement, in committee

[42]*Pravda* and *Izvestiia*, December 20, 1969. [*CDSP* XXII, no. 1, pp. 3–4.]

[43]*Izvestiia*, April 27, 1968. [*CDSP* XX, no. 17, p. 23.]

[44]*Ibid.*

does not strike at the legitimacy of the system as fundamentally as a single hand raised in open dissent during a vote of the Supreme Soviet.

According to a newspaper account of hearings in the Budget Committee in 1967:

> Short, businesslike reports and discussion in these committees are often transformed into heated, prolonged arguments, and in answer to some weighty evidence one can hear a no less weighty rebuttal. This is fully understandable . . . [for] behind each line of the over-all plan lies the fate of a whole branch of the economy, the prospective development of huge areas of the country.[45]

The same report went on to describe what was presumably a typical scene in the committee:

> The report of Comrade Apriatkin called forth a lively discussion. Especially many arguments arose concerning one of the recommendations of the Ministry of Geology. The [Planning and Budget] Committee emphasized the necessity of thorough explorations for oil and gas reserves in the European part of the U.S.S.R. Here 80 percent of the users of fuel are found. Deputy G. V. Zubarev arose ιo oppose this point in the report:
>
> "As is well-known, the addition of a cubic meter of gas reserves from the eastern part of the country is several times cheaper than from the west. [However] pipelines for gas and oil are very expensive. It seems to me that we must consider the question of drawing the users closer to the place where fuel is extracted. Major new enterprises must be situated primarily in the east, and not in the European part of the country."
>
> This view of the problem also brought forth objections. "It is impermissible to counterpose the western part of the country to the east," said M. A. Iasnov. "All areas must be developed normally." . . .
>
> Such probing, serious discussions were conducted for each section of the plan: by examining all sides of the question and weighing all the pros and cons. Not one of the unresolved problems, not a single principal shortcoming escaped attention. This is a typical case.[46]

While such sessions are unlikely to produce many changes in the budget or in legislation, they do serve to raise issues, and bring the views of affected interests to the attention of the government. Aside from those changes brought about by the committees' co-reports, in cases where draft legislation is published, committee examination of the draft always produces a considerable number of detailed changes. For example, the draft text of the Public

---

[45] "Glavnyi plan strany," *Izvestiia*, October 7, 1967. See also: the report in *Izvestiia*, December 11, 1966, which mentions "heated arguments with representatives of the departments and ministries" in committee hearings on the budget, and sharp disagreements on a report prepared by a sub-committee concerning reorganization of the precast reinforced concrete industry; and another account in *Izvestiia* (January 9, 1966) which mentions "a lively exchange of opinions."

[46] *Ibid.*

Health Principles code mentioned previously, containing 55 articles, was finally adopted with 111 changes after being examined by the Public Health and Social Welfare Committee. Most of the changes, however, involved small adjustments of the wording for improved textual accuracy, such as the replacement of the word "medicine" by the phrase "curative and diagnostic means."[47] Although these changes are not monumental, they do represent an improvement in the legislation not unlike the improvements long credited to the Standing Committees of the British Parliament. Furthermore, many of the changes show clear evidence of the involvement of specialized and expert interests (in this case, the medical and public health professionals) in the final stages of the consultation process.

In cases such as the Public Health Code, where the political responsibility of the party leadership is not engaged, the Standing Committees perform some useful functions for the leadership. Through the Committees' activity, the effectiveness of the bill is apparently enhanced, while at the same time its legitimacy and prospects of affective acceptance are improved. Indeed, the role of the Standing Committees has advanced to a sufficient stage of reality for Soviet legal specialists to disagree over it, particularly in regard to the relationship between the Presidium of the Supreme Soviet and the Committees in the intervals between sessions.[48]

Within the limited confines of their delegated authority, the British and Soviet committees perform useful functions for the representative assembly and ultimately the political leadership of the country. They cannot, however, solve the basic dilemma of representation in a modern, industrial society. By their organization and composition, they supply an extra measure of expertise and time to permit the representative assembly some small surveillance over the making of rules for society. But they have not the resources to confront the administrators, executives and bureaucrats consistently on terms of equality. In neither system do committee members have a staff to carry out investigations and briefings, to better prepare members for their confrontations with the government. These are severe limitations to which must be added, in the Soviet case, the ultimate limitation of a one-party system. As we have already seen, this party is not a "monolith," as is often claimed by its propagandists, but even with the existence of diverse factions and groupings,

---

[47] *Pravda* and *Izvestiia*, December 1969. [*CDSP* XXII, no. 1, pp. 7-13.]

[48] O. Ye. Kutafin, writing in the main Soviet legal journal, took the unorthodox position that the Standing Committees "are subordinate solely to the chairman of the chambers in the intervals between sessions" and that "making the Standing Committees responsible to the Presidium of the Supreme Soviet contradicts the very nature of the Standing Committees." He was rebutted by L. Mandelshtam in *Izvestiia*, who replied that "O. Kutafins's article contained a wrong interpretation of important questions . . . and gave a distorted picture of the state practice of the Presidium . . . and the . . . committees." The debate is contained in *CDSP* XVIII, no. 30, pp. 17-22.

the absence of a legitimate opposition and the lack of any realistic threat of a "backbench revolt" in the CPSU reduces the influence of committees over the government.

REPRESENTATION AND RESPONSIVENESS

From a functional point of view, the Supreme Soviet and the British Parliament are more alike than is commonly acknowledged. As legislatures, they both normally play a minor role, mainly confined to improvements in legislative draftsmanship, accomplished through committees. Their major function in this regard is to legitimize legislation, to make it authoritative and, in Beer's phrase, "to mobilize consent" for it. In neither case, however, is the representative assembly *supposed* to act as a legislature in any fuller sense, according to the normative principles of legitimacy established for the institution.

Aside from legislation, the main functions of these representative assemblies concern the two-way flow of political communication between regime and people so that, on the one hand, the people can respond appropriately to the government and, on the other hand, the government can maintain its sensitivity to pressures for change. While there are many criticisms of these assemblies by those who would wish more for them, this accretion of regime responsiveness may be all that can be reasonably expected of a representative assembly under conditions of a modern industrial society.

By any measure of effectiveness, the British Parliament is clearly superior to the Supreme Soviet in providing open channels of communication. Because opposition is legitimate and organized, and because dissent, discouragement, and disagreement are legitimate and thus capable of open expression, the British system can provide more effective and accurate channels for transmission of negative feedback. The limitations on such negative communications hampers the Soviet government's attempts to correct mistaken or misapplied policies.

A modern industrial society requires a high degree of coordination between its parts, and the political regime must inevitably undertake to provide that essential coordination through regulation and control. To do this effectively, it must have information on the results of its past actions, and some knowledge of the views and attitudes of those who will be affected by any new action. The British Parliament does provide a considerable amount of such information, and although the information is sometimes very "noisy" (i.e., full of contradictory signals and static), it does usually provide—along with information from other sources such as the press and opinion polls—a basis for action, or for prudent inaction.

The deficiency of the Soviet regime in this regard is not as extreme as is sometimes imagined, for there are some possibilities for feedback flow from lower levels of the bureaucracy and from partially separate channels such as the press and the network of soviets—but it remains a deficiency, nevertheless. The recent trend toward more "public discussion" over pending legislation and the increased role of the Standing Committees of the Supreme Soviet may represent an attempt to overcome this handicap without raising the frightening spectre of an organized opposition or legitimized dissent on the fundamental premises of the regime.

In the absence of a legitimate opposition, however, there is no Soviet organization which can consistently adopt a critical attitude toward the government's performance and program—in fact, there is a vested interest in all parts of the party-state organization to reduce and restrict criticism. Even within legitimate areas of criticism (such as the failure of lower level bureaucrats to carry out directives of the leadership), there are endless possibilities for suppressing and avoiding criticism. As *Pravda* recently noted in exposing one provincial party organization:

> *Pravda* receives quite a few letters from working people. . . . The editors have forwarded many pointed and important letters to the province Party committee for verification, consideration and the taking of the necessary steps. Sometimes attempts to brush aside criticism or to present matters as though nothing had happened are encountered in this process.[49]

This problem is endemic to the system. Lower level bureaucrats are really only emulating their superiors when they seek to suppress criticism, and bureaucratic careers are generally made by successful emulation. Since the structure of the Soviet system excludes all autonomous sub-structures, the only possible effective criticism is criticism sanctioned or directed from above, and thus only the very top level can avoid it entirely. The major problem, however, is not the absence of criticism, but the routinization of criticism into a sterile formula. Formalized criticism and self-criticism can and does become a substitute for effective criticism. After an exposé, *Pravda* may report that "measures have been taken," but the net result usually is simply a minor variant of the *status quo ante.* The attempt to construct a monolithic system and instill monolithic thought tends to dry up the wellsprings of independent ideas and action, so that the system is not self-correcting. When the Soviet ship of state receives a mistaken or confusing order from its captain, there is a tendency to steer doggedly into familiar rocky shoals, and then blame some lowly helmsman rather than the captain and his staff.

Ultimately, the role of representative assemblies in the process of governing society is delimited in both systems by the structure of the party system. Thus it is the party system in Great Britain that determines the format of parliamentary activity. Two highly cohesive groups, the majority in government and the minority in opposition, debate the virtues and defects of gov-

[49]*Pravda* January 28, 1970. [*CDSP* XXII, no. 4, p. 9.]

ernment policies and proposals within a large consensus on the legitimate means and ends of political action. The effect of party organization is to limit the role of Parliament as an independent body by binding its members either to the present government leaders or to the past and future government leaders. But the relationship also binds the leaders to some lesser extent, and in this lies the vestigial powers of Parliament: a symbiotic relationship of leaders who must sometimes follow, and followers who can sometimes lead.

The Supreme Soviet is more severely restricted by the party system embedded within it. This is partly the result of the absence of a legitimate opposition outside the CPSU and partly the result of tighter restrictions on legitimate expression of dissent within the Party itself. As in the British case, the party organization determines the format of parliamentary activity, with very limited (and thus legitimate) criticism of the government expressed in discussion periods, and one solid bloc of votes (instead of two) formalizing parliamentary approval of government policies. Even in this case, however, the government cannot afford to disregard the views of those who will be affected by its policies, and in this fact lies the *only* vestige of power that can be ascribed to the Supreme Soviet. As in the case of the British Parliament, it is the power of influence over the actions of political leaders, but unlike the British case, it requires support from within the "collective" leadership itself to be effective in altering policy. The ultimate sanction that followers can impose over leaders in the Soviet system is poor performance—perfunctory implementation of and lethargic reaction to the leadership's policies—the most wasteful and demoralizing way of assuring long-term responsiveness of the party-state.

These considerations naturally lead to a closer examination of the policy-making process in the two countries. In the next chapter we shall examine how policies are made and adjusted in both systems through the complex interaction of leaders, administrators, and citizens—all reacting to the sometimes complementary and sometimes contradictory requirements of practical necessities, objective self-interests, and principles of legitimacy.

Legitimacy,
Leadership,
and Policy-Making

Up to this point, the discussion has centered on institutions that do not make policies. At most, they provide significant inputs to the policy process (i.e., they have strong influence); at their more normal least, they have little or no discernible effect on this process. This is simply one way of alluding to the fact that in modern industrial societies, such as the British and Soviet, policies—or what passes for policies—are formulated and authorized in a variety of ways, dependent on the nature of the subject under consideration. It is not possible to specify a single policy process for either the Soviet or British government, for they are both characterized by a multiplicity of procedures, some of which are more or less typical for the resolution of particular kinds of problems. But there is much evidence to suggest that many matters are decided, or in some sense resolved, in an *ad hoc*, fortuitous, almost accidental way.

While this may be disconcerting and disheartening to the analyst, it should not be unexpected. Governmental structures arise and develop in response to more or less regularly recurring functions assumed by the government in relation to society. Such structures may long outlast their original functions, and such is the force of inertia that a structure may long outlast *any* discernible function—except perhaps as a legitimacy-supporting symbol. Many policies are developed, however, not in response to regularly recurring functions, but in response to unique combinations of circumstances, and this type of policy will require unique combinations of governmental structures to respond appropriately.

Policies are, essentially, governmental responses to perceived problems. It is clear that such perceptions involve the values of the observer, for there must be something in a given condition which is perceived as undesirable (a value judgment) in order for that condition to be considered a problem. Poverty, a high birth rate, or any number of given conditions of a population may be viewed as problems or as the normal condition of humanity, or as great benefits. This is because a problem can only arise if one has established a goal—an abstract conception of something better—against which the present is measured. If a given condition is viewed as inevitable or beneficial, there cannot be any such measurement. The goal does not have to be anything as grand and glorious as the communist society of universal brotherhood; it may be something as immediate and mundane as water purification.

Both perceptions of the present and goals for the future are affected by values, and values are often strongly influenced—if not determined—by culture. The culture establishes norms against which conditions are evaluated, and if one can speak of political culture as that aspect of the total culture which relates to politically relevant values,[1] then it is clear that the political culture of a country can have a great effect on the policies that are made by a government, not only in determining the choices made by the policy-makers, but in determining which questions are brought into the arena for consideration.

The values which derive from political culture are important in determining whether or not a policy will be formulated, for it is not unusual for governments to display splendid indifference toward certain environmental conditions until reference to cultural values reveals these conditions to the public's conscience as problems. Both British and Soviet societies are high-consensus societies, but one aspect of this situation is that a high value is placed on political activity which does not disturb the consensus. In both countries, governmental inaction can be the result of an insufficient consensus on the existence or severity of a problem, or lack of a sufficient consensus on either the means to achieve a consensual goal, or on the goal itself. Policies which might be dictated by efficiency norms (such as, for example, devaluation of the pound sterling, or in the Soviet case, permitting market mechanisms to affect prices) are resisted and forestalled by contrary values held by those in leadership positions. Paralysis or incremental, minimally responsive policies are often the result when such a value conflict exists.

---

[1] For an excellent discussion of political culture, see Gabriel Almond and Sidney Verba, *The Civic Culture: Political Attitudes and Democracy in Five Nations* (Boston: Little, Brown and Co., 1965), pp. 1–44.

A preference for incremental policies and a "muddling through" approach to problems is heightened by the extreme complexity of policy-making procedures in these two massive governmental structures, by the staffing procedures used to fill positions of policy significance in the structure, and by the very nature of the problems which arise in modern, industrial society. The conservatism which characterizes policy-making in these countries is directly related to the specialization of expertise and personnel which characterizes social organization as a whole, and the political structure in particular. Common reference to consensual values is insufficient to establish preferences among policy alternatives. Knowledge that is technical and experience that is deep but narrow are often prerequisites—or thought to be prerequisites—for determining optimal policies. The very extensive involvement of government in the social and economic activities of a complex, industrialized society means quite simply that the government must be capable of apprehending the esoteric arguments of specialists in a wide range of highly trained occupations. To accomplish this, the administrative structures must recruit men who can deal with outside specialists effectively.

One outcome of this specialization is that policy becomes diffused over a wide range of subject areas. Each specialized governmental group in interaction with corresponding outside specialists defines the extent and direction of government involvement in a sector of socio-economic activity. The whole of this multi-faceted activity may not quite equal the sum of its parts, for the opportunities for inconsistencies and contradictions are everywhere apparent. As governmental structures proliferate, the difficulties of coordination grow, and the attention of ever higher levels of the government turns to problems of administration. This in itself is a formidable obstacle to long-range policy-making. In addition, bureaucratic structures develop characteristic "institutional points of view"—normative attitudes towards the limits of the possible—which are passed along to all newcomers as they are socialized into the institution. Such traditions act as powerful brakes on innovation, particularly when coupled with norms of conformity to the group and harmony within the group. As the recent history of both Great Britain and the Soviet Union shows, conflict is far more likely to appear—when it appears at all—among different governmental organizations (each "representing" its client group of outside specialists) than among members of a single governmental organization.

The scope and complexity of economic activity in the modern industrial society has led to the necessity in both countries of governmental long-range planning, in addition to short-range regulative techniques. The penchant for planning in the Soviet Union is one of the few authentic legacies of Karl Marx still operative there. The "conscious" application of Marxian "scientific" economics is considered indispensable for rapid and efficient development. In Great Britain, the growing acceptance of Keynesian economics—even by the Conservatives—has legitimized government involvement in short-term regulation and financial manipulation. Over-all planning has also been increasingly accepted as a possible remedy for Britain's relatively slow economic growth, balance of payments problems, and regional lags in economic development.

In all its plans, regulations and laws, the government formulates policy as admixtures of efficiency and value orientations. The efficiency is provided, presumably, by expert analyses, by data accumulation, by technical studies and reports. Much of this information is feedback—data on the effects of past policies and activities—and there may also be projections and forecasts, presumably based on "objective" criteria. The unintended consequences of past policies may necessitate new adjustments, and changes in the environment constantly require revisions in even the most successful policies of the past. The flow of technical information is supposed to be value-neutral, but in practice it is very difficult, if not impossible, to avoid implicit normative judgments in the selection and presentation of data.

In both systems, a distinction is often made between specialists and generalists: the former transmitting expert information and judgments to the latter, who use consensual values (such as the "public interest") in making decisions. Such distinctions are always clearer in theory than practice, although the hierarchical structure of governmental organs does roughly resemble this distinction if one assumes that the men at each organizational apex are generalists and their subordinates are specialists. Of course, this sharp distinction is not found in practice, for, sooner or later, generalists must become specialized to some degree by training or experience. It is more realistic, therefore, to speak of different degrees of specialization at different levels of the structure.

The specialization or structural differentiation required of these governments is a product of the specialization inherent in a modern industrial society and of the instrumental conception of governments as a mechanism for satisfying the increasing material expectations of the population. The more advanced these societies become in production techniques, the more coordination is required to obtain efficiency, and the more government is called in to provide the coordination. The legal distinction between government ownership and private (shareholders') ownership of producing units is not of great significance in this regard. Soviet and British managers play similar roles in "lobbying" for managerial points of view, most particularly for maximum role autonomy within the economic system.[2]

Policies are developed in many different segments of the political structure, and there is generally some correspondence between the subject of policy and the specialization of the policy-making organ. This correspondence

---

[2]Given the common tie of party membership and the narrow limits of legitimate dissent in the Soviet Union, the amount of role independence there is bound to be far more restricted than in Britain. The common factor, however, is the leverage which expertise gives to specialist groups in asserting their claims to independence from political controls.

seems most consistent in the kind of policy-making achieved through the government's regulative capacity—the issuing of administrative rules and regulations. Such outputs are the routine function of specialized agencies of government and are essentially similar in both countries. But policies even within such routine subject areas are occasionally created by other means, if the particular subject has greater than ordinary *political salience.* The amount of political salience cannot be measured by any simple yardstick. Some factors which may increase the salience of a political problem, raising it to the level of an *issue*, are:

1. the proportion of the population affected;
2. the intensity of effect on a segment of the population;
3. the extent to which the matter touches on (or conflicts with) legitimizing principles of the regime;
4. the extent to which the matter receives publicity;
5. the extent to which the matter is a subject of controversy.

The more any one of these factors is connected with a problem, the greater the chances for the matter becoming an issue, and the greater the chances that the normal policy-making procedures will be superseded by a procedure on a higher level of the organizational pyramid. To the extent that higher levels are more likely to have generalized policy outlooks, the result of increasing the political salience of a problem in either society is the removal of the decision from the normal specialist procedures and the substitution of more politically visible, generalist procedures. This process of raising the level of decision-making occurs in a small percentage of cases, but presumably the most important cases are among them. The relationship between salience and policy-making procedure is demonstrated by numerous cases from the recent history of both countries.

In both countries, for example, the routine regulation of certain industries contributing to air and water pollution has been shifted, at least for a time, to higher levels when the public-health implications of pollution have raised questions outside the normal competence of the regulatory agencies. Publicity has been generated, because the pollution is thought to create a potential health hazard for the entire population and an immediate danger to certain segments of the population (and to some specific forms of life). It is precisely in such cases that conflict can arise between different segments of the governmental structure. In the example just mentioned, the routine production goals of one segment comes into conflict with the public-health and conservationist goals of other segments, and the conflict must be resolved by higher levels, sufficiently generalized to encompass both goal orientations.

LEADERSHIP STRUCTURE

Although governmental structures performing policy functions are highly complex and variegated, one can, for the purpose of description, distinguish four structural tiers, as shown in Table V.1, which are differentiated by their roles in the decision-making process: the *primary leader, leadership core, national leadership,* and *administration.*

The Primary Leader in the Soviet system is the General-Secretary of the CPSU, a fact which both symbolizes and gives reality to the assertion that the Party is the central policy-making hierarchy of the Soviet governmental system. Just as important, the General-Secretary usually does not, and certainly need not, hold any important position within the Soviet state structure. This is because the entire state structure, up to and including the U.S.S.R. Council of Ministers, is placed in roughly the same legitimized functional role as the Civil Service in Great Britain: as thoroughly competent and policy-neutral implementers of policies laid down by the party leadership. The present General-Secretary, Leonid Brezhnev, is ceremonially included in the Presidium of the U.S.S.R. Supreme Soviet, but he is not a member of the more important Council of Ministers (the rough *constitutional* equivalent of the British Cabinet).

The British primary leader is the Prime Minister and, like the Soviet leader, he is the head of his party. Unlike the Soviet leader, however, the authority of his position is derived almost wholly from the legitimacy of the state structure, and not from the legitimacy of the party in the public consensus. Leadership is legitimized in the British system by the electoral process, and the growth in the power of the Prime Minister in the last several decades has been accompanied by the growing importance of the choice between Prime Ministerial candidates as a prime factor in the outcome of elections. The Prime Minister is always at very least a man of proven popularity—at least

Table V.1

Leadership Tiers in Great Britain and the Soviet Union

Leadership Tier	Institution of Government		Policy-Making Roles[1]
	Soviet Union	Great Britain	
Primary leader	General-Secretary of CPSU	Prime Minister	Ultimate decision
Leadership core	Politburo of CPSU	Cabinet	Decision
National leadership	Central Committee of CPSU	Parliament[2]	Influence
Administration	Party-State *apparat*	Ministries and Departments of Government	Regulation and expert opinion

[1] These terms are intended to suggest characteristic policy-making roles as discussed in the text
[2] Including the entire House of Commons and the most active members of the House of Lords

at the beginning of his tenure in office. The vote-getting ability of a Prime Minister contributes strongly to his authority over his colleagues, just as repeated failures of a party leader to attain office will weaken his authority.

In the Soviet system, the policy-making leadership is not legitimized by a popular electoral process, although elections are used to legitimize the state structure. The leadership is legitimized through the doctrine that the Party has special abilities to utilize the science of Marxism-Leninism in the solution of social and economic problems, and that the internal organization of the Party maximizes its ability to employ its special talents. Despite the many years of Stalin's predominance, and the apotheosis of Lenin as founding genius of the regime, the idea of a single leader, standing at the head of the Party, has not been legitimized as a permanent feature of the Party structure. Partly as a reaction to the unlovely consequences of Stalinism, and partly as a response to the needs of the post-Khrushchev leadership group, the contemporary doctrine ascribes the major responsibility of leadership to the Party as a whole, and legitimizes the notion of "collective leadership" as the appropriate form for internal direction of the Party's affairs.[3]

> The principle of collectivism defines the very essence and historical significance of the Communist Party, its nature and character; and [this principle] expresses the objective and immutable truth that the people are the creators of history.[4]

Whether or not Stalin makes his way back into the history books from his present status as a quasi-unperson, the reaction against his method of personal rule, the notorious "cult of personality," seems to persist. A modest edition of Leonid Brezhnev's collected utterances has appeared, but the Soviet press has not given him the prominence that was once accorded even to Nikita Khrushchev. Judging from all outward signs, the Soviet leaders have in the years since Khrushchev's fall (in 1964) worked out a *modus vivendi* which limits the role of the General-Secretary to being "first among equals." The limitations on the General-Secretary's role—at least as seen by other leaders—have been clearly described in a *Pravda* article:

> The secretary of a Party committee is not a boss; he is not invested with the right to command. He is merely the senior person in an agency of collective leadership elected by Communists. He bears greater responsibility than the others. But in the decision of questions he has no more than the same rights as the other members of the committee.[5]

The legitimization of particular leaders in the past always involved the claim that he had special qualities of near superhuman genius which made it

---

[3]This matter is discussed more fully in my article, "New Factors of Stability in Soviet Collective Leadership," *World Politics* XIX, no. 4 (July 1967), pp. 563–81.

[4]P. A. Rodionov, *Kollektivnost'–vysshii printsip partiinogo rukovodstva* (Moscow: Izd-vo politicheskoi literatury, 1967), p. 6.

[5]F. Petrenko, *Pravda*, July 20, 1966. [*CDSP* XVIII, no. 29, p. 27.]

objectively necessary to place the entire leadership in his hands. There seems no inclination to make this patently inaccurate claim for Brezhnev, or any other current leader, although the role of leadership in general is upheld by such statements as:

> Our party has always protected, is protecting and will protect the authority of its leaders, for without high authority of experienced and tempered leaders, brought forward by the Party and people themselves in the course of struggle for communism, it is unthinkable that there would be discipline and organization, and without these, it is impossible to move forward.[6]

Thus the legitimization of leadership is based on the "objective necessity" for centralized and unified command. This necessity is contained within the Leninist concept of organization, democratic centralism, which

> includes the dialectical unity of two opposites, one of which is centralism and the other, the most widespread internal party democracy. . . . The fact that the leadership of the Party is carried out by a single center permits all the Party's work to be subjected to a single will, and gives its policies and methods a single direction, and based on concrete tasks, leads to a more effective use of Party forces.[7]

As can be seen from this quite typical statement, the Soviet explanation of leadership is structural in format, and is not based on any special talents claimed for the particular men who happen to fill leadership positions. The General-Secretary and his colleagues are portrayed as very popular and very sincere—and very self-effacing. Their personalities, family lives, personal interests—in short, all the data that would reveal them as composed of flesh and blood—are omitted from public references to them. Their public statements are apparently carefully composed to avoid any hint of inconsistency or originality. The result of this effort has been that the cult of personality has been transformed into the cult of impersonality, and the entire leadership has been coated in a medium gray tint, quite fitting for Moscow's wintry weather.

The second tier of leadership in the Soviet Union, the Politburo, is composed, at present, of fifteen members and six alternates. The number of members and the composition of the Politburo is apparently decided through a bargaining procedure among the existing members. Entry to the Politburo is thus effected by co-optation, and although the General-Secretary presumably has more weight than the others in changing the composition, it would appear from the record of the post-Khrushchev leadership that the General-Secretary is either unable or unwilling to bring in his own supporters exclusively. The Politburo has been remarkably stable since 1964, and has survived economic failures and the Czech crisis intact. Of the four additional full members of the

[6] Rodionov, *Kollektivnost'*, p. 30.
[7] *Ibid.*, pp. 17, 21.

Politburo announced in 1971, three had previously been candidate Politburo members and one had been a Secretary of the Central Committee. There were twenty-five very familiar faces in the Politburo and Secretariat announced at the 24th Party Congress in 1971.

This disinclination to change the membership of the Politburo is apparently the result of a delicate balance of powers within the existing group. In such a situation, new entrants can realistically be viewed as a potential threat to the prerogatives and powers of some existing members. Existing rivalries and alignments can also be disturbed from the present equilibrium by new entrants. On the other hand, the average age of the present full members is 62 and the youngest is 53. Since they are all thoroughly mortal, it can be expected that the present members will eventually be forced to assure continuity of leadership as death and disease take their toll. Replacement of incapacitated members is easier (or less threatening) than enlargement of the Politburo, since the balance can be preserved through co-optation of departed members' protégés.

All the members of the Politburo hold other important positions in the Party or state structures. These positions absorb most of their time and energy, and provide them with differing policy perspectives, drawn from the institutional interests with which they are identified. The conflict of these interests, of group interests, and possibly of personalities within the Politburo is the essence of leadership-core politics as it is conducted in the Soviet Union. As we shall see, the relationships among members of the Politburo, that is, the factional alignments, are likely to shift on different issues because of the cross-cutting responsibilities of the leaders.

In Great Britain, the second tier of leadership is the Cabinet. While several experiments with unusually small Cabinets have been attempted in the past, recent Cabinets have varied between 17 and 25 members. The determination of its size and the selection of its members lies with the Prime Minister. He has considerable discretion in making these choices, although there will usually be a number of important party leaders who cannot be safely excluded.[8] Although a few of these leaders will "choose themselves," the discretionary power of appointment and dismissal from the Government does give the Prime Minister considerable potential power over the other Cabinet members, and has been a factor in elevating his authority over them. In this regard, the Prime Minister enjoys powers which would be the envy of his Soviet counterpart. As often happens, however, the power of potential coercion is so persuasive that it need rarely be used.

---

[8] Sir Ivor Jennings writes: "Most of the leading party members, indeed, choose themselves. The nucleus of the Cabinet exists before the Prime Minister begins to draw up lists. His task is to give these leaders appropriate places and they themselves have much to say about their own offices." *Cabinet Government*, 3rd ed. (Cambridge: Cambridge University Press, 1969), p. 68.

The question of whether British government is still directed by a collective leadership or whether it has become a near-dictatorship of the Prime Minister has been a matter of debate in Britain in recent years. One school of thought contends that the era of Cabinet government has ended in Great Britain, and been transformed into the era of Prime Ministerial government.[9] Others contend that the Prime Minister's powers have been greatly exaggerated, and that he is still subject to the same kinds of constraint that characterized earlier Prime Ministers.[10] As in most debates of this kind, both sides can make telling points by referring to cases which illustrate different Prime Ministerial styles of leadership. The fact that there is merit in both arguments indicates that the relationship between the Prime Minister and the Cabinet is quite flexible. A strong, domineering Prime Ministerial personality will make the most of his potential powers, while a consensus-seeking, less self-assured Prime Minister will shrink from using the weapons at his disposal. Lord Morrison has said: "I have served under three Prime Ministers, each of whom had his own technique. Largely it is a matter of personality."[11]

The relationship between first and second tiers of leadership is not well defined in either system. There are no specific constitutional or legal provisions which define the relationship, and since it must necessarily be an informal, personal, face-to-face interaction, hidden from view by strong traditions of secrecy, the variations on the basic theme are endless. The fact that the Prime Minister enjoys more power over his colleagues than the General-Secretary does over his seems indisputable. Aside from the power to hire and fire his colleagues, the Prime Minister also can claim to be an important factor in the electoral success of his party, and he receives considerable attention from the mass media, to the point where he becomes the personification of the entire Government team ("the Wilson Government," "the Heath Government," etc.). On the other hand, the General-Secretary has no independent base of power, other than the continued goodwill of his colleagues. He must, in fact, be continually wary of undermining his position by alienating too many of his collegial comrades. Certainly this is the lesson he would have to learn from the sad experience of Nikita Khrushchev in 1964. Since the General-Secretary cannot beat his rivals, he must, in effect, join them by seeking consensus on issues, moderating factional disputes, and finding compromises between conflicting policy viewpoints. If he has learned from Khrushchev's experience, he would avoid being identified with innovations

[9] See R. H. S. Crossman, "Introduction," to Walter Bagehot, *The English Constitution* (New York: Cornell University Press, 1963), and John P. Mackintosh, *The British Cabinet*, 2nd ed. (London: Methuen, 1968).

[10] See G. W. Jones, "The Prime Minister's Power," *Parliamentary Affairs* XVIII, no. 2 (Spring 1965), pp. 167–85.

[11] Rt. Hon. Lord Morrison, *Government and Parliament: A Survey from the Inside*, 3rd. ed. (London: Oxford University Press, 1964), pp. 19–20.

which, when they fail, become "adventurism" and "harebrained scheming," and convert the innovator into the scapegoat. Given his rather tenuous position vis-à-vis the other leaders, and his primary constituency and power base in the conservative upper Party *apparat*, the General-Secretary's interest in self-preservation would seem to dictate a policy of caution, consensus, and conservatism. All the available evidence shows that this, indeed, has been Leonid Brezhnev's approach to politics since 1964.

British and Soviet concepts of individual and collective responsibility within the leadership core are remarkably similar. In both systems, all future-directed policies are legitimized as the collective decision of the entire leadership core. Politburo and Cabinet face the world with a façade of perfect unanimity. No member of the leadership core is permitted to state publicly any reservations concerning a policy of the leadership, and in fact each member is supposed to support policy with a show of enthusiasm. Of course, in both countries one may detect different degrees of enthusiasm in the public remarks of leaders and this may be taken as a sign of discord within the leadership. Even when there is discord, the responsibility of the entire collective leadership for future-directed policies is maintained. Meetings of the leadership core are thus conducted in the strictest secrecy, and records of these proceedings become classified documents. Neither leadership group is likely to admit its past errors in over-all policy, so that acceptance of collective responsibility is made immeasurably easier by excluding the element of collective guilt.

Individual responsibility is brought into play either by publicly identified personal indiscretions, or by egregiously poor performance in a section of the administration under the responsibility of a particular leader. When individual responsibility is invoked, the offending member is excised from the group, and the other leaders, in effect, deny their responsibility in that particular case. Individual responsibility has been applied very sparingly in recent years, in both Britain and the Soviet Union. In Britain, individual responsibility may be brought into play by a scandal, such as the famous Profumo Affair, the result of which is resignation and disgrace. But more often it is the rationale behind a Prime Minister's decision to reshuffle Cabinet appointments or re-organize the Cabinet structure. In the Soviet Union, the ax of individual responsibility has not been applied to Politburo members since the ouster of Khrushchev, but it has been applied to lower-ranking officials in the Party and state structure with considerable frequency.[12] Furthermore, the cult of impersonality shields the Politburo members from publicity about their per-

---

[12] It can be argued that the loss of important posts by A. Shelepin and N. Podgornyi, while both retained membership in the Politburo, represents a case of individual responsibility. It seems more likely, however, that the motivation was personal rivalry rather than poor performance. See Michel Tatu, *Power in the Kremlin: From Khrushchev to Kosygin* (New York: Viking Press, 1967), pp. 499, 503.

sonal failings or private indiscretions, especially when they are of the Profumo type.

Recruitment into the leadership core is conducted through different channels in the two systems, a fact which helps to explain the rather different leadership types one finds in the Politburo and Cabinet. Politburo members are recruited from the administrative structure, with Party *apparat* members (*apparatchiki*) the dominant group. The result is to place at the top of the structure men who have extensive experience in the non-public, bureaucratic politics which characterizes the entire Soviet system, including the Politburo. There is, in other words, no discontinuity between the skills required for upward mobility in the recruitment channel and the skills required of a Politburo member.

Recruitment to the Cabinet, on the other hand, comes almost exclusively from the membership of Parliament. Most often the attributes which achieve success for members of Parliament are skill in debate and public oratory, loyalty to the party leadership, ability to get along well with parliamentary colleagues, demonstrated energy and responsibility in performing minor tasks, and at least the surface appearance of knowledge and intelligence. While all of these attributes may be very useful to a Cabinet member, the absence of direct experience in the administrative organization of government may in some cases be a handicap. The Conservative Party, which has had great success since World War II in achieving and retaining governmental power, has had greater opportunity to train prospective Cabinet members by apprenticing them as junior members of the Government. Such apprenticeship partly compensates for the lack of continuous and direct experience in the roles which are required of a Cabinet member.[13] However, if one is primarily concerned with the administrative aspects of a Cabinet member's job, there is some cause for concern that the recruitment pattern does not provide sufficient experience for the Cabinet appointee. Whatever freshness of vision he may provide as an outsider, he must also learn how to use the administrative machinery to his own ends and he must be determined to persevere and penetrate all obstacles. On the other hand, it is certainly not true that a Cabinet member is only, or even mainly, an administrator. He must also continue to be a politician and to use his parliamentary skills and experience as a public figure to advocate and defend his Government's policies. It is, in fact, this combination of public and administrative skills that is so difficult to find, and there are numerous examples of failure in either category.[14]

[13] The number of appointments in Government below Cabinet rank has continuously grown, and now is over one hundred.

[14] Both kinds of failure are usually signaled by changes in the Government initiated by the Prime Minister, and only rarely and capriciously by the application of the doctrine of individual responsibility. For the latter case, see S. E. Finer, "The Individual Responsibility of Ministers," *Public Administration* XXXIV (Winter 1956), pp. 377–96.

The third tier of National Leadership in the Soviet Union is the Central Committee of the CPSU. The Central Committee is national in scope, 38.9 percent of its members coming from the Party *apparat* at republic and regional levels, and another 7.4 percent with positions in the state *apparat* at those levels.[15] Another 14.8 percent are members of the central Party and state *apparat*, thus providing a majority of Central Committee members who are full-time professionals in the administrative politics of the regional and central party-state organization. Membership in the Central Committee is a sign of an individual's relative importance, rather than being important, in itself, for the extra powers it gives. Among the 195 full members of the Central Committee are the most important political figures in the country (and the 165 candidate members rank just below them)—not because they are members, but because their primary positions in the party-state *apparat*, or in economic management, the military, or other fields entitle them to membership.

The Central Committee acts as a pool from which Politburo members are drawn, the penultimate step to the summit. The present full members of the Politburo spent an average of seven years as members of the Central Committee before their promotion.

Central Committee membership is decided by the Politburo, apparently with some care for preserving the dominance of *apparatchiki*. This, however, is the expected result of such a co-optative procedure, for the men at the top are likely to have the highest regard and trust for—and the closest personal ties and community of views with—those men below them who are following the same career patterns, and whose outlook is being shaped by the same experiences which molded the top leaders. Over the years, however, Central Committee membership has gone increasingly to those *apparatchiki* who have considerable prior experience outside the Party in professional, technical, and management careers.[16] Within this group, it is likely that some attention is given to preserving the Politburo's balance of forces, by including some associates (or protégés) of each Politburo member in the Central Committee. Although something can be gleaned by tracing career lines in detail, the web of personal relationships between Politburo and Central Committee members is too complex and too obscured by secrecy to draw firm conclusions.[17]

[15] The figures are from Frederic Fleron, "Career Types in the Soviet Political Leadership," in R. Barry Farrell, ed., *Political Leadership in Eastern Europe and the Soviet Union* (Chicago: Aldine Publishing Co., 1970), p. 113.

[16] *Ibid.*, p. 125.

[17] Nevertheless, this sort of analysis can be stimulating and quite useful in understanding some aspects of Soviet politics, as is demonstrated by such works as Michel Tatu's *Power in the Kremlin*, Robert Conquest's *Power and Policy in the U.S.S.R.* (New York: St. Martin's Press, 1961), and Sidney Ploss's *Conflict and Decision-Making in Soviet Russia* (Princeton: Princeton University Press, 1965).

The National Leadership tier in the British system is the total active membership of Parliament, but especially the House of Commons. In a fashion similar to the Soviet case, this group of men forms the pool out of which the leadership core is drawn. The party division bifurcates the group, providing two separate channels of co-optation into alternating leadership cores. As in the Soviet case, this method of selection is likely to perpetuate the characteristics of the existing leadership groups, but unlike the Soviet case, there is no consideration given to the institutional connections of candidates for promotion—since there usually are none.

There are some other contrasts, the greatest being that the National Leadership in Britain elects the two candidates for Prime Minister by choosing, in separate party caucuses, the two party leaders. This choice is made only on the resignation or incapacitation of an existing leader,[18] but as in matters of greater import, the power to give implies the power to take away, and there are a number of examples of pressure from below forcing a party leader to resign.[19] Of course, the Soviet system provides no regular mechanism for election of the Party leader by the Central Committee. But leadership disputes within the Politburo, if they reach an impasse, may be appealed to the Central Committee, as apparently happened in 1957 and 1964.

Although these two national leaderships are similarly situated in the policy-making process, they obviously perform very different continuous functions for their systems. The Soviet national leadership is primarily a regionally based, intermediate link in the Party's chain of command. Its main function is to initiate and supervise the fulfillment of plans and directives from the central leadership (the Politburo and Secretariat in Moscow). The continuous and largely non-policy functions of the British national leadership are those of representation, as described in the previous chapter. This great difference in continuous functions of the two national leaderships helps to explain the quite different sort of influence that they exert on the policy process (see *infra*, p. 155).

The fourth tier in the policy-making structure is the administration, which in Great Britain is the Civil Service, and in the Soviet Union is the party-state *apparat.* These large bureaucracies are charged with the day-to-day responsibilities for implementation of government policies. This activity involves the setting of regulations within guidelines established by the "political" leadership, enforcement and supervision of these regulations and adjudication of disputes arising from them, the collection of data concerning past

---

[18]In contrast to the Conservative Party, the rules of the Parliamentary Labour Party require the Leader to stand for election annually. These elections, however, are rarely contested and there is no case of an incumbent being defeated.

[19]For a thorough review and analysis of these cases, see R. T. McKenzie, *British Political Parties*, 2nd ed. (London: Heinemann, 1964), pp. 21–55, 297–386.

performance and environmental conditions affecting policies, dissemination of information and coordination of governmental activities, and preparation of proposals and suggestions for new policies.

The guiding principle of the administrative tiers in both countries is loyalty to the party leadership in power. In Great Britain, of course, this means freedom from strong partisan prejudices, so that the Civil Servant can faithfully execute the policies of whichever party is temporarily in power. It has been able to achieve this neutrality to the satisfaction of both party leaderships. The Soviet administration is legitimized as the loyal follower of the Party's directions—strong partisan prejudices are an absolute requirement in this case. Its partisan loyalty is assured by requiring party membership for all responsible state officials, and by constant observation and evaluation by the Party *apparat*, which controls the table of organization (*nomenklatura*) of each department of the state, and the list of promotions and demotions within the state hierarchy.

In common with bureaucratic structures in other countries, the Soviet and British administrative tiers can best be described as hierarchies of expert knowledge and experience. Both through formal education and through years of work in specific fields of government activity, members of this tier acquire considerably more specialized expertise than the party leadership tiers.[20] This knowledge is theoretically at the willing disposal of the party leadership, but it does give special advantages to the administrator in influencing and altering policies initiated by the relatively inexpert political leaders. This influence on policy is mainly exerted by the upper levels of the administrative tier, which has the most continuous contact with the political leadership. The highest level of the British Civil Service consists of the almost 3,000 members of the Administrative Class and the top administrators in a few departments (such as the Foreign Office and Inland Revenue) which have a semi-independent Civil Service organization. The upper levels of the Soviet administrative tier can conveniently be taken as the Chairmen and Deputy Chairmen of the U.S.S.R. Council of Ministers, the heads and deputy heads of the ninety-three U.S.S.R. ministries and state committees, and the Chairmen and Deputy Chairmen of the Council of Ministers of the fifteen union republics. The pattern of recruitment to these upper levels is quite different in the two countries. Entrance to the Administrative Class in Britain can be either by promotion from the lower Executive Class or by direct admission through comprehensive examination and interview procedures. Most Administrative Class officers, especially at the very highest levels (Permanent Secretaries and Deputy Secretaries), have been direct entrants and a great majority of these have been educated at the two

[20]This characteristic was emphasized by Max Weber in *The Theory of Social and Economic Organization*, ed. Talcott Parsons (New York: The Free Press, 1964), pp. 329 ff.

preeminent English universities, Oxford and Cambridge.[21] A high proportion of "Oxbridge" university graduates seems characteristic of both Civil Servants and Ministers in the Government; a study in 1957 showed that 68.5 percent of the top 77 Civil Servants and 71.5 percent of Government Ministers had graduated from one of these two universities.[22] Having the same alma mater certainly does not assure that men will be lifelong friends or have identical attitudes toward political problems, but the common educational background (and the implication of common social background) increases the probability of long-standing acquaintanceships between these two groups and makes communication and harmonious collaboration easier and more natural. The situation is described by H. E. Dale as follows:

> A high official [i.e., civil servant] especially if he was educated at Oxford or Cambridge, is likely to have in Parliament a fair number of old acquaintances, and some friends, perhaps men whom he has known from boyhood or early youth, and calls by their Christian names or nicknames. He meets them at his club or in private society; he may stay with them at their country cottages (if they possess such amenities) during weekends, or take holidays with them.[23]

Particularly when a Conservative Government is in power, "Cabinet Ministers . . . and their civil servants are not naturally separated by any wide differences of social habit and intellectual training. If not educated at the same schools, they have been at the same universities and have taken there the same kind of curriculum, they belong to the same clubs, they speak the same dialect of English."[24] Although recruitment is effected by different means, and career experiences have diverged, this common background—when it exists—can be very helpful in bridging the gap between men whose personalities have led them to prefer quite disparate careers.

The same kind of result is achieved in the Soviet system by instituting a common channel of recruitment for both state and party workers. It is not unusual for an individual to cross over from one hierarchy to the other as he

---

[21] Whether this is due to the quality of applicants from Oxford and Cambridge, or the quality of the examination procedure, is open to question. In the period 1957–63, 85 percent of those admitted directly to the Administrative Class were from Oxford or Cambridge, and one of every six Oxbridge applicants was accepted, while only one in 26 applicants from other universities was admitted. See "Sixth Report from the Estimates Committee, Session 1964 – 65: Recruitment to the Civil Service," H. C. 308 (1965), p. 29.

[22] Tom Lupton and C. Shirley Wilson, "The Social Background and Connections of 'Top Decision Makers,' " in Richard Rose, ed., *Policy-Making in Britain: A Reader in Government* (London: Macmillan, 1969), p. 11.

[23] H. E. Dale, "Parliament in Relation to the Civil Service," in Lord Campion et al., *Parliament: A Survey* (London: Allen and Unwin, 1952), p. 136. See also his *The Higher Civil Service of Great Britain* (Oxford: Oxford University Press, 1942), p. 143.

[24] Dale, *The Higher Civil Service. . .* , p. 128.

advances his career. The sharp British distinction between the role of the Civil Servant and the role of the politician is not rigorously observed in the Soviet system. However, a similar functional division between policy making and policy implementation is achieved by the creation of two separate but parallel hierarchical institutions: the Party and the state. Contrary to the British practice, only a small proportion of the Party leaders (about 13 percent of the CPSU Central Committee) work directly and primarily in the state structure. Despite this institutional separation, the strong common indoctrination in *partiinost'* ("party spirit"), and the common values and interests of careerists in both hierarchies create the same foundation for harmonious interaction that exists in the British system. Of course, neither common background nor common value and goal premises are sufficient to eliminate the possibility of conflict arising between the two groups—as is most amply evidenced by the vicissitudes of Soviet politics over the years.

In both systems, a distinction is made between the "political" tiers—the leader, leadership core, and national leadership—and the administration, but both systems have had difficulty in maintaining the theoretical boundary line. The role of the administrator cannot be isolated from politics, despite the best intentions of all concerned. The administrator provides inputs of recommendations and data to the political policy process, and his closeness to the subject and experience give added weight to his judgments.

On the other hand, it is considerd illegitimate for the administrator to *make* the decision, for despite his expertise, only the party leaders are authorized in theory to make the final choice between the alternatives. In neither country does the administrative tier have the legitimate function of determining governmental policy, and in fact the inferior position of administrators in relation to party leadership tiers is a hallowed part of the legitimizing doctrines of both political systems. A former Minister, Mr. Patrick Gordon-Walker has written: "In some ways, a Minister's Department is his refuge. Here he is master in his own house."[25] Soviet statements are quite explicit concerning the superiority of the Party to the state structure: "Besides the Communist Party, armed with Marxist-Leninist theory, knowledge of the laws of social development, strong unity of its ranks, and its close ties with the masses of the people, there is not, and there cannot be, any other political organization which would be able successfully to coordinate the operation of all state and public organizations, consistently consider and combine the interests and needs of all classes and social groups, all nations and nationalities, [and] all generations of our society."[26]

[25] Rt. Hon. Patrick Gordon-Walker, M.P., "On Being a Cabinet Minister," in Rose, *Policy-Making in Britain*, p. 124.

[26] *Gosudarstvennoe pravo SSSR* (Moscow: Izd-vo "IUridicheskaia literatura," 1967), p. 145.

Although the party leadership tiers can legitimately triumph in any overt confrontation with administrators, the task of implementing policies always gives the administrative tier the possibility of consciously sabotaging the policies forced on it, or unconsciously interpreting the ensuing general directives in such a way as to deflect the effects of the policy in the direction of administrative prejudices or simple administrative convenience. Furthermore, as in the other tiers, it would be a gross over-simplification to assume that the entire administrative structure is united in its views. Perhaps more than the other tiers, because of its size and deep involvement in developing and protecting specialized segments of the economy (and corresponding specialized interests), the administrative tier is likely to be divided in its opinions on the effects of policy.

Finally, it should be pointed out that while the administration tier has advantages of expertise and experience in relation to the party-based tiers above it, there is a constant circulation of officials within the administration of both countries—and this tends to weaken the claim to special knowledge of those who rise in the structure. Indeed, if one considers only the upper levels of the administrative tier, the term "expert" may have to be highly qualified. The British Civil Service has been typified at the highest levels by the generalist administrator, who combined "an attitude of effortless superiority . . . with cultured skepticism."[27] Theoretically, the generalist is one who can put policy proposals in the broadest perspective, who can see the widest implications in any changes that are suggested. He may see hidden dangers which specialists are apt to overlook. His influence is thus largely conservative in nature, but this has fit prevailing British preferences for policies of gradual, evolutionary change.

Generalists, of course, cannot be expected to have deep, specialized knowledge of a particular subject area. The method of recruitment and training of the Administrative Class of the British Civil Service makes such specialization very difficult, and therefore very rare. This lack of expertise at the upper levels has led to many criticisms of the Civil Service as inadequate to deal with the complicated problems of the modern state.[28] Aside from recruitment patterns, the emergence of generalists at higher levels of the admin-

---

[27]Thomas Balogh, "The Apotheosis of the Dilettante: The Establishment of Mandarins," in Hugh Thomas, ed., *Crisis in the Civil Service* (London: Anthony Blond, 1968), p. 12.

[28]For example, Thomas Balogh writes: "In fields in which specialized knowledge or training is required to carry on a sustained argument, the absence of such specialized knowledge invariably leads—not to the absence of theorizing, to "hard-headed realistic empiricism"—but to jejune meditations based on a set of simple theology and beliefs, if not on some long-since exploded fallacy" (*ibid.*, p. 17). A major critique of the Civil Service which emphasized this problem, was presented in 1968 to the House of Commons by a Select Committee of inquiry under the chairmanship of Lord Fulton (Cmnd. 3638).

istration is in part the outgrowth of the nature of hierarchical organization. As K. C. Wheare has put it:

> When we look at the way in which offices are organized, both in the government and outside it, we find that, as a general rule, officials at the top or head of the office are not experts; they are usually general practitioners. This is in most cases a consequence of necessity, for those at the top must deal with a wider range of questions than those lower down and they are bound to be less expert.[29]

Thus the upper-level British administrator usually does not have an advantage of trained subject expertise over the party leader appointed as a Minister, although he usually is somewhat less ignorant of the subject than his political superior. What he does have is administrative experience, usually within the very department which he heads.

Upper-level Soviet state administrators are likely to have more specialized or even vocational education in the fields which they administer. A career in the Soviet state bureaucracy usually begins with training at one of the many scientific-technical institutes which provide a highly specialized, production-oriented education. Although horizontal shifts are not unknown, there is also a greater tendency for Soviet state administrators to remain in one technically specialized vertical channel throughout a career. To some extent, this is necessitated by the more direct and comprehensive involvement of the state in economic management. In education and experience, state administrators can usually claim more expertise than their opposite numbers in the Party *apparat*. The relationship is thus broadly similar to that of the British Ministers and their Civil Servants.

POLICY-MAKING SCENARIOS

As already mentioned, there are very many different kinds of governmental actions that can be characterized as policy making, and in fact policies can even be the latent and unintended consequence of government actions. The governmental machinery of the modern industrial state is so vast, so complex, that there is almost an endless variety of policy-making possibilities, some of which seem to be totally fortuitous. Despite the obvious difficulties of classification, the picture can be considerably clarified by distinguishing policies according to the governmental institutions which become involved in the policy-making process.

On the highest level of generality, one can divide policies into two broad categories: those that involve the party leadership tiers and those that involve only the administrative tier. The important factor in determining whether a

---

[29]K. C. Wheare, *Government by Committee: An Essay on the British Constitution* (Oxford: Oxford University Press, 1955), p. 16.

policy will be brought up to the party leadership is the degree to which those in the system consider it an *issue*, using some (partly instinctive) criteria for measuring its political salience. In both systems, the legitimacy of administrative policy-making is limited to politically non-salient matters, to matters which are not deemed sufficiently important to concern the higher tiers.

Policies are not always embodied in specific written texts. The administrative tier in particular may set policy directions by the subtle emphases which it imparts to the implementation of established rules. The government's priorities relating to resource allocation are especially likely to be indicated by indirect means—such as, for example, a reduced allocation for a government agency or a subsidy for a particular industry.

Policies are always related to change, but sometimes they are attempts to create or accelerate change (and thus *active* policies), and at other times they are attempts to cope with change that has already occurred (and thus *reactive*). Even reactive policies have potentially active side effects, which may be as unwelcome to the policy-makers as they are unexpected. The unintended fall-out from past policies usually requires further adjustments through a series of reactive policies.

Policy-making is generally and rightly thought to involve some element of conflict. The conflict may be between different leaders, governmental institutions, interest groups, or segments of the population, and any combination of these and other human associations. The conflict may also be between differing opinions concerning the relative merits of policy alternatives, without strong connection to particular groups or persons. The important thing is that two or more alternatives exist and are actively considered, since in the case where only one possibility for action exists (or is thought to exist by all concerned) the procedures for policy-making are shortcircuited.

The policy-making process can be clarified by associating it with the four tiers of the leadership structure (see Chart V.1). Each tier has characteristic or modal policy-making processes, which we shall call policy-making scenarios. Yet, most policies are produced by a process of continuous interaction among these tiers until a decision (or some other less definite resolution) is made. A decision is in one sense an attempt to resolve existing policy conflicts by selecting one of several policy alternatives, by combining features of different policy proposals in a compromise, or by postponing a decision to a more propitious time. The process is complicated by the fact that governments cannot deal with each policy in isolation from other aspects of its general program. Conflicts often arise, not because of disputes over the merits of a particular policy, but because two perfectly acceptable policies seem in some respects to be incompatible with one another, or with the over-all objectives of the government. These policies are most likely to be "kicked upstairs," for they inevitably involve conflict between two or more governmental institutions as rival sponsors of policies in their own area of competence. In such a

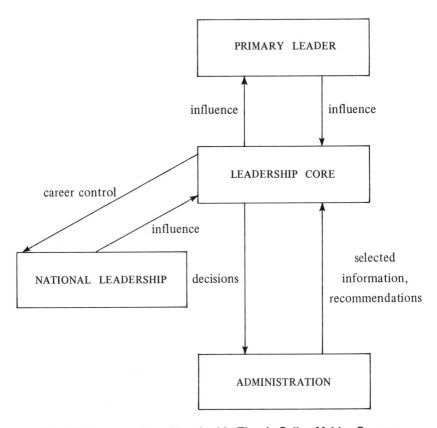

Chart V.1. Interaction of Leadership Tiers in Policy-Making Process.

case, resolution of conflict involves setting priorities in terms of over-all objectives, a task which can only be performed by an institution whose authority encompasses the rival sponsors.

As a general rule, the more conflict is generated by policy proposals, the higher is the level on which the conflict will be resolved. The decisive level for a particular policy is the highest level at which two or more alternatives are proposed and actively considered. After the decision has been reached, policies are often authorized by ratification through a legitimizing process, such as passage of a bill through the representative assembly, or formal acceptance by the leadership core.

For descriptive purposes, let us consider several of the most characteristic policy-making scenarios of the British and Soviet systems. These scenarios do not, by any means, exhaust all of the possibilities, but they are models which fit a large number of cases in the recent history of both countries.

1. **The Administrative Tier Scenario**: Administration, very much like adjudication, includes the making of decisions based upon existing rules. Administrators in both countries are often called upon to issue detailed regulations within general guidelines established by the party leaders. The issuing of regulations is so widespread in the administrative tier, and their political salience is considered so low, that the party leadership tiers are often entirely ignorant of their contents. Such regulations are, for the most part, unknown also to the general public. It is not surprising that this should be so, for in both countries the sheer bulk of such regulations is staggering.

In Great Britain, administrative regulations, or "delegated legislation," are issued under the authority of covering statutes as Statutory Instruments. A single statute can set off a whole avalanche of Statutory Instruments, as is indicated by the fact that in 1968 only 77 statutes were passed by Parliament, while the administrative tier issued 2,077 Statutory Instruments.

At the national level of the Soviet government, the situation is quite similar. Laws (*zakony*) passed by the full Supreme Soviet form a very small portion of the authoritative rules issued by the regime. Edicts (*ukazy*) issued by the Presidium of the Supreme Soviet are more numerous, but they too are far from the major portion of rules—and most of them concern awards, promotions, demotions, and place-name changes. The bulk of regulatory acts are decrees (*postanovlenie*) issued by the highest level of the administrative tier, the Council of Ministers. According to one estimate for the period 1945–65, for each law passed, there were 50 edicts issued and 285 decrees approved, many of them unpublished and virtually unobtainable. As a yearly average for this period, it is estimated that 510 statutes and edicts were issued and 2870 decrees authorized by the Council of Ministers.[30] Although decrees are supposed to be issued only in conformity with existing laws and edicts, it is unlikely that this requirement receives any greater attention than any other legal restrictions on the power of the Soviet leadership.

The British system, on the other hand, does provide a mechanism for review of Statutory Instruments by members of the representative assembly. This is accomplished in two ways: about half of all Statutory Instruments are "laid on the table" before the House of Commons for a period usually of 40 days, during which the House may act to annul them; and a Select Committee on Statutory Instruments is established for each session to review all Instruments to assure that they are within the terms of the authorizing legislation, that they have been issued promptly, and that they are clear in meaning. The work of this committee certainly seems to show that the vast majority of Statutory Instruments are drawn with due regard for proper procedure and

---

[30] See Dietrich A. Loeber, "Legal Rules 'For Internal Use Only'," *International and Comparative Law Quarterly*, vol. 19 (January 1970), pp. 74–77.

substantive intent of the authorizing legislation; of 10,232 Instruments examined from 1944 to 1959 only 120 were reported to the House for deficiencies.[31]

The regulations issued by the administrative tier make exciting reading for very few people in the system. This is because the vast majority of regulations concern the establishment of norms, procedures, and standards for production and distribution, and as such they affect very few people vitally and very many others only indirectly. Judging from the available evidence, the regulations are often drawn up partly in consultation with the affected groups. This is done to assure that the regulations are established within empirically sound limits and to assure the group's cooperation. Obviously, the government administrators wish to draw on the greater expertise of the practitioners in various fields of production, and the practitioners in return receive due consideration for their views. The administrative tier may also perform a judicial function when different economic interests are in conflict or citizen complaints are received. In all of this activity, its attention is directed to an essentially conservative task: the fitting of each new problem and concern into the fabric of existing procedures and policies. It is in this sense, rather than as conscious philosophical conservatives, that bureaucracies may be said to resist change.

2. **The National Leadership Scenario**: The most significant policy-making functions of the national leadership tier are performed in conjunction with the other leadership tiers. In neither country does the national leadership meet as a group to decide issues (in the sense already presented of resolving conflict by selecting from the range of possible alternatives). Both Soviet and British national leaderships lack cohesion and common interests which would permit them to exercise real power commensurate with their high authority. (It would, of course, be legitimate for the national leadership to dismiss the entire leadership core and replace it with another more to its liking.) Lacking real possibilities for translating its authority into real power, the national leadership in both countries acts as a transmission belt of influences from geographic and economic sectors to the leadership core.

3. **The Leadership Core Scenario**: In both the Soviet Union and Great Britain, the leadership cores are collective leadership groups, which operate under similar norms of behavior. Collective responsibility for major decisions, modified by somewhat inconsistent norms of individual responsibility for glaring errors, secrecy of the decision-making process, and a public

---

[31] John E. Kersell, *Parliamentary Supervision of Delegated Legislation* (London: Stevens, 1960), p. 170.

show of unanimity—these characteristics apply to both groups equally. Within the leadership core, each member is assigned administrative responsibility for a specific area of public interest. Supervision of a segment of the administrative tier is a major task for most—but not quite all—core members. This supervisory specialization is linked to specialization in the decision-making sphere. Policy initiatives in a specific subject area are generally expected to come from the core member whose supervisory role includes that area.

This division of responsibility is beneficial to the leadership core in two ways. First, it helps to avoid continual conflict within the group by systematically giving each member a leading role in formulating policies on a rotational basis. Although the core member may be quite inexpert in comparison with his subordinates in the administrative tier and outside specialists, he is, after a short time, more knowledgeable about affairs in his own domain than the other core members. At the very least, his superior access to information, to briefs prepared by his subordinates, will give him significant advantages when policies in his area of competence are discussed by the group. Thus the likelihood is increased that the other members will acquiesce in policies proposed by the relatively expert member. In effect, a shifting pattern of deference, depending on the subject discussed, is established in the group according to the established division of responsibility.

The second possible advantage of this system is that it provides the member with an opportunity to become more proficient in dealing with the problems of his subject area and coping with his own administrative staff. This opportunity is considerably lessened, however, in British practice by rather rapid turnover, caused both by the alternation of parties in consequence of elections, and the reshuffling of Cabinets which occurs within the lifetime of each Government.

Major administrative assignments and changes are always publicly announced in Britain. The British Cabinet, however, has for many years been divided into a series of subject committees (both standing committees and temporary *ad hoc* groups) to examine policies in areas which require coordination between Ministries. Committee designations and assignments are kept secret—a secrecy that is legitimized by the doctrine of collective responsibility and enforced by the Official Secrets Act. Yet it is well known that certain committees such as the Defense Committee, Atomic Energy Committee, Home Economics Committee, Legislation Committee, and Future Legislation Committee have been established by recent Governments to the point where they "have practically become parts of the Constitution."[32] Policy decisions taken by Cabinet committees have even more weight than those proposed by individual Ministers, and it is even less likely that there will be serious opposi-

---

[32] Gordon-Walker, "On Being a Cabinet Minister," p. 122.

tion to the proposal in the full Cabinet, since the Cabinet members most affected by the proposal have already assented to it in the committee stage.

The use of Cabinet committees is but one example of a notable characteristic of British Cabinets: that *Cabinets are conflict-avoidance mechanisms*, that all their procedures and norms of behavior are directed toward assent, mutually supportive behavior, and a pervasive "team spirit." Numerous accounts by former Cabinet members lead to this conclusion. Lord Morrison, who served in three Cabinets, has written:

> To describe the Ministerial contributions [in Cabinet meetings] as speeches would not be quite right. They are, or at any rate should be, to the point and in the nature of quiet, well-considered remarks, calculated to lead the Cabinet in the direction desired. . . . Personalities and bad temper are unusual and would certainly be discouraged, because it is very necessary for the Cabinet to be and to feel like a team, collectively concerned with the public interest. . . . So in due course we reach the point where what is called the Conclusion has to be reached. Now this is not done by voting, for the holding up of hands or the calling of "Aye" and "No" would not only be regarded as a breach of Cabinet decorum but also be felt to symbolize and demonstrate, nakedly and unashamedly, a lack of Cabinet unity and solidarity which is always deprecated. In most cases the Prime Minister is able, with the assent of the Cabinet, to state that the general view would appear to be so and so, and that is duly recorded in the Conclusions as the decison reached. . . . In the exceptional case of the Cabinet being somewhat acutely divided and strong views being held on a matter of particular difficulty . . . it may be right to let the decision stand and go ahead, but it may be better to suggest that in view of the sharp division of opinion Ministers should think about the discussion and defer a final decision until a later meeting.[33]

Patrick Gordon-Walker, who has held four different Cabinet posts, writes in the same vein:

> There are no resolutions or set propositions before the Cabinet; no voting system—just talk. Members discuss until a consensus of opinion is arrived at. When he thinks fit, the Prime Minister will sum up the views of his colleagues as they have emerged . . . silence signifies assent—not necessarily precise agreement, but acceptance of the prevailing view. . . . On even rarer occasions—perhaps never at all in the life of a Government—the Prime Minister may "collect the voices": ask each member in turn to say "yes" or "no" and count up the result. . . . A Cabinet that has to resort to this sort of voting is in all likelihood near the end of its days.[34]

Despite this elaborate etiquette, directed toward assuring "acceptance of the prevailing view," disputes can arise between Cabinet members, but they

---

[33] Morrison, *Government and Parliament*, pp. 19–20.

[34] Gordon-Walker, "On Being a Cabinet Minister," p. 120.

rarely loom so large as to threaten the unity of the Cabinet. A Minister who fundamentally disagrees "on a matter of principle" with his Cabinet colleagues, must either swallow his disquiet, or resign from the Cabinet—but resignation in modern times has usually been the quickest and surest path to political obscurity.[35] A man who resigns from the Cabinet because of a disagreement is likely to be viewed by his colleagues with everlasting distrust—so deep is the team spirit embedded in British political norms. As Jennings notes, "a minister who resigns on the ground of disagreement must, if his political ambition is to be further realized, either form a new party or join the Opposition."[36]

But the bulk of Cabinet business is not likely to involve Ministers in discussions or disagreements on principles. The matters are more mundane, and the judgments more pragmatic. On this level of discussion, the procedure is nicely tailored to the quietening of disagreements or even doubts. In addition to the conflict-avoidance procedures mentioned by Morrison and Gordon-Walker, there is the unifying effect of years of association in the same party, with its code of team-work and solidarity before the opposing party. Particularly when a Prime Minister is strong and dominates his Cabinet:

> It is very hard for a minister who begins to have doubts to intervene with effect. He has insufficient knowledge, he is always too late, and is contending with the Prime Minister and the men whom the latter has elevated to a position of trust. Also, when decisions have been taken, there is little that can be done other than protest in the secrecy of the Cabinet or resign.[37]

If so much effort is expended on avoiding conflict, can it be said that the Cabinet actually makes policy decisions? This certainly is not the view of John P. Mackintosh, whose statement was just quoted, for he writes:

> The Cabinet does not make policy. Decisions are taken at various levels and if the Prime Minister is inactive little is done and most of the plans come from ministers, departments or Cabinet committees. But a successful, strong and opinionated Prime Minister can put his impress on a whole government. His ideas will be worked out either by himself or with a few colleagues. . . . It is easiest for such a Premier to conduct affairs with the aid of the departmental ministers concerned, and the *Cabinet falls into place as a forum for informing his colleagues of decisions that have been taken.*[38]

---

[35] See R. K. Alderman and J. A. Cross, *The Tactics of Resignation: A Study in British Cabinet Government* (London: Routledge and Kegan Paul, 1967).

[36] Jennings, *Cabinet Government*, p. 264.

[37] John P. Mackintosh, *The British Cabinet*, p. 484.

[38] *Ibid.*, p. 483. Emphasis added.

For the bulk of Cabinet work, Mackintosh's view seems substantially correct. The appearance of an item on the agenda of a Cabinet usually signifies a *fait accompli*: the senior members and most directly affected members of the Cabinet have already agreed on a course of action, for which Cabinet endorsement is now sought. Samuel Brittan, in his excellent study of the British Treasury, reports that:

> The Cabinet itself hears the Budget only the day before the Chancellor announces it to the House. . . . The real reason why the Cabinet can do so little on Budget eve is not because it is technically impossible but because it has not been in on the key discussions and hears for the first time the Chancellor's arguments. It is then too late to thrash the whole matter out afresh.[39]

In most cases, particularly involving legislation, a Cabinet committee will have worked out all the necessary compromises between different departmental views before the matter reaches the Cabinet. In such cases, "subsequent Cabinet discussion is rarely necessary."[40] In those cases where the policy seems of secondary importance, for the most part involving a single department, the chief obstacle to the measure may be the problem of finding parliamentary time for the passage of a bill. Because parliamentary time is always in short supply, relatively non-controversial bills of lesser importance may wait on line through several sessions before being scheduled in a Government's legislative program. The task of developing a sessional legislative program, and determining the programmatic priorities which this implies, falls to the Future Legislation Committee of the Cabinet, which was created to help "the Cabinet to escape Departmental pressure in determining legislature priorities."[41] A bill which passes this hurdle, and is approved by the Legislation Committee of the Cabinet, is unlikely to be seriously opposed when it appears on the agenda of the full Cabinet.

An additional factor, which tends to reduce the policy-making role of the Cabinet, is the existence of an "inner Cabinet," a small circle of usually senior Cabinet members who have the Prime Minister's confidence and friendship, and who are likely to discuss issues with the Prime Minister more frequently than the others, in both formal and informal settings. Many Cabinets have had such an inner circle of Prime Ministerial cronies, and the knowledge that such a group has agreed on a policy is likely to abbreviate Cabinet discussion of the matter considerably.

Thus, in most matters put forward by a British Government, the full Cabinet is not the decisive decision-making institution. It may be a court of

---

[39] Samuel Brittan, *The Treasury under the Tories, 1951–1964* (Baltimore: Penguin Books, 1964), pp. 111–12.

[40] Jennings, *Cabinet Government*, p. 261.

[41] S. A. Walkland, *The Legislative Process in Great Britain* (London: Allen & Unwin, 1968), p. 60.

last resort on particularly thorny matters, and it may unaccustomedly decide a course of action in a sudden crisis, when there has not been sufficient time for a smaller group to prepare a *fait accompli*—but for the most part it is simply a convenient meeting of busy political executives, where they can keep "in touch with all the various lines of activity and . . . give the work of the government a measure of unity."[42]

Very little is known about the internal procedures of the CPSU Politburo, and most of that has been gained by inference from external evidence. This is particularly true of the period since Nikita Khrushchev was pensioned, since the present leadership seems more intent than ever to obscure its internal workings. It has never been Soviet practice to announce Politburo meetings or to discuss the important role of the Politburo in Soviet politics.[43] More recently, even the external signs by which one could detect the rising or falling fortunes of individual Kremlin luminaries have been expunged from press reports.[44] This has made life much more difficult for Western Kremlinologists, while concurrently life has become somewhat easier—at least more secure—for Politburo members.

Nikita Khrushchev, during his troubled tenure in office as First Secretary, was somewhat more obliging in revealing something about Politburo procedure than any of its present members. In an interview with Turner Catledge, then editor of *The New York Times*, in May 1957, Khrushchev said the following:

> [The Politburo] meets regularly at least once a week. . . . More often than not, when questions are examined at meetings of the [Politburo] different points of view are expressed, as the members . . . strive to examine the problem under discussion as thoroughly as possible. During the discussions, the members . . . usually arrive at a unanimous point of view. If on

[42]Mackintosh, *The British Cabinet*, p. 384. (Page reference is for the first edition, published in 1962.)

[43]As just one of countless examples, one could cite the textbook published by the Academy of Sciences, *The Political Organization of Soviet Society*, which contains just one passing reference to the political role of the Politburo. *Politicheskaia organizatsiia sovetskogo obshchestva* (Moscow: "Nauka," 1967).

[44]For example, the names of Politburo members used to be published in order of importance, a procedure which delighted Kremlinologists. Nowadays, the list of names is invariably given in alphabetical order. The sole exception to this rule is the verbal announcement of the proposed Politburo line-up given by the General-Secretary to the select audience at the Party Congresses. Brezhnev has taken the "liberty" of announcing his colleagues in the apparent order of his preferences. In 1971 this order was: Brezhnev, Podgornyi, Kosygin, Suslov, Kirilenko, Pel'she, Mazurov, Polianskii, Shelest, Voronov, Shelepin, Grishin, Kunaiev, Shcherbitskii, Kulakov. It is significant, however, that in the Soviet press version of Brezhnev's speech the list is printed in "normal" alphabetical order. Thus Brezhnev's ranking is not authoritative and is probably more an indication of closeness to the General-Secretary than power in the Kremlin (although the two are probably connected to some degree). In any case, the Soviet public is never given anything but a strictly alphabetical listing of Politburo members.

some question unanimity cannot be reached, the problem is decided by a simple majority vote.

Of course, very heated debates sometimes arise. But that is quite natural in a democratic discussion.[45]

From this account, one gains the impression that life in the Khrushchevian Politburo was rather more turbulent than it has been in the British Cabinet of recent years. At the time of the interview, the turbulence must have been particularly high, for it was only a few weeks later that a majority of the Politburo (then called the Presidium) voted to remove Khrushchev, a decision that was subsequently reversed by the Central Committee. The leaders of this attempted anti-Khrushchev coup (the so-called "Anti-Party Group") were later revealed to have opposed Khrushchev's policies over a period of "three or four years," and this no doubt led to the "heated debates" to which Khrushchev referred in his interview.[46]

There are reasonable grounds for suspecting that the leadership turmoil of the Khrushchev years has been reduced considerably under Brezhnev's leadership. One reason for this supposition is the evidence of greatly increased stability in the membership of the Politburo (and other leadership organs such as the Central Committee and Council of Ministers). This security of tenure implies, at the very least, that debates have not in recent years been so heated that a critical confrontation between Politburo factions has occurred. Furthermore, the relatively cautious and conservative approach which the Politburo has taken to many issues would seem to indicate that consensual compromises have been sought within the group—perhaps to avoid such confrontations.[47]

On the other hand, compromise solutions are only required when conflict exists, and there is still evidence of such internal disagreements within the Politburo. (A most notable case was the wavering of the Politburo in the months before the decision was made to invade Czechoslovakia in August, 1968.) What has apparently changed, however, is the degree to which such conflict is permitted to disrupt the relations and working arrangements between Politburo members. In other words, a new set of norms, regulating conduct of Politburo members and setting limits on the methods by which conflict is resolved have been tacitly accepted by the leadership—primarily

[45] *N. S. Khrushchev, Speeches and Interviews on World Problems, 1957* (Moscow: Foreign Languages Publishing House, 1958), pp. 53–57.

[46] See the resolution of the Central Committee Plenum, *Pravda*, July 4, 1957 [*CDSP* IX, no. 23, p. 5].

[47] A good example of this approach was the Politburo solution to the problem of economic reform, where it fully accepted neither the proposals of the reformers (Liberman, Birman, et al.) nor the warnings of the most conservative elements. The program which was adopted was clearly a compromise.

because the new, more gentlemanly rules of the Soviet political game enhance the personal security of each leader.

One can only speculate about the scene inside the Politburo meeting room. It can be safely assumed that the General-Secretary, Leonid Brezhnev, chairs the meeting, although it is impossible to know the extent to which he dominates the meetings. It is difficult to avoid the conclusion that his influence over his colleagues is likely to be less than that of the British Prime Minister over his Cabinet. The General-Secretary does not appoint the members of the Politburo, nor can he dismiss those members who displease him. The Prime Minister has both of these powers, within limits imposed by the probable political consequences. It is important to recall that the most sweeping leadership purge of the last decade was carried out not by Khrushchev or Brezhnev, but by Harold Macmillan in 1962.

The General-Secretary's position seems less secure than the Prime Minister's position in several other respects as well. To a much greater extent, the General-Secretary depends on the support of his colleagues, for he has no other basis for his power—save a desperate appeal to the Central Committee such as Khrushchev employed in 1957 successfully, and in 1964 unsuccessfully. The British Prime Minister has a following in the country and in the Party, demonstrated by his successful leadership of the party to governmental power. A serious move by the Cabinet to unseat him—even if unsuccessful—would so weaken and divide the party that the odds of its winning a subsequent election would be too low for even the London bookmakers to calculate. A Politburo majority, on the other hand, can carry on quite well without the General-Secretary. It need only be certain of carrying a majority of the Central Committee—the last and decisive constituency for resolving such conflicts. Thus, the potential for removing a General-Secretary is always present in Soviet politics, while such a threat hardly applies to the Prime Minister at all. When Prime Ministers have resigned, it has been because they have lost the confidence of a large number of supporters outside the Cabinet and, in fact, on several recent occasions of this rare event (Neville Chamberlain's resignation in 1940, Anthony Eden's in 1957, Harold Macmillan's in 1963 and Alex Douglas-Home's in 1965), the Prime Minister apparently retained the support of his Cabinet despite widespread disaffection outside.

Judging from such considerations, one might imagine the General-Secretary dealing very cautiously with his comrades on the Politburo. They, in turn, are likely to pay some deference to him on condition of his remaining first among *equals.* The lack of precision in this relationship no doubt creates tensions, but the existence of a common bond of Party loyalty, the hallowed *partiinost'*, and common bureaucratic training probably serves to relieve the tension somewhat. Clearly, the other Politburo members have played a role in preventing Brezhnev from receiving the kind of publicity that was accorded to Khrushchev. Some of Brezhnev's speeches are not even published, and he is rarely given special credit or mention for the many "successes" credited to the Party as a whole.

Under current conditions, it is highly unlikely that any General-Secretary would make a major decision without gaining the assent and endorsement of the Politburo. In fact, Khrushchev's short-lived attempt to circumvent the Politburo was both an indication of his growing estrangement from his colleagues in it, and a major contributing factor in his eventual downfall. On other occasions, even during foreign crises such as the Hungarian and Polish "events" of 1956, the Cuban missile crisis of 1962, and the Czechoslovakian crisis in 1968, the Party leader has clearly acted within a collegial process, avoiding the appearance of playing an independent role. The only analogous British crisis of recent decades, the Suez campaign of 1956, was apparently decided by Anthony Eden without even informing the Cabinet until the last moment.[48] Given the constraints on his policy-making prerogatives, it is virtually inconceivable that a General-Secretary would attempt such a serious venture without prior Politburo approval.

It is quite possible that the Politburo "decision-makers" are restrained from actually making decisions to an even greater extent than the members of a British Cabinet. As in the Cabinet, the Politburo members have divided the responsibilities so that the same considerations of relative expertise apply: each member is likely to be paid his share of deference by the others as his area of specialization is reached on the agenda. Technical considerations are likely to weigh more heavily on the Politburo than on the British Cabinet, because of the vast compass of the Soviet economic and social planning effort. Of course, there is no way of knowing whether conflict-avoidance is as much a part of Politburo interaction as it is of Cabinet interaction, but such a characteristic would certainly not be inconsistent with all that is known about the Politburo. In both leadership cores, the requirement of collective responsibility and public unanimity makes internal conflict and contention something that all members would wish to avoid if at all possible. It is no less disturbing to a Politburo member than a Cabinet member to participate in violent disagreements behind closed doors and yet be forced to support the opposing majority's point of view before the public—even to call it a wise or brilliant or perfect solution to the problem. In addition, the close working relationships and the minimum necessary degree of mutual trust necessary to discharge the Politburo's responsibilities would be severely taxed, if not destroyed, by intense, emotional disputes. The tenuous balance of forces within the Politburo, *upon which the security of each member depends*, would be

---

[48] See Paul Johnson, *The Suez War* (London: MacGibbon and Kee, 1957) and Randolph Churchill, *The Rise and Fall of Sir Anthony Eden* (London: MacGibbon and Kee, 1959).

threatened by heated disputes and by the formation of relatively permanent factions within the Politburo. For these reasons it seems likely that conflict-avoidance would operate within the Politburo as it does in the Cabinet: depersonalized, technically-oriented discussions of issues, each member striving to maintain a cool, detached, analytical approach, which leaves many avenues of face-saving escape if one's position is not supported. This cautious, dispassionate approach is most likely to lead to the sort of compromises and stability which have become characteristic of the Politburo in recent years.

* * *

The policy-making process as a whole involves the interaction of the various leadership tiers with each other, and their interaction with social and economic interests outside the governmental structure. The scenarios already presented have provided a description of the part which each leadership tier plays in itself, as part of the process in its many possible variations. It need hardly be said that these tiers do not operate in isolation from each other, but are linked together by chains of interaction replete with the flow of political communications, pressures, influences and authority. It is therefore important to examine the policy process in larger scope, by considering several scenarios of tier interaction.

4. **Scenario of Leadership Core and National Leadership Interaction**: Interaction between the leadership core and the national leadership is a continuous process in both systems. Neither national leadership makes political decisions, but both can play a significant role in influencing the decisions of the leadership core. In both countries, the national leaderships form a pool of younger talent out of which future leadership cores will be drawn. National leaders will naturally pay some deference to members of the leadership core, although this is somewhat less necessary in Britain. In both systems, the national leadership is co-opted into the leadership core from above, a consideration which produces some degree of deference out of career ambitions. Party loyalty, which ties together these two tiers, demands that the national leadership follow the policy leads of the leadership core, and the party provides disciplinary weapons to be used against consistently recalcitrant members.

Thus a superficial look at these systems would indicate that discipline and cohesion are so high that the leadership cores could be said to control the national leaderships, by persuasion or threat, to such an extent that the national leaders play an insignificant role in policy-making. Such a view, however, is inaccurate, for it misses the more subtle, barely palpable flow of influences from below to the top. Neither the Politburo nor the Cabinet makes policy in splendid isolation from the political currents which swirl around them. Indeed, the very fact that their members have risen so high is an indication that they are particularly adept at detecting those influences and moving in the required direction. The ambition, skills, and sensitivity which have propelled these men to the top naturally includes the desire to "do a good job," to be thought well of by their colleagues, lower-ranking supporters and perhaps even by future generations of historians—this last probably a forlorn hope at best! There is considerable evidence to show that in both countries the leadership core continuously strives to gain the active and enthusiastic support of the national leadership, and in the process the core is influenced by the opinions and information which it receives from below.

Ernest Marples, reflecting on the hectic "dog's life" which he led as Minister of Transport, found solace in the thought that:

> These continual deputations, interviews, consultations, letters and protests may often be a waste of time, but they also create a curious and intangible intimacy between the rulers and the ruled. The public must never be given an excuse for thinking that the members of its Government inhabit a superior and impenetrable world where it can knock but never enter.
>
> What is more, the democratic process is not just a one-way traffic. A good Minister is a Minister who can lead but is always going back to the grass roots. He should remember that he is not dealing with ruthless profit and loss, but with the lives of ordinary men and women.[49]

M.P.'s, who are legitimized as representatives of these grass roots, are most active in seeking out Ministers to present the views of constituencies or interests. As Marples notes, "the tradition is that a Minister must keep open house for every member of the Commons."[50]

British Cabinets, regardless of which party is in power, regularly gather information on the opinions of their backbench supporters. This is done through personal contacts, and through the liaison efforts of the Government Whip's Office. The Whip's Office collects information on the Members' voting records, public statements as reported in the press, and privately expressed opinions. The Cabinet depends on this information to forewarn it of widespread disaffection with Government policies. The parliamentary contingents of both parties are organized in subject committees of backbenchers which regularly meet to consider policy questions. The opinions expressed in those closed-door sessions are communicated to the party leadership, either by Whips in attendance or by the taking of minutes. As several studies have shown, widespread and intense backbench dissatisfaction with a Government proposal exerts the strongest possible pressure on the Cabinet to withdraw or

---

[49] Rt. Hon. Ernest Marples, "A Dog's Life in the Ministry," in Rose, *Policy-Making in Britain*, p. 130.

[50] *Ibid.*, p. 129.

substantially modify the policy.[51] It is not the backbenchers nor the front-benchers of the Opposition party which the Government fears, but the loss of support from its own parliamentary rank-and-file. Faced by opposition from within, the Cabinet can insist on its policy and pressure its own backbenchers into providing the necessary majority votes. But the costs are high: a significant depletion of party unity and morale, and a public display of disarray which always tends to weaken public confidence in the Government. Most Governments will be reluctant to pay such a price, and in any case there must be compelling reasons to force the Cabinet into such an uncomfortable position. In fact, one mark of a successful Cabinet is its ability accurately to predict backbench reactions and so to avoid these situations.

On the other hand, the Government's ability to persuade, cajole, and convince its supporters of the necessity of a policy should not be underestimated. On many questions of lesser political salience, the opposition of a small group, no matter how intense, is likely to be overwhelmed by the indifferent support of the large majority. In such matters, the Government can and does have its way. If its majority is large enough, it can afford to be more tolerant of open backbench rebellions, and indeed is likely to suffer more of them, for with a large majority, backbenchers can display more independence without endangering the existence of the Government. With a small majority, Governments are less likely to force contentious issues, and more likely to insist on strict party discipline; but under such conditions, potential rebels—no matter what they may say to newspaper reporters or their wives—are almost certain to follow the Government Whips into the division lobbies.[52] This is simply one example of the circular flow of influences and pressures between the British national leadership and leadership core. Both groups have an over-riding interest in preserving and, in fact, strengthening the Government in the face of attacks by the opposition party. Leaders want their followers to be loyal, but the followers also want to be loyal to their leaders. The Government's backbenches are often the source of disagreement and occasionally of rebellion, but always within the confines of a tacit understanding: when the life of a Government is at stake, the requirement of party loyalty transcends all other contrary considerations. Only in extreme cases—when the Government's very existence is threatened—will the top leaders take punitive action against a rebellious backbencher. Robert J. Jackson's thorough study of backbench rebellions concludes with a very apt statement of the relationship between discipline and rebellion:

---

[51] For examples of decisive backbench pressure, see Ronald Butt, *The Power of Parliament* (London: Constable, 1967).

[52] See Robert J. Jackson, *Rebels and Whips: An Analysis of Dissension, Discipline and Cohesion in British Political Parties* (New York: St. Martin's Press, 1968), p. 189.

The revolts that occurred in parliament and the very few punishments that were used against the recalcitrants were important in the dialogue between party leaders and followers. It is through the interaction of informal rebel groups with parties' formal groups and leaders that policy evolves. Since a party is a vessel for reconciling diverse interests it is not surprising to find that individual Members sometimes think it necessary for them to revolt while at the same time they do not desire to harm their party. Nor is it surprising to discover that although party leaders threaten to punish recalcitrants they usually think that it is impractical to take any action against them.[53]

The threat of rebellion by the Government's backbenchers and the threat of disciplinary action by the Government are dialectical components of the British parties' responsiveness, flexibility, and cohesion. But these threats are the more powerful the *less* they are used. In the normal circumstances, which after all are the substance of British politics, the individual M.P. follows his leaders out of a generalized *partiinost'* and lack of self-interest in the matters at hand. Nigel Nicolson (who lost his seat in a dispute with his local constituency association) has written:

> In the great majority of cases [the MP] does not feel the need to think at all, if the matter is unimportant to his constituents or uninteresting to him personally. He gladly follows the lead given by the leaders of his parliamentary party, whether in or out of office, because he shares their general outlook and trusts them not to depart from it in the details of policy for which they are responsible. If atomic energy or coalmining, about which I know nothing, are under discussion, it would not occur to me to take a stand against the party line.[54]

The relationship between these two tiers in the CPSU is considerably more one-sided—although not totally so, as is sometimes suggested. What role (if any) the Central Committee plays in Soviet policy-making is certainly far from clear. During Khrushchev's tenure, verbatim reports of plenary sessions of the Central Committee were reported in the press, complete with Khrushchev's many interruptions, admonitions and bits of advice. Since Khrushchev's removal, plenary sessions have not been fully reported—occasionally not even announced—so it is not clear whether Brezhnev's promise (in 1966) of an "enhanced role for plenary sessions of the CPSU Central Committee" has materialized.[55] The secrecy which has surrounded recent meetings of the Central Committee might very well be an indication that relatively open and frank articulation of diverse views is now permitted there. Such a develop-

[53] *Ibid.*, p. 308.

[54] Nigel Nicolson, *People and Parliament* (London: Weidenfeld and Nicolson, 1958), p. 71.

[55] "Report of the Central Committee to the 23rd Congress of the Communist Party of the Soviet Union," *Pravda* and *Izvestiia*, March 30, 1966. [*CDSP* XVIII, no. 13, p. 4.]

ment would not be inconsistent with prevailing doctrines of legitimacy or with the development of interest group articulation in Soviet politics. Indeed, it may be highly significant that some Central Committee sessions have apparently adjourned without publishing a single document, neither a keynote speech nor a set of directives or resolutions.

In our analysis of British parties it was pointed out that British national leaders always have a potential threat of withdrawal of support, which causes the leadership core to consider very carefully the likely reactions of their followers to all policy proposals. Clearly, the Soviet national leadership does not possess this threat of withdrawal of political support—but the question remains: does not the success or failure of a Soviet policy depend to a large extent on the enthusiasm and motivation of the national leadership, who in any event will be responsible for fulfilling it? The Central Committee members are somewhat closer to the problems that must be resolved by policies than are the members of the Politburo. Politburo members wish to develop policies which will work, which will produce the desired result, and to do this they must depend on information and advice that reaches them from lower echelons. It is highly likely that they seek such advice and information from their subordinates in the Central Committee and Central Committee Secretariat. Once again, this requirement establishes a circular flow of influences, with Central Committee members playing an indirect role in formulating policies. Since both Central Committee and Politburo members have the same generalized goals and probably similar perceptions of immediate problems, Central Committee members are likely to be drawn into policy discussions as advisers on the practicability of alternative policy proposals.

In recent years, the role of lower echelons has been enhanced by the characteristically cautious approach of the Politburo to the problems of economic reform. Rather than introduce these reforms by sweeping decrees and wholesale reorganization, the Politburo has preferred an incremental approach. First the new method is tried out experimentally by a few firms, and then, if successful results are obtained, an increasing number of enterprises are gradually brought under the new system.[56] The widespread use of this incremental approach is probably a reaction to the characteristic Khrushchev technique of plunging ahead with major reorganizations before acquiring adequate information on the probable results. Certainly it fits well with the characteristic conservatism and businesslike, managerial approach of the post-Khrushchev leadership. Whatever the reasons may be for its wider use, incrementalism carries the strong implication that the policy-making influence of the lower echelons, and particularly the Central Committee, is greatly

---

[56] This procedure has been used for the increased application of "economic accountability" (*khozraschet*), material incentives in agriculture, "direct links" between producers and sellers, profitability as a measure of enterprise performance, and the so-called "Shchekino experiment" of increasing production while reducing the work force.

enhanced. By basing far-reaching decisions on the results of small-scale experiments, the Politburo is clearly being guided by a flow of information from below, by a "pragmatic" approach to problem-solving, placing great emphasis on adjusting policies in conformance with empirical results. Incremental, pragmatic problem-solving emphasizes the dependence of the leadership core on the national leadership—just as Khrushchev's more romantic, grandiose policies eventually caused the national leadership to be demoralized and disenchanted with his antics.

From the outside, it appears that the Central Committee plays a policy-making role much the same as that defined by Walter Bagehot for the nineteenth-century English monarch: "the right to be consulted, the right to encourage, and the right to warn."[57] The British national leadership plays a similar role, using more open techniques based on the greater legitimacy of dissent. Its greater threat potential would seem to make it more influential than the Soviet national leadership, but its lesser expertise and greater isolation from administrative structures at least implies a reduced influence. It is impossible to assign weights, to measure the relative influence of these two national leaderships. The avid reader of British political history will know a number of cases which appear to demonstrate the great influence of the national leadership—and many other cases which apparently demonstrate the opposite. There are no cases in Soviet political history which clearly delineate the policy-making role of the Central Committee (except perhaps in the crises of Khrushchev's leadership in 1957 and 1964). One can only hope that in the future more information will be openly divulged, or that bureaucratic laxity will increase in the agencies of Soviet censorship.

5. **Scenario of Party Leadership and Administration Interaction:** Although the functional division of responsibilities between these tiers is quite sharp in the abstract, actual practice tends to blur the distinction. Formulation and execution of policies are better seen as parts of the same continuous process than as distinct, separable, and identifiable functions. In the process of implementing a policy, administrators must often make interpretations which substantially affect the outcome, and there are usually many lacunae in over-all plans which must be filled by administrative decisions. Thus implementation is to some degree a derivative form of policy-making. On the other hand, the formulation of policy is often based on the experience of implementing similar policies in the past. Most "new" policies are simply changes in old policies, changes that appear necessary because the return flow of

[57]Walter Bagehot, *The English Constitution*, p. 111. Of course, this does not mean that the English monarch played the same policy implementation role as Central Committee members do today. The similarity is in the limits imposed on *overt* policy-affecting activity. As has been pointed out, Central Committee members are involved in the execution of policies on a regional basis, and this activity adds to their possibilities of affecting policies indirectly, as well as to the influence of their "encouragements" and "warnings."

"feedback" information indicates that existing policies have not resolved the problems perceived by the policy-makers.

The problem of acquiring accurate feedback information is greatly increased in the Soviet Union by the absence of legitimized, autonomous organizations outside the party-state *apparat*. The highly integrated party-state bureaucracy, with its Leninist chain of command from higher to lower levels, faces a perennial problem of acquiring accurate feedback, for in a system of co-optation from above, lower bureaucrats will always have a personal interest in camouflaging problems, hiding failures, and reporting successes. Because of the substantial risks involved in taking responsibility for any project, lower bureaucrats generally seek the protection of higher levels to cover the possibility of failure.

Of course, these tendencies are not characteristic of Soviet bureaucracy alone, but their dysfunctional consequences are magnified in the Soviet case by the absence of outside, independent checking organizations. Starting in Lenin's time, there have been attempts to meet this problem, at least to the extent of exposing venal or indolent officials, through a series of party or "workers'" control commissions. These attempts have all failed. The commissions could not remain independent of the monolithic *apparat* structure, because they were inevitably a threat to the *apparatchiki*—and potentially a powerful political weapon.

The system is not entirely helpless in this respect, however. Apparently scandalous situations in localities are regularly revealed, as higher-level officials attempt to escape responsibility by castigating their subordinates. Aside from corruption, the main sins uncovered in such exposes are "bureaucratism" (excessive attention to paperwork and failure to check on actual conditions), "petty tutelage and substitution" (the tendency of party officials to become too involved in day-to-day state administration), and simple failure to achieve the output quotas set by the plan.

Indeed, one of the chief causes of violations of Soviet administrative norms is the plan itself. The setting of unrealistic, over-optimistic quotas forces responsible *apparatchiki* into some desperate juggling and trading of their assigned resources. An example of this tactic was given by Brezhnev in his speech to the October 1968 Central Committee Plenum:

> In Azerbaidzhan ... of the funds provided in 1967 for agriculture, the sum of 3,100,000 rubles was transferred to the construction of a subway and housing in the city of Baku. In Moldavia, an attempt was made to transfer 2,900,000 rubles, also from funds earmarked for agriculture, to the construction of a railroad; the justification given, incidentally, was that the railroad will be built through a rural locality. A highly dubious argument![58]

[58] *Pravda*, October 31, 1968. [*CDSP* XX, no. 44, p. 7.] Things apparently got worse in these two union republics, for major scandals were revealed in both during 1970. See *CDSP* XXII, no. 12 and 24.

The exigencies of plan fulfillment are the main element in defining the relationship between the Soviet leadership core, national leadership, and administration. Soviet politics to a large extent concerns the pulling and tugging of regional *apparatchiki* to acquire higher resource allocations and more "reasonable" output quotas from central agencies. Public references to this quiet, continuous struggle for scarce resources appear quite often. Of the 37 regional party and state *apparatchiki* who spoke at the Twenty-Third Congress, 28 mentioned a conflict with central planning authorities over some detail affecting their area. Taking as an example the speech by V. Ye. Chernyshev (a Party First Secretary from the Maritime Territory), we find the following clear references to the resource allocation struggle:

> Maritime Territory can give the country a great deal of tin, lead, and other very important materials. But in order to do this it is necessary to create a complex of factories. . . . We are counting on the U.S.S.R. State Planning Committee and the appropriate ministries to take an interest in this area. . . .
>
> We proposed that the new five-year plan provide for the construction of irrigation systems for 100,000 hectares of rice. However, the U.S.S.R. State Planning Committee has cut this figure to 30,000 hectares. Such a rate of development of rice planting is in our view insufficient.[59]

Mikhail Sholokhov, the well-known writer, described the situation somewhat more graphically:

> Our province officials go to Moscow and get now one thing, now another. Looking at them, I also go. But, naturally, my sights are lower: One time I might try to wangle a school, another time some shingles or timber for collective farm construction. So I go to the Minister: "Comrade Minister, please give me 3,000 shingles for collective farm cow and calf sheds!" And the Minister answers: "But you know we have a planned economy. You've already received everything you're supposed to according to the plan." I say to him: "I understand, but the cows, not to mention the calves, don't understand why they have to get wet in the fall rains and freeze in the winter."[60]

In this struggle over scarce resource allocation we find another dimension of the specialist-generalist distinction. Members of the lower echelons (national leadership and administration) represent *special interests*, either regional or economic. Their conflict over resource allocation is resolved by the members of the leadership core, who necessarily represent the *general interest*. By virtue of their institutional affiliation, the men in the Politburo must reconcile conflicting, legitimate claims on the limited supply of available resources in order to produce a reasonably realistic plan. Most of the recon-

---

[59] *Pravda*, April 1, 1966. [*CDSP* XVIII, no. 15, p. 15.]
[60] *Pravda*, April 2, 1966. [*CDSP* XVIII, no. 16, p. 27.]

ciliation takes place in the offices of the ministries and at the State Planning Committee (*Gosplan*), but it is likely that important disputes reach the Politburo as the court of last resort.

The politics of planning brings the collective leadership in the Politburo into a continuous round of consultations and negotiations with both special- ists and special interest representatives. Marxist-Leninist doctrine legitimizes only "rational" and "scientific" decision-making, and thus emphasizes the importance of expert calculations in determining courses of action. "Sub- jectivism," or willful, capricious, uninformed decision-making is considered a serious malady for a leader, and was an important charge directed against Khrushchev at the time of his removal. The collective leadership's procedure in formulating some important agricultural policies in 1965 was described by a Leningrad party *apparatchik*, V. S. Tolstikov, as follows:

All the members of the Presidium [i.e., Politburo] of the CPSU Central Committee, the Secretaries of the CPSU Central Committee and Comrade Brezhnev . . . before submitting proposals for the consideration of the plenary session, did a colossal job of studying the actual state of affairs in agriculture in all regions of our country and in all the branches of the national economy linked with the development of agricultural production *and consulted a large group of farm specialists and leaders, scientists, economists, and Party and Soviet workers.*[61]

That these procedures give the national leadership and administrative tiers great opportunities for influencing decisions seems undeniable. The extent to which these tiers seize the opportunity will depend to some extent on the personal relationship, institutional affiliations, and career prospects of the lower and higher leaders involved in the consultations. If the desire of the lower *apparatchik* to shed responsibility is paramount, he would be less likely to press specific proposals, for which he could later be held accountable. Of course, higher leaders also wish to cover themselves against future responsi- bility by striving for a consensus of the leadership and basing themselves to the fullest extent possible on expert, "scientific" opinions.

A comparison with the situation in Great Britain once again reveals some striking similarities. The British Government has increasingly become involved in areas of the economy once left in private hands. Both British parties have accepted the necessity for some sort of economic planning (although the Labour Party appears more deeply committed to it). Through such agencies as the Economic Planning Board and the National Economic Development Council, attempts—not entirely successful, it must be admitted—to develop coordinated economic plans have been made. In addition, the government, either directly or indirectly, employs millions of workers, and the yearly

[61]V. S. Tolstikov in *Pravda*, March 31, 1966. [*CDSP* XVIII, no. 13, p. 20.] Emphasis added.

Budget has widespread repercussions in all sectors of the economy. It is still true that as economic planner, employer, manager, and regulator, the British government does not play the same totally encompassing role as the Soviet party-state structure. But with central government revenue at approximately one-third the net national income, and with the proportion increasing, British government can certainly be seen as *the* main factor in economic development.

Just as in Soviet politics, a major part of British politics concerns the struggle for the allocation of scarce resources. The party leadership tiers in the government adopt over-all economic policy goals, such as increased economic growth and foreign-trade surpluses; the particularistic demands of various economic interests must be blended into these over-all objectives. The optimal policy is one which seems reasonably certain of attaining the objective while at least partially accommodating the interests involved. It need hardly be said that these two optimal policy characteristics are often difficult to obtain simultaneously.

The relationship between the party leadership tiers and the administrative tiers is structured to a large extent by this continual process of mixing and blending particular, special interests into the general policy of the Government. On the surface of the Government there lies a patina of party leaders, some one hundred of them, who are constitutionally responsible to Parliament for all Government policies. Below this thin layer there is the substance, the body of the Government: the thousands of Civil Servants who remain as the party leaders come and go. The relationship between Civil Servants and Ministers is a very complex one. Just as in marriage, legal requirements define only the outer form of the relationship, but the personalities of individuals determine its actual substance. The marriage of Civil Servants and Ministers is not always a happy one. Aside from personality mismatches, which usually cause a discreet transfer of the Civil Servant, there can be conflicts over policy. These conflicts are usually over means rather than ends of policy, for Civil Servants are trained, and constitutionally required, to accept the policy goals of whichever party leadership team is temporarily in office. Cases of overt obstruction by Civil Servants are extremely rare.[62] Yet the question remains: What are the respective policy-making roles of the top Civil Servants and Ministers?

The clearest limitation on the Minister's involvement is that of time, combined with the immense volume of activity in all departments of govern-

---

[62] They are not, however, unknown. The story is still told of the Parliamentary Counsel who detested the policies of Lloyd George, but could not bring himself to the point of violating the Civil Service code of faithful service to the Government. "The struggle in his heart found a curious outlet: he said it was impossible to cast these ideas into statutory form, and, as no-one else could do it, the work was held up for months." Sir Edward Playfair, "Minister or Civil Servant?" *Public Administration*, XLIII (Autumn 1965), p. 266.

ment. Despite the hectic pace of Ministerial life, most of them simply find it impossible to keep abreast of the entire range of departmental operations. An eminent Civil Servant has written that he was struck by "how limited in number . . . were the topics on which a minister could keep himself regularly informed and take the important decisions." He continued:

> It was not a question of energy or will. All the ministers under whom I served worked long hours and worked hard. It was the result of the sheer volume of business and the extreme variety of matters it concerned. In consequence while the minister was responsible for all that was done, most things were done without his knowledge.[63]

The things that are done without the Minister's knowledge are usually matters of low political salience, but there are cases, such as the famous Crichel Downs Affair, in which a Minister may feel compelled to take responsibility for administrative errors that occurred without his knowledge and which only later become matters of high political salience.[64] In most such matters, however, it is probably advantageous to the Ministry that the Minister remains ignorant, for if he acquainted himself with all such low priority details, he would not have sufficient time for his major function of coordinating departmental policy with that of the Government, "and if he immerses himself in departmental duties he becomes not a minister but a very senior administrator."[65]

On questions of higher political salience, the Minister is necessarily informed, and takes part in formulating the policy, but there is some difference of opinion on how well informed he is, and whether he plays a decisive, independent role in policy-making. The flow of information is vital to the determination of policies, if they are to be rational approaches to empirically relevant problems. This information flows upward through the administrative structure to the Minister, but at each remove from its source, it is distilled, abridged, and clarified for the easier understanding of the inexpert man at the top. Honest and conscientious Civil Servants attempt to prepare a "brief" (the word is highly descriptive) on a complex matter, in which all sorts of technical arguments, committee discussions, negotiations, expert opinions, and the like are accurately reduced to the few pages which the overburdened Minister can find time to read. Not even inflexible honesty and conscience can prevent some distortions from entering such an attenuated communications link to the top. This fact is acknowledged among both the critics and practitioners of the administration tier. Among the former, Thomas Balogh writes: "The fact is that in internal administration and policy, and external

---

[63] Sir Oliver Franks, as quoted in Jennings, *Cabinet Government*, p. 119.

[64] For a discussion of the Crichel Downs Affair, see Geoffrey Kingdon Fry, *Statesmen in Disguise: The Changing Role of the Administrative Class of the British Home Civil Service, 1853–1966* (London: Macmillan, 1969), pp. 257–64.

[65] Jennings, *Cabinet Government*, p. 119.

relations, ministers of both parties had no chance of mastering the growing troubles as they were at best not supplied with all the facts, and at worst supplied with misleading appreciations."[66] A former Minister, Sir Edward Boyle, recalled a few cases "where fairly senior officials have kept the Minister in the dark, or have tended to keep him in the dark, about the fact that there was quite a lot of debate further down the line" in the Ministry.[67] Aside from suppression or manipulation of information, which most would admit is a rarity, there are numerous opportunities for administrative prejudices or preferences to appear before the Minister in the guise of seemingly objective, empirically-based evidence. "What is the difference, the great human bridge, between 'should' and 'is'?" asks a former senior Civil Servant, Sir Edward Playfair. "Very often, unfortunately, civil servants do not recognize it themselves. They wrap up preferences in formal terms."[68]

The input from the administrative tier to the Minister is not only ostensibly value-neutral information, for it is the acknowledged function of senior Civil Servants to impart their advice and views to the Minister. Playfair writes that it is a "universal civil service axiom" that "the civil servant must present the alternatives but he must come down on one side or the other; otherwise the Minister is left floating."[69] Under such conditions, the personality, the skill, the determination and the expertise of the Minister must all be of a rather high order for him to resist the pressure and pursue his own preferences. His resolve to do so will be immeasurably strengthened, of course, if the policy is strongly supported by the party leadership, and has high priority there. Still, one cannot escape the conclusion that in the ordinary case, the Minister, who rarely knows much about the subject, and who is merely passing through the Ministry in the course of a varied political career, is all too easily persuaded by the gentle blandishments from below. Samuel Brittan, in his study of the Treasury, sums up the usual situation with admirable felicity:

> Politicians may prevaricate, they may accelerate (but how rarely!), they may tone down, or add verbal gloss. . . . But the one thing ministers, especially Chancellors, are rarely able to do effectively is to question the analysis on which the advice given to them is based. And having accepted the analysis they are ninety per cent of the way towards accepting the policies implied by the advice, in one form or another, sooner or later.[70]

Both Ministers and civil servants perceive their relationship through the prism of legitimizing doctrines that define their respective roles: the Minister

---

[66] Balogh, "Apotheosis of the Dilettante," p. 26.

[67] Sir Edward Boyle, "Ministers or Civil Servants?" *Public Administration*, XLIII (Autumn, 1965).

[68] Playfair, "Minister or Civil Servant?"

[69] Ibid.

[70] Brittan, *Treasury under the Tories*, p. 305.

decides issues, and civil servants faithfully execute the ensuing policies. To quote Sir Edward Playfair once more: "The good civil servant subordinates himself totally to the Minister's decision but speaks out frankly when and only when advice and criticism is helpful or necessary; the good Minister listens with care to all the advice and criticism which he gets and then makes up his own mind."[71] Such a definition, of course, still leaves open the question of who is to determine "when advice and criticism is helpful or necessary" and whether it is possible for the "good" Minister to "make up his own mind," when his own mind is empty of judgments from sources that are independent of administrative advice.

The primary direction of influence exerted by the administration tier on policy-making is toward a cautious, careful conservatism. Changes may be unsettling to an established and confortable routine. Established procedures are like a security blanket for middle-ranking administrators, protecting them from contingencies and reducing the tensions of choice that arise from new situations. Even the more innovative administrators can become affected by the positive value which regularly repeated practices seem to acquire over time. "This is the way it has always been done" can very easily become equivalent to "this is the way it should always be done." Civil servants themselves readily admit this tendency. Sir James Dunnett, former Permanent Secretary to the Ministry of Transport, once acknowledged, without undue concern, that "we are in the Civil Service perhaps inclined to be a little conservative; once an organization has been set up in a certain way we are perhaps inclined to let it run on in that way without too much self-examination."[72] The way that the Foreign Office "runs on" is described by Lord Strang, who was its Permanent Under-Secretary:

> The rules of procedure for the conduct of business in the Foreign Office are laid down in detail in an Order Book; and this, together with the traditional practices passed on from seniors to juniors down the years, determines the methods by which work is done and the spirit in which it is done. The Order Book is a comprehensive compendium which contains a body of instructions ranging from the rules of draftsmanship formulated by Sir Thomas Sanderson, Permanent Under-Secretary at the end of the nineteenth century . . .[73]

Minds finely honed on the procedures of the Order Book or its equivalent, attuned to the delicate etiquette of the organization, to its hoary customs and

---

[71] Playfair, "Minister or Civil Servant?" p. 268.

[72] Sir James Dunnett, "The Civil Service Administrator and the Expert," *Public Administration* XXXIX (Autumn 1961), p. 227.

[73] Lord Strang, "Permanent Under-Secretary," in Rose, *Policy-Making in Britain*, p. 134. The Permanent Under-Secretary in the Foreign Office is equivalent to the Permanent Secretary in other departments.

usages, minds trained to be wary of the consequences of action rather than to welcome them—this is the image of the administrator which seeps through the description by Lord Strang and others.[74]

The implications of this characteristic for policy-making are extremely important. If the Minister is unsure of himself or effectively dominated by his senior Civil Servant, and if the department has an established "department policy" which it pursues doggedly over the years without either particular success or particular calamity, the result can easily be a slow slide toward eventual disaster. The exceptionally able and determined Minister can indeed put his impress on an entire department, although even he will find his pristine principles eroded by the pressures focused on him from all sides. He must spend much of his time in Parliament, acting as spokesman for his Ministry or for the Government, and additional time must be found for the public relations chores which all Ministers must cheerfully endure. Precious little time is left for consideration of immediate policy, to say nothing of long-range planning or in-depth studies of existing policies. Thus, in matters of policy:

> The role of the minister is largely confined to that of choosing between alternatives as presented to him by his senior official, or perhaps officials. Unless he is very tough, and persistent, and energetic, or unless he has his own advisers outside the official chain of command, he will be lucky if he can discover much or anything about the options which have been ruled out on the way. . . . Out of all the things a minister might want to do, or hope to do, he is likely to be told he can't do some at all, or that "as a matter of fact, Minister, the choice lies between these two." Of course, it is not a matter of fact, but of opinion, but few ministers are likely to know this, or to have the knowledge, the energy, the *time*, to push their opinion against that of their permanent officials.[75]

In much if not all of this, the Soviet party leader might knowingly sympathize with his British counterpart. Their structural situations are quite similar. Both have the function of preparing policies in a specified area for approval by the entire leadership core; both have relatively permanent, if not expert, administrative structures below them which prepare all the materials from which policies must be drawn; and both must take responsibility for a multitude of administrative activities which they have neither the time nor energy to check. The built-in limitations on innovation and the conservative bent of relatively permanent bureaucratic structures act as a brake on responsive policies in both countries, but the British system contains greater possibilities for the inflow of fresh ideas through the alternation of party leader-

---

[74] See Brittan, *Treasury under Tories.*

[75] Roger Opie, "The Making of Economic Policy," in Thomas, *Crisis in the Civil Service*, p. 71.

ships and the increasing use of independent, non-administrative "brain trusts" of personal advisers drawn primarily from academic and business life.

Yet, whatever theoretical advantages the British system might have in introducing innovative ideas, it has not in practice been much more successful than the Soviet system in breaking the chains of economic orthodoxy. Perhaps the most positive thing that can be said about economic policy in both countries is that it has been consistent; new ideas have been hammered down to fit the mold of traditional administrative views, and economic policy has drifted through a series of minor reforms. Not even the more widespread use of outside advisers helped the Wilson Government very much in freshening its supply of economic policies.[76] In both countries, the continuous struggle for allocation of scarce resources, in the form of government expenditures and priorities established through regulations, absorbs the attention and saps the energies of administrative and party leadership tiers. Max Nicholson's criticism of British policy-making applies just as well to the Soviet system:

> No adequate and enduring provision has been made for studying existing or for anticipating future problems in public affairs, and for taking timely and sound dispositions to deal with them. Where important issues, such as the need for technological education or the need for planning, are raised by others they have habitually been ignored or tackled on a too-little-and-too-late basis by both politicians and administrators. The System robustly provides that the blind shall lead the blind.[77]

6. **Scenario of Outside-Interest Interaction with Leadership Tiers:** All of the leadership tiers interact with economic interests which are outside the governmental and party structure but which play a continuous and essential role in policy-making. In both countries, the continuous consultations and negotiations between government and outside interests is considered a legitimate and necessary facet of governmental activity.

In Great Britain, the consultative process is legitimized as part of the representative process, whereby the views of affected groups are brought to the attention of government, and the cooperation of these groups with government policies is obtained. As a standard British work on the subject avers:

> The government's concern in the various activities of the citizens has laid upon it the necessity of sounding opinions as a guide to action, for the opinions of those concerned is a fact of the situation with which the government has to deal. But the sounding of opinions generally must prove such a difficult task that the government has resorted to the easier

[76] See Samuel Brittan, "The Irregulars," in Rose, *Policy-Making in Britain*, pp. 329–37.

[77] Max Nicholson, *The System: The Misgovernment of Modern Britain* (London: Hodder and Stoughton, 1967), p. 163.

method of consulting various representative organizations. . . . In a society in which the major demands appear to have been satisfied, both the main political parties realize the necessity of securing co-operation from all sections of society. The government seeks by consultation to build up where possible a responsive attitude to its proposals. It seeks co-operation and elimination of open discontent.[78]

The legitimacy of these consultations has achieved such a high consensus in Britain that the omission of consultations in the preparatory stages of legislative or regulatory drafting can be employed as a persuasive argument against the rules that ensue.

It is also widely felt that government rules are likely to be unworkable or impractical if they are drawn without due consideration for the superior experience and professional expertise of the affected groups. Organized groups can often supply information, statistics, expert testimony that may be very useful in avoiding unintended consequences of new rules. But the economic interests which perform necessary functions in the modern, industrial society also have a potential threat which adds greatly to their bargaining power: the threat of withdrawal of their cooperation in carrying out the government's aims. The group can threaten to deny the government its "advice, acquiescence, and approval—which can cause, to put it mildly, 'administrative difficulties' and which, by anticipation, endow the group with bargaining power in its relations with government."[79]

Obviously, a Soviet economic interest cannot employ the threat of withdrawal overtly, for the legitimizing doctrines hold that all interests are inherently, harmoniously united in the policies of the CPSU. But only the most superficial observer would contend that these doctrines rule out indirect threats of non-cooperation which, in the long run, can be just as effective in bending policies to the advantage of the affected groups. The experience of the Soviet government since its inception has been that economic goals of the regime can be achieved only by establishing appropriate incentives for the functional groups whose working cooperation is required for success. Where incentives have been low, as in agriculture, the result has been persistent failure; where incentives have been relatively high, as in certain industrial fields and in Siberian development, the results have been much closer to

---

[78] J. D. Stewart, *British Pressure Groups: Their Role in Relation to the House of Commons* (Oxford: Oxford University Press, 1958), pp. 6–7. S. A. Walkland contends that "a general consensus on the legitimacy of organized interests having a voice in public policy explains the widespread practice of consultation with pressure groups more satisfactorily than reference to the practical technical and political benefits which governments gain from it." *The Legislative Process in Great Britain* (London: Allen and Unwin, 1968), p. 43.

[79] Samuel H. Beer, *British Politics in the Collectivist Age* (New York: Alfred A. Knopf, 1966), p. 331.

expectations. Based on this experience, the need for incentives has been incorporated in legitimizing doctrines under the heading of the requirement for "material self-interest in the results of production."[80] It is the legitimized requirement for material self-interest which is the essence of the threat of withdrawal used by Soviet economic interests. Once it is acknowledged by the leaders that people work well only when offered sufficient incentives, it becomes a simple matter for a spokesman of an interest to advocate a greater allocation of resources to his group in order to assure that it will diligently achieve the planned production goals.

The example of Soviet agriculture illustrates this relationship quite well. In the period between Stalin's death and 1959, increased expenditures in agriculture and increased incentives for the collective farmers brought a steady upsurge in agricultural production. From 1959 to the end of the Khrushchev era, the pattern was one of decreased incentives and agricultural stagnation.[81] One of Brezhnev's first moves upon replacing Khrushchev as party leader was to condemn his predecessor for "actions of a purely willful nature" and for "administration by fiat" in the field of agriculture. Brezhnev's reforms (of March 1965) were primarily directed toward increasing incentives by raising state prices paid to collective and state farms for compulsory deliveries, and lowering compulsory delivery quotas to permit even greater bonuses for above-quota deliveries. He publicly acknowledged the importance of incentives for achieving the planned goals: "The chief thing now consists in resolutely putting an end to subjectivism in the practice of managing socialist agriculture and in making broad use of economic and moral incentives in all sectors of the production activity of the collective and state farms."[82] By all accounts, the results were a predictable increase in harvest yields, some of them achieving new records for Soviet agriculture.

Given this kind of passive threat of withdrawal of full working capacity and given the recognized legitimacy of material incentives in any scheme for increased productivity, it is highly likely that group representatives—they could be factory managers, collective farm chairmen, *raikom* chairmen, etc.— could argue with members of the administration or national leadership that the existing or planned allocation of resources does not provide sufficient incentives for the production groups involved. Certainly the major thrust of

---

[80] For a Soviet discussion of material self-interest, see V. S. Naidenov, "Printsip material'noi zainteresovannosti–printsip stroitel'stva kommunizma," *Voprosy filosofii*, no. 5, 1962; and I. Ia. Oblomskaia, "Razvitie material'noi zainteresovannosti kak ekonomicheskoi kategorii pri perekhode k kommunizmu," *Vestnik moskovskogo universiteta (filosofiia)*, no. 3, 1963.

[81] For an excellent review of agricultural policy and performance during this period, see Nancy Nimitz, "The Lean Years," *Problems of Communism* XIV, no. 3 (May–June 1965), pp. 10–22.

[82] *Pravda*, March 27, 1965. [*CDSP* XVII, no. 12, p. 11.]

Professor Liberman's by-now-famous proposals for industrial reform involved the setting of more appropriate performance indicators so that incentives could be rationally restructured.

The point is that both British and Soviet governments must work in close cooperation with many production groups that alone can supply the vital professional, productive expertise required to fulfill the government's plans. It is a situation of mutual dependency. The government can always command, but commands do not usually generate enthusiasm and maximum efforts. The government needs feedback from below, and it does not want to alienate any substantial group whose productive efforts are required. The symbiotic relationship of government and functional interests in both countries is an essential part of the policy-making process, and a useful part in that it helps the government to be responsive to the needs of *organized* groups with recognized productive functions in society. While it may be argued that Soviet groups do not have the same regular access to the policy process and the same freedom of action that British groups undoubtedly possess, there is convincing evidence to show that Soviet groups have sufficient access and independence to play a meaningful and sometimes decisive role in the formulation of policy.[83] In permitting this access, the Party leadership is simply responding to the requirements of managing a modern industrial society, a task made all the more difficult by its insistence on controlling everything in the name of "building communism." Indeed, failure to provide adequate access, and thus failure to be adequately responsive to the changing needs of society, could very well lead to a degeneration of the system—a fate predicted by the Soviet historian Andrei Amalrik and by some Western scholars.[84]

While it may be true that the Soviet system provides insufficient access to the party leadership tiers for organized interests, it may equally be true that the British system provides too much. The desire to accommodate all interests, to gain their approval and avoid conflict with them at all costs, can lead to stagnation of policy just as easily as insufficient group access. A close, warm, and enduring relationship between the rule-makers and the ruled can effectively prevent the issuance of regulations that are necessary for the protection of the general public interest, but distasteful to the most closely affected interest groups. It is difficult to imagine such distasteful regulations being promulgated if the procedure is that described by a former Lord Chancellor to the House of Lords:

[83] For a perceptive discussion of group involvement in policymaking, see Joel Schwartz and William Keech, "Group Influence and the Policy Process in the Soviet Union," *American Political Science Review* LXII, no. 3 (September 1968).

[84] See Andrei Amalrik, "Will the Soviet Union Survive Until 1984?" *Survey*, no. 73 (Autumn 1969); and Zbigniew Brzezinski, *Dilemmas of Change in Soviet Politics* (New York: Columbia University Press, 1969).

We no longer promulgate the regulations or rules in the Gazette and wait for representations to be made. We go to the trade or interest concerned and deal with it by getting them around the table, hearing what they have to say and then drafting the rules after obtaining their views.[85]

If all interests are to be accommodated, the result is hardly likely to be a coordinated policy which meets the needs of the present and accurately anticipates the problems of the future. Kenneth Waltz paints the picture in the most somber terms:

[In England] all interests are regarded as legitimate: the problem of policymakers is to arrive at a compromise among them, to find an accommodation that all will accept. Since the aim of the government is less to control than to accommodate, it is unfashionable, or bad form, to set interests in opposition publicly so that, by a dialectical process, a resolution can be achieved. The objective instead is to strike a compromise that all of the important interests in conflict can live with. Thus each program is at the moment acceptable, but the result taken in summation over a period of years is chaotic.[86]

But the real danger in both systems is not that of imminent collapse or chaotic policies. Neither system has achieved a brilliant record of responsiveness to the human needs of their populations, but both systems have apparently achieved an adequate record—adequate, that is, for a high consensus society and for a very high stability of political institutions. And in this lies the danger, for it may be possible to muddle through indefinitely, with indifferent success, satisfying just enough needs to keep legitimacy intact, and yet failing to deal with serious problems, and particularly the problems of the unorganized sections of the population.

PUBLIC OPINION AND INERTIAL GUIDANCE

In much of their policy-making processes, the Soviet and British governments operate along the lines of the *corporatist state*: dealing with people organized into functional groups, seeing its major function as the harmonious coordination of all the parts into a smoothly working mechanism. The influence of a generalized undifferentiated public opinion on the government's policies is more difficult to detect, and far more difficult to assess.

Public opinion has political salience only if it is known by those who are involved in determining policies. In the modern industrial society, with its

---

[85] Walkland, *Legislative Process in Great Britain*, p. 19.

[86] Kenneth N. Waltz, *Foreign Policy and Democratic Politics: The American and British Experience* (Boston: Little, Brown, 1967), p. 165.

large and varied population, the signals must be strong and unambiguous for the leadership to receive them. Of course, a single public opinion does not exist, for "the public" is never of one mind on any matter of public policy. On some matters, however, a dominant and intense opinion of a large but unmeasured segment of the public can have a significant impact on the direction of policy.

Methods for determining the opinions of the public are not well developed in either country. Polls are used in increasing numbers by British leaders, although the failure of polls to predict the outcome of the 1970 General Election has tended to discredit this technique somewhat. The mass media and contacts with representatives may also provide some feedback information, as may the communications of various organizations representing a group or espousing a cause. Taken all together, however, these channels of information about the public mind provide a cloudy picture at best, and a distorted picture at worst. In such a situation, it is entirely possible that a "general public outcry" against a government proposal, reported in the press, may simply be a well-run public relations campaign of an organized interest.

In the Soviet Union the leadership is even more hampered in gathering information on public opinion. Confidential reports from the bureaucracy, particularly from the secret police (the KGB), may give some information, but this channel is not reliable for reasons already discussed. The mass media are far less useful for this purpose; representatives are mainly concerned with local grievances, and even personal contacts (on inspection tours, for example) cannot be freed of the distorting influence of subordinate-superordinate relations.

The situation would be very serious for the Soviet regime, and yet an important problem for the British, if these governments needed to know public opinion to formulate the bulk of their policies. In point of fact, they don't. The situation would still be troublesome if a public opinion existed on these matters. In point of fact, it doesn't. The great bulk of government policies concern matters of no direct concern to the undifferentiated public. The impact is too small to disturb public tranquillity. In such matters, the administrative tier, "representing" the public interest, is likely to settle the matter through consultations with a specialized functional interest group (or groups).

Even in matters of greater scope, where seemingly grave issues are at stake, the state of public opinion may have no bearing on the outcome. Regardless of the question, about one-quarter of those polled in Britain "don't know." It is likely that ignorance is even more widespread in the Soviet population. Amongst those who are better informed, British polls show that only a small proportion have intense feelings about particular policies. It is all the less likely that Soviet citizens adopt strong views on political matters, where they are totally impotent, not only to affect the outcome, but even to articulate unorthodox opinions.

The absence of strong feelings, of public information, of unambiguous communications of opinion and of reliable channels for such communication leaves the leadership tiers considerable leeway in making policy in the large majority of cases. In the Soviet Union there simply are no other cases; a truly independent public opinion can never be openly expressed, and all independent opinions are forced underground, where they have no discernible effect on policy. But in Great Britain, independent opinions are often publicly expressed, and they do seem occasionally to have some effect on the course of public affairs. The flow of influences, however, is not all in one direction. As Jennings reminds us: "On the one hand . . . we find that the Government is very susceptible to public opinion; on the other hand we find public opinion very susceptible to persuasion by the Government."[87] The existence of the mass media permits the opinions of leaders to influence the public far more than it permits the views of the public to influence the leaders. Even without any conscious attempt to manipulate public opinion, the publicity given to the views of men in authoritative public positions is bound to affect the views of many citizens.

Even more important than this is the *inertia* of public opinion in Great Britain. The public does not change its opinions rapidly, but it forgets them rather easily.[88] Citizens are not likely to be aroused about policies in such fields as foreign policy, which ordinarily do not directly touch on their personal lives and fortunes. It may be, as Kenneth Waltz asserts, that "public opinion, which is not an obstacle to immediate acts and specific programs, nevertheless exerts a gentle pressure that over a period of years encourages tendencies and tends to shape policies."[89] But the public opinion of which Professor Waltz speaks is not the opinion of the mass public, the ultimate distillation of opinions from each section of the population. The opinions of the mass public are no doubt an important incentive to the Government to provide a maximum degree of domestic economic prosperity, and to avoid threatening conflicts, both domestic and foreign. Beyond this, in all the many matters which confront a government during its tenure and which only indirectly affect tranquillity and prosperity, the government can be influenced only by the views of those who actively seek to influence it and who, by

[87]Sir Ivor Jennings, *Parliament*, 2nd ed. (Cambridge: Cambridge University Press, 1957), p. 525.

[88]With this in mind, *The Economist* (June 27, 1970, p. 11) helpfully reminded the new Prime Minister, Edward Heath, of an old axiom of British politics that all the unpopular measures a Government wishes to enact should be disposed of during its first year and a half in office.

[89]Waltz, *Foreign Policy*, p. 174.

virtue of background and position in society, have a status which assures them ready access to the political leadership.

Access and receptivity to influence are made easier by common educational and social backgrounds, and reinforced by the fact that "they tend to an extraordinary degree to lead physically contiguous lives. They speak a very similar language of ideas, they read the same newspapers, they belong to the same narrow range of clubs, they have been members of the same or equivalent schools, universities and regiments and are inclined to perpetuate sentimental and even institutionalized associations with them."[90] They can and often do differ on particular policy questions, but the effect of this homogeneity of background and life style can and often does tend to limit the range of alternatives considered by the influential groups, in the same way that the leadership tiers are limited.

The similarities with the Soviet system on this point are unmistakable. Soviet interest groups are quite different from the British, but they display the same homogeneity of background and outlook. Once again, differences on immediate policies and priorities do occur between these different groups, but there is a common, binding core of beliefs and attitudes, reinforced by very similar life styles and experiences, which hold these groups together and limit their horizons.[91]

This relative homogeneity and stability of Soviet policy-makers and policy influencers may, indeed, be the chief cause of the unimaginative conservatism of their policies. To a lesser extent, the same can be said of the British. A public sufficiently satisfied to be ridden with indifferent inertia, and a political system sufficiently capable to guide this inertia through endless incremental adjustments—this seems to be the over-riding impact of the situation in both countries.

[90] David Vital, *The Making of British Foreign Policy* (London: Allen and Unwin, 1968), p. 83.

[91] See Jeremy Azrael, *Managerial Power and Soviet Politics* (Cambridge: Harvard University Press, 1966), pp. 167–72.

VI

Similarities and Differences

The preceding analysis has focused on the underlying similarities—in legimitizing doctrines and political processes between two systems that have often been thought to occupy opposite poles in the spectrum of political systems over the world. It is important to illuminate the similarities precisely because the differences between the Soviet and British systems have so often been exaggerated. Political leaders in both countries have been prime contributors to this exaggeration. British and Soviet leaders are apparently united in the belief that their two countries are separated by a vast gulf of divergent principles and practices. Traditions, some with deep historical roots, tend to emphasize each country's uniqueness, often combined with a presumption of superiority. The differences between the two countries are magnified additionally by a great deal of common ignorance and prejudice on both sides, multiplied on the Soviet side by the regime's thoroughgoing efforts to keep its citizens uninformed or misinformed about life in Great Britain and the West in general.[1]

The similarities that have been discussed in previous chapters fall into two categories: similarities in legitimizing doctrines and similarities in actual political processes. In the Soviet Union, the Marxist notion of

[1] A good example of this attempt at "disinformation" by the Soviet regime is a book by V. Osipov entitled *Britaniia 60-e gody* [Britain in the 60's] (Moscow: Izd-vo politicheskoi literatury, 1967).

an equal and democratic society, freed from the distortions of unequal, capitalist property relations, has been adopted as the basis of the Soviet state's legitimacy. It is still accepted there that the state will wither away, just as Marx and Engels predicted, but in the meantime the state has been transformed from an instrument of the dictatorship of the proletariat to a "state of the whole people."[2]

In Great Britain the notion of an *equal* society has not gained as much widespread acceptance as the idea of a *just* society, giving equal protection of the laws to all its citizens, and a state which exists for limited ends and which limits its means accordingly. Government by consent of the governed is a principle that has been carved out of several centuries of English constitutional history; elections periodically supply the governed's consent, although the choices provided by elections have been quite limited in recent times. In any case, the legitimacy of the Government in Great Britain rests upon this popular choice.

The idea that the people rule through representative organs of government is firmly established as a legitimizing principle of the state in both countries, along with the concept that the party in power is the choice of the people and is responsive to the people's best interests, whether expressed or not. In neither country does one find a serious challenge to the basic structure and processes of government, although less fundamental organizational changes occur rather often. Both systems are stable, within our previous definition of gradual, orderly change, and are supported by a very wide social consensus. The processes whereby policies of the government are formulated, legitimized, and implemented have also been shown to bear certain striking and significant similarities.

Yet, against these similarities, one must counterpose some equally important differences, which bear particularly on the relationship of the individual citizen to the government. The Soviet government tries to *mold* its citizens; the British government tries to please and impress its citizens. The Soviet citizen is the subject of government policy, while the British citizen is the object of such policy. The legitimacy of both governments is ultimately based upon a concept of "service" to the people, but the British government tries to do its best for people as they are, while the Soviet government tries to "improve" the people, to make them worthy of truly "communist" policies.

---

[2]This is a highly illogical formulation—as the Chinese have vigorously pointed out—because the state, according to Marx's analysis, exists solely as an instrument of the dominant class, enforcing unequal class (or property) relations. Once a society reaches a higher level of organization, the need for the state disappears, since there is no class conflict, and the state thus withers away. Thus a "state of the whole people," in a self-proclaimed socialist society "building communism" seems a "revisionist" anomaly. For the Chinese critique of this idea, see the *Red Flag* editorial, "Long Live Leninism!" (April 16, 1960).

A good example of this distinction is the question of wage incentives in industrial production and services. The British government has bargained with various labor groups in recent years, often conceding settlements that have contributed to the spiral of inflation. It is simply an accepted proposition in Britain that people work for material rewards, and that one must deal with material demands realistically, through negotiations leading to a compromise settlement. In the Soviet case, however, the government has repeatedly attempted to substitute "moral" incentives for material rewards, giving decorations to "heroes" of production and red banners to "brigades of communist labor," incessantly inculcating standards of "communist morality" which involve social altruism and work for the benefit of society without calculating one's own interests. Far from being simply a cynical, money-saving scheme of the CPSU leadership, this emphasis on moral incentives springs from the Marxist-Leninist concept of "consciousness," which implies that people of a truly communist society understand that their personal interests are completely in harmony with the interests of others, that "work is a joy and man's greatest happiness when it is work for the good of the community." The current crop of Soviet people must be improved until everyone achieves this level of consciousness. Until that time, the leadership concedes some material incentives, reluctantly noting that they seem to spur production far better than red banners and plaques.

The contrasts in this and other respects can be traced to differing concepts of the goals of the political system. To the Soviet leadership, politics is the process by which an ultimate state of social and economic perfection is uncovered by a progression of defined historical stages. The British government, thoroughly disbelieving in perfection as an attainable goal, assumes that out of a thousand compromises, the passage of time, and the accumulation of experience, something rather satisfactory will probably ensue. Always skeptical of any "final solution," always reluctant to tamper with the way things have been done, and always aware that there are at least two sides to every issue, it has raised "the loyal opposition" to a valued place in the governmental structure, even paying its leader a salary out of the public coffers.

In policy-making, the dynamism which should spring from the utopian goals of the Soviet system has been thoroughly dissipated by the overwhelming bureaucratic norms of the party-state structure. In this regard, the Soviet system is no less conservative than the British. The idea that there is one Indivisible Truth, One Correct Solution to every problem—an idea which can certainly be traced to Lenin himself—has produced an intolerance for dissent and an insistence on orthodoxy in thought and action which have been detrimental to the development of the system *even within its own terms*. The performance of the British system can be faulted in many respects, but it contains within itself the possibility of self-correction through the internal flow of information, facilitated by the presence of legitimate centers for the collection and dissemination of negative data and criticism: the opposition party, autonomous organized interests, and an independent press.

The Soviet system, on the other hand, is a good example (in Karl Deutsch's terms) of a system which is deficient in providing feedback information, and which often thereby fails to be self-steering.[3] To some extent the Soviet leadership's failure to correct deficient policy may be attributed to ideological preconceptions which effectively eliminate the most appropriate corrective actions. But the Soviet leadership has shown remarkable ingenuity in detouring around these preconceptions when convinced of the necessity. The tendency of the bureaucracy to supply positive, supportive feedback and to attenuate negative feedback must also be considered a factor in the repeated failure of Soviet policy to adjust to changing conditions and past shortcomings.

Thus the restriction of information flow and the silencing of negative feedback, which have been typically seen as immoral (illegitimate) in the West, can also be seen as a structural defect of the Soviet system which leads to inefficiency. It is precisely because of this, however, that the regime is constantly under pressure to open the channels of communication. The regime claims that its organization of society is more efficient than other systems, and measures its performance in terms of material output, economic growth and similar empirical standards. Organized, expert groups which accept the goals of the regime can thus claim a place in the determination of policies in the name of efficiency.[4] Competing claims for the distribution of scarce resources are continually presented to the Party leadership, and the more specialized groups—be they doctors, lawyers, the military, or economic managers—continually attempt to establish some degree of professional autonomy. Since efficiency is a criterion, and since empirical measurements are used, each specialized group has a persuasive argument for determining its own methods and standards, based on its near monopoly of expertise and special talent. It is this process which tends to "liberalize" Soviet society, despite the fears and warnings of the more conservative members of the Party leadership. But the Party leadership is not a conservative monolith standing in opposition to group pressures. These leaders also specialize to some degree and tend to identify with the needs of the interests in their area of supervision. This situation leads to a process of bargaining and accommodation in the short run, but also implies the possibility of gradual liberalization of society in the longer perspective.

Liberalization does not necessarily mean freedom of expression for individuals outside their areas of specialization. The Party finds it necessary to

---

[3]See Karl Deutsch, *The Nerves of Government* (New York: The Free Press, 1966), especially Chapters 5 and 11.

[4]See Jeremy Azrael, *Managerial Power and Soviet Politics* (Cambridge: Harvard University Press, 1966).

provide private channels of communication for interest groups in order to achieve its own goals, but its legitimate position as the "only necessary" party would be threatened by the open articulation of divergent views on policy matters. It is, however, very difficult in the long run to maintain the precarious balance between the narrower and wider forms of liberalization.

Open articulation of diverse views on policy issues is a basic characteristic of the British system, which differs sharply with the Soviet norm; but the distinction is in practice somewhat lessened by the fact that even in Britain the views that are actually expressed are largely within the value consensus of the major parties. Views outside this consensus can be openly articulated with impunity, but they are not as widely circulated. There is a circular flow of cause and effect here: the existing consensus makes the population less receptive to non-consensual messages; the population's unresponsiveness to these non-consensual messages makes it less likely that they will circulate widely, and the lack of wide circulation for non-consensual views in turn reinforces the consensus.

In both countries, the most important facts about the public at large are the apathy with which it faces public issues, and the high consensus within it supporting the regime's legitimacy. Taken together, these attributes give the political leadership the greatest possible freedom of action to determine policies. Ironically, in both cases, the leadership is restricted less by the opinions or desires of the mass public than by its own organization, by the interaction between the various leadership tiers, by the bureaucratic norms which pervade the policy-making process, and by the ultimate self-limitations of its own concepts of legitimate political action. Both leaderships view their role as "service" to the people and measure their performance in terms of "benefits" which they bestow on the public. It is in these terms, and these terms alone, that their power is legitimized.

Within the "power structure" of government we have found a similar division into four leadership tiers for policy-making, a similarity which is to some extent dictated by the necessities of governing an industrialized mass-society. But there were also some highly significant differences: the bifurcation of the British leadership into two alternate teams, the location of the primary leader, leadership core, and national leadership within the Party structure in the Soviet Union and within the state structure in Great Britain. We have noted that the "higher" tiers are likely to be involved in determining policies that are judged to have higher political salience, and that in fact the locus of decision-makers varies inversely with political salience. Particularly in matters of lower political salience, and most particularly in matters relating to the allocation of scarce resources, the functional interest groups, spawned in the very process of creating an industrial mass-society, play a great role in determining the outcome. In both societies, the close cooperation of government and these interests is legitimized primarily as the means to achieving social harmony and practical efficiency.

The two systems share a considerable disparity between their doctrines of legitimate political power and the actual, operational distribution of policy-making power within the structure. In both countries, the legitimization of the state is based on popular sovereignty as expressed indirectly through assemblies of people's representatives. In both countries, the myth is sedulously propagated that the representative assembly is sovereign, plenipotentiary, the very center of government. Yet, in practice, policy in matters of high political salience is formulated within the leadership core, and in matters of low salience, within the administration. On occasion, the British representative assembly can influence policies (particularly through the effective National Leadership of the moment, the majority members), and in this respect its power is somewhat more tangible than its Soviet counterpart. Yet, it is impossible to argue that the British Parliament in recent times has played a significant, or even a continuously relevant role in the making of British policy. Whatever subsidiary functions one may ascribe to it, its chief modern function is to legitimize rules and to give them authority. This function it shares with the Supreme Soviet.

While the opinions and desires of the mass public do not play a direct role in determining policy, it is still true that policies must contain sufficient incentives or rewards to generate the responses from the affected part of the population required for success. In this way, the public passively imposes some limitations on the policy alternatives selected by the leadership—although there is no assurance that the leaders will accurately gauge the "public mood" in this respect.

One of the central themes of this book is that the nature of the modern, industrialized mass-society, its sheer size, its diversity of occupational roles, its diffusion of public responses, and its concentration of effort on private, material rewards, have created a remarkably similar environment within which the Soviet and British political systems must operate. The adaptations of these systems to the common elements in their environments have engendered the similarities we have noted in their policy-making processes and in their legitimizing doctrines. The differences remain, and they are still important. They relate, for the most part, to the differing goals of the regimes, and to differing concepts of the legitimate scope of means used to achieve the ends of government. Still, if one were to include the large "private" industrial enterprises in Britain within the over-all governing structures of society—and there are good reasons for doing so—the differences between the British and Soviet systems would be considerably reduced.

THE IMPORTANCE OF BEING LEGITIMATE

One of the hallmarks of a successful political system is that it acquires a consensus on its legitimacy, and thereby imparts authority to its structures (which become institutions) and to its rules (which become laws). In the modern, industrialized mass-society, the acquisition of legitimacy by the government is crucial, because the government, in allocating scarce resources to the myriad of functional groups, must disappoint and frustrate some of their instrumental goals. The stability of the political system depends on the acquisition of legitimacy to the point where it becomes a consensus value.

Legitimacy is acquired through the sufficient satisfaction of instrumental demands over time, the provision of sufficient personal and national security, and—most importantly—through the political socialization process in which the regime's legitimizing doctrines are inculcated in younger generations.

To what extent have the British and Soviet regimes succeeded in establishing their legitimacy with the mass public? According to our earlier definition, legitimacy requires an emotional attachment of the individual to the regime, an attachment of loyalty and sentiment that goes beyond the mere calculation of regime performance and personal gain. It may well be, as Robert Presthus has suggested, that the relatively less numerous "upward-mobiles" accept regime values most readily, while the more numerous "indifferents"—in this case the mass of the population—remain relatively passive.[5] In the very least case, the success of regime legitimization can be measured by the degree to which it paralyzes all tendencies to opposition and renders potential dissentients passively, outwardly obedient to the regime's minimal demands for political conformity. Legitimizing doctrines have succeeded if they foster an upward-mobile elite which ardently believes in them, and a mass public which is so disarmed by them that it can be "inertially guided" by the regime's leaders. A nation of true believers, of devoted regime supporters, is not found in either country, nor is it really needed. Although the Soviet system strives for such a society, it seems as far from the goal as the British, who do not even want it.

In fact, both regimes appear to have achieved considerably more than this minimum of support from their citizenry. An affective relationship to the basic, ostensible values of these regimes—their legitimizing doctrines—is probably more widespread than is satisfaction with government performance. Relative indifference to the particulars of politics and relative passivity to the policies of the moment do not necessarily mean that a few, simple, "homely truths" about the regime's virtues have not been learned early in life. Patriotism, flags, ceremonies, and the entire panoply of propaganda keep such truths alive, even when the government's efficiency falls.

The chief virtue of a high-consensus society is that it assures regime stability. The chief danger is that it tends toward excessive policy stability or, put the other way, toward insufficient flexibility and innovation in policy-making. Both the virtues and the dangers are amply shown by the recent

[5] See Robert Presthus, *The Organizational Society* (New York: Alfred A. Knopf, 1962).

history of the Soviet and British systems. If citizens judged their governments on instrumental efficiency grounds alone, it is doubtful that either government would have survived the very first Day of Judgment.

But perhaps one should not stress too much the judgments made by the mass population. More important are the judgments rendered by the leaders themselves, and the political, professional, and managerial elites, those who most thoroughly accept the values of the regime and who are most motivated to achieve through those values. There is a profound truth in Alfred Meyer's observation:

> In sounding off in ideological fashion, Soviet leaders are not talking to us or to the "masses," but are talking to each other or, much more important, primarily to themselves. Soviet ideology is not only communication with others. It is also a monologue in which the leaders compulsively engage. We might refer to this mass monologue as a process of self-legitimization, a continual attempt on the part of the rulers to convince *themselves* of their legitimacy.[6]

A NOTE ON CONVERGENCE

One of the main themes of this book has been the underlying similarities of the British and Soviet systems of government. A possible explanation of this similarity is the theory of convergence, which, simply stated, holds that developed nations of the communist and non-communist world are converging into a single type of post-industrial welfare state. In some respects, convergence seems a plausible description of the apparent developments of the past several decades. These decades have seen a notable transformation of the established Western state systems from *laissez faire* to welfare, and more recently, a retreat of the Soviet Union from the ramparts of revolution to the quest for more chemical fertilizers, plastics, and Fiat automobiles, a comfortable style of life that seems familiar and friendly to the West.

While the preceding analysis certainly carries implications that bear on the notion of convergence, the term has not been used primarily because it is a dynamic, developmental term, which suggests not only that the two systems are similar but that they are moving toward ever greater similarity. That the British and Soviet systems might in time appear essentially identical cannot be ruled out, but it does seem highly improbable. The convergence idea implies that common features of industrialized mass-societies compel adaptation of the political system along identical lines, whereas it seems more likely that, for every given set of environmental conditions and problems, there are several broadly similar alternatives that can serve as approximate solutions.

---

[6] Alfred G. Meyer, "The Functions of Ideology in the Soviet Political System: A Speculative Essay Designed to Provoke Discussion," *Soviet Studies* XVII, no. 3 (January 1966), p. 280.

Furthermore, the goals of the regime, the priorities which it establishes partly as the result of its history and traditions, may cause it to choose different solutions from the limited range of alternatives than another regime confronted with the same set of conditions.

In light of this, it might be more realistic to view convergence as an asymptotic relationship, reaching unity only at an infinite point in time, and with a decent distance maintained between the two systems for the foreseeable future. Whether one views this speculative suggestion as hopeful or depressing depends on one's evaluation of current trends in these industrial mass-societies, including man's ever-increasing capabilities for self-destruction through careless folly as well as through purposeful self-delusion.

Index

Index

THE JOHNS HOPKINS UNIVERSITY PRESS

This book was composed in Press Roman text by
Jones Composition Company. It was printed on
60–lb. Sebago Regular stock by Universal
Lithographers, Inc. and bound by L. H. Jenkins, Inc.
in Interlaken Matte cloth.

Library of Congress Cataloging in Publication Data

Gilison, Jerome M   1935–
   British and Soviet politics.

   Includes bibliographical references.
   1. Great Britain—Politics and government—1945– 2. Russia—Politics and government—
1945– I. Title.

JN234.G55 1972   320.3   72–4017
ISBN 0–8018–0710–7